DATE
WITH THE
DEVIL

DATE
WITH THE
DEVIL

DON LASSETER
WITH RONALD E. BOWERS

P

PINNACLE BOOKS
Kensington Publishing Corp.
http://www.kensingtonbooks.com

Some names have been changed to protect the privacy of individuals connected to this story.

PINNACLE BOOKS are published by

Kensington Publishing Corp.
119 West 40th Street
New York, NY 10018

All Kensington titles, imprints and distributed lines are available at special quantity discounts for bulk purchases for sales promotions, premiums, fund-raising, and educational or institutional use. Special book excerpts or customized printings can also be created to fit specific needs. For details, write or phone the office of the Kensington Special Sales Manager: Kensington Publishing Corp., 119 West 40th Street, New York, NY 10018. Attn: Special Sales Department, Phone: 1-800-221-2647.

Pinnacle and the P logo Reg. U.S. Pat. & TM Off.

ISBN-13: 978-0-7860-2035-5
ISBN-10: 0-7860-2035-0

First Printing: June 2012

10 9 8 7 6 5 4 3 2 1

Printed in the United States of America

CHAPTER 1
DANGER IN DAGGETT

Shimmering heat waves radiated from the endless desert floor as Allura McGehay sped along the I-40 Freeway, ten miles east of Barstow, California. By midmorning, when she steered her green Dodge Dakota pickup onto the remote Nebo Street off-ramp, outside temperatures had already skyrocketed above the 100-degree mark.

The attractive young woman drove about a half mile north on the two-lane road, approaching a round, wide-sweeping arc that would take her once more in an easterly direction. She had routinely made the big right turn countless times in trips to the rustic village of Daggett, only four more miles from the curve.

Suddenly, directly in front of her, Allura caught sight of another car careening around the bend and speeding directly toward her—in her lane!

Driving in the vast Mojave Desert has always been dangerous. Grinding, high-speed collisions are often fatal. Getting stranded in the 25,000 square miles of emptiness could expose hapless victims to life-threatening temperatures reaching 120 degrees.

The region is heavily traveled by commuters from Southern California. Barstow, about ninety miles from Hollywood, is a dividing point with an important "Y" intersection. Gamblers and fun seekers heading for Las Vegas stay on Interstate 15, slanting slightly northeast. Other travelers bound for Arizona, New Mexico, Texas, Oklahoma, and beyond veer directly east onto Interstate 40, which retraces much of old Route 66, the historic "Mother Road." Songwriter Bobby Troup, paying tribute to the legendary two-lane artery in his popular 1946 song, "(Get Your Kicks on) Route 66," made mention of Barstow.

Allura had none of this on her mind as she turned off I-40, heading for the diminutive town of Daggett, which sits astride the original Route 66. A community of fewer than two hundred residents, plus another one thousand in the surrounding region, Daggett had seen better days. Its rusting and battered remnants sit silently baking in the desert, surrounded by miles of sand, sage, and creosote bush. First established in the late 1800s as a silver and borax mining center, Daggett had enjoyed a period of glory when the Santa Fe Railroad built tracks paralleling the Mother Road. Now skeletons of long-abandoned service stations mark former havens for travelers; fenced and boarded buildings stand empty, and weed-choked yards overflow with scabrous, dead vehicles. The unincorporated town still maintains a U.S. Post Office, staffed by one person. Allura had friends in one of the more pleasant sections of Daggett, and wanted to pay a visit on that sizzling Saturday morning, June 16, 2007.

The speeding car hurtling toward Allura's pickup didn't slow or swerve. She wrenched her steering wheel to the right, barely avoiding a disastrous head-on collision, and came to a heart-thudding halt. The jerk who forced her off the road never even bothered to stop.

Shaken and trembling, Allura struggled to catch her breath. Her pickup sat leaning to the right in the soft, sandy shoulder less than fifty yards from the portion of road marked as HISTORIC ROUTE 66. After a few moments, when her pulse stopped pounding, she felt composed enough to continue on her way. With the engine still running, Allura pressed her foot on the accelerator, only to feel her rear tires spin in the sand. She gave it a little more gas, and gained nothing in forward momentum. Backing up proved equally futile. Two more attempts to escape only sank the wheels deeper into the desiccated earth.

Allura glanced around at the familiar terrain. Back toward Barstow, she could see a few buildings stretched across a military base in the far distance, separated from her by flat, scorched, boundless miles of sand and ubiquitous creosote bush. The opposite direction, toward Daggett, offered more of the same. In her forward view, Allura scanned an outcropping of tan-colored rolling hills stretching across the remote horizon. On a yonder slope, she could make out giant white letters decorating a hillside and spelling out CALICO. They marked the site of a ghost town by that name.

Approximately twenty yards behind her vehicle, the desert was creased by a "wash," a shallow, dry streambed for flash floods, no more than two feet deep and about twelve yards wide. A concrete bridge passed over it, completely indistinguishable due to the absence of side rails. Motorists don't even know they have driven over a bridge. The sandy ditch, which hadn't been wet in many months, was littered with sun-bleached detritus, including old tires, broken pieces of plywood, and plastic bottles. It could also be the home of rattlesnakes, coyotes, scorpions, and a myriad of other creatures Allura would prefer not to encounter.

Not yet panicked, but feeling a crawling sensation of concern, Allura weighed her options. First she flipped her cell phone open, only to see the message, *No service*. Damn!

The intense, searing heat and scorching sun made the possibility of walking into Daggett a dangerous prospect, especially without any water to carry along. And a shapely young woman hiking alone in the desert could face other frightening or life-endangering perils.

Another possibility would be to hope that someone in the scant passing traffic might stop and offer assistance. But not every citizen of this region would be a Good Samaritan. Allura knew the chances of rape, or even worse, could not be ignored.

She glanced into her rearview mirror and felt her heart speed up again, trying to leap through her throat. A pickup truck slowed and came to a halt a few yards behind her. She could barely make out the features of the driver, a man with a shaved head, wearing a black pullover shirt.

As always, appearances can be deceiving. The pickup's driver, Christopher DeWitt, a U.S. Marine dressed in civilian clothing, had nothing but the purest of motives, simply wanting to help. Allura felt the weight of the world lift when he smiled, gave her a friendly wave, stepped out of his vehicle, and walked up to her window.

"Look's like you're stuck," he drawled. "Let's see if we can get you out of this pickle. When I give you the signal, ease down on the accelerator and I'll try pushing from behind. I can't do it with my truck, 'cause I would sink into this sand just like you did."

Christopher centered himself at the rear of Allura's truck, facing backward with his hands in a position to lift the bed as much as he could. He yelled, "Go ahead."

Allura gently pressed the floor pedal. The tires did nothing but send two rooster tails of sand and dust into the air on both sides of DeWitt.

Within a few minutes, another Samaritan halted and offered to help. Robert LaFond—stocky, goateed, and shaved head, also wearing a black T-shirt—joined Christopher in grunting, lifting, and pushing. Both men worked up a lather of perspiration with no positive results. They tried rocking the

Dodge forward and backward, but it stubbornly remained in place like a recalcitrant mule. If anything, Allura's truck just embedded itself deeper in the sand.

"I think we need to pick up some rocks or sticks and put them in front of the rear tires," Christopher suggested. Robert volunteered to see what he could find. A quick scan of the barren terrain showed a complete absence of any useful stones. He decided to extend his survey down into the gully, where rushing water of long ago might have uncovered rocks, boards, sticks, or anything that could be jammed under Allura's tires to help them gain traction.

The hot, blinding sun caused Robert to shade his eyes by using his hands as a visor. As he glanced about, he thought he saw the brilliant glint of something golden near the concrete wall of the low bridge. Taking a few steps closer, Robert felt a rush of horror grip his gut.

To the stunned young man, it appeared that a blackened human arm extended from the shadows under the bridge. The golden flash looked like it came from a wristwatch encircling the mummified wrist.

Clutched by a mixture of fear and dread, he couldn't force his legs to move any closer to the dreadful apparition. Spinning around, Robert raced back up to tell Christopher what he thought he had discovered.

As a combat veteran, having served in Iraq, DeWitt had seen his share of dead bodies. The experience had not numbed his sensitivity, but looking at a corpse didn't send him reeling, as it would most people. Christopher ambled down the gentle slope, approached the spot described by Robert, and knew that they had indeed discovered the remains of a human being.

The body had obviously been exposed to desert heat for quite some time. Christopher couldn't even be certain about the deceased person's sex, but he thought it probably a woman due to the long blond hair and what looked like a tank top and bra wadded under the armpits.

She lay facedown in a tight fetal position with the legs cramped under the torso in a compressed kneeling posture. Flimsy shorts, once white but now darkly smudged, partially covered the posterior. The left arm extended out from under the bridge shadow, and a gold-colored wristwatch gleamed brightly in the sun. It contrasted sharply against the blackened skin. What was left of the fleshless face was turned toward the watch. The right arm, bent in a relaxed position, reclined on the dirt above the disheveled hair.

Decomposition had blackened every inch of the remaining flesh, while all fluids from her body had drained into the sand, darkening it beneath her.

Christopher trudged back up the rise and confirmed to Robert and Allura that they had found a dead person. LaFond had no interest in having another look, but Allura couldn't resist the terrible temptation to see for herself. Rather than descend into the gully, she walked back to the bridge, leaned over the edge far enough to spot the watch-bearing arm, and felt repulsion wash through her entire body. She made it back to her vehicle before giving in to nausea and throwing up.

Christopher popped his cell phone open. Unlike Allura's, his connected immediately. He called 911 to report the grisly discovery.

San Bernardino County Sheriff's deputy Doug Alexander pulled up to the scene a few minutes after eleven o'clock. The sun, approaching its midday zenith on that Saturday, June 16, 2007, seemed to sap out all of the oxygen from the air supply. As Alexander climbed out of his patrol car, Robert LaFond trotted over to describe what they had found. In his subsequent report, Alexander wrote, *I asked him to explain to me what was going on and he pointed to a green Dodge Dakota pickup truck which was stuck in the dirt shoulder on the east side of Nebo Street.*

LaFond dutifully spieled out the events about seeing the body under the bridge and DeWitt's verification that it was a human corpse.

The deputy took notes, thanked Robert LaFond, and spoke to Christopher Dewitt. His story complemented LaFond's. Alexander asked the men to show him the body. In typical cop speak language, he noted, *I left my marked sheriff's unit in the roadway with my emergency lights on, and walked to the east side of the roadway and over a small mound of dirt in a wash where I looked down and observed what I recognized as a deceased or dead body which appeared to be female.*

Alexander immediately notified his watch commander, Corporal Marie Spain. She left the station in Barstow, accompanied by Deputy Gary Hart. Upon arrival at the bridge, Hart secured the entire perimeter with yellow crime scene tape. Spain notified the Homicide Division.

CHAPTER 2
"THIS IS MY SISTER"

One hundred miles southwest of Daggett, where California coastal breezes cooled the atmosphere, Robin Henson sensed something terribly wrong. Kristin, her younger sister, hadn't responded to e-mails, phone calls, or text messages for more than a week. It certainly was not the first time they had been out of communication for extended periods of time, but this separation felt different. Through their shared childhood, their young-adult years, and into their thirties and early forties, Robin and "Kristi" had always been connected by more than personal visits, telephones, texting, or old-fashioned mail correspondence. Affectionate bonds between them transcended the physical and bordered on telepathic transmissions. But even those circuits had gone strangely silent.

In Robin's home, near the western border of Los Angeles County, and a fifteen-minute drive from the ocean, an ethereal emptiness filled the rooms like a gloomy fog. It gripped her heart and soul. Psychic links between the pair had existed since their early childhood in New York and Massachusetts.

Robin's young-adult daughters, Jessica and Julia, also felt the melancholy vacuum.

Troubling prescience for Robin had started on Thursday, May 31, 2007, Memorial Day, sixteen days before Allura McGehay found herself in desert danger. The date also happened to be Jessica's twenty-first birthday. Robin had wanted to invite everyone to a family celebration for that holiday, but Kristin hadn't responded. That didn't fit her normal pattern of enthusiastic participation in family functions.

In the following days, Robin's growing worry turned into deep anxiety. She and her second stepfather, Peter Means, who remained connected to the now-grown children, spoke by telephone or text-messaged daily, praying that nothing disastrous had happened. They hoped that rough spots in the life of Kristi, also known as "Krissy," had been left behind her.

Early childhood for Robin and Kristin had been difficult, exacerbated by frequent moves and family turbulence. Their mother, Marie, had delivered Robin and her male twin, Richard, in Glens Falls, New York, three years before Kristin arrived on May 6, 1969. Later recalling the beauty of her baby sister, Robin said, "She was just this cute, chubby little thing with gorgeous hair, plump cheeks, and a great smile. Sugar and spice. Sweet and nice. We had the chicken pox when Kristin was about six months old and she had only one teeny-tiny pockmark on that darling little face."

Their father, Rick Arlington, found it necessary to repeatedly uproot his wife and kids, due to his job, and migrate to different cities. They lived in Lake George, Utica, Syracuse, and Albany before moving to Massachusetts. Working as a nurse, Marie hated the ongoing failure to settle down and find stability somewhere. Stressful disagreements between Rick and Marie grew into irreconcilable differences, and before Kristin's second birthday, led to a divorce. Marie soon remarried and the children began adjusting to a father figure with a different surname: Baldwin. They also gained a new sibling in 1972, another girl. Stephanie's birth would be the final addition.

The second marriage also crashed and burned within a few years. Painful discord between parents overflows onto children, making their existence miserable too. Living in New Hartford, New York, they longed for a place of peace and serenity, where they could live like other kids they met in school. Fortunately, it came with their mother's third husband.

Marie had grown up in Vermont. In the seventh grade, she had met classmate Peter Means and later dated him while they attended high school together. After the Baldwin marriage ended in divorce, Marie attended her high-school reunion, where she and Peter felt the embers of romance warm up again. Means would later recall, "I was living in Massachusetts, working for a company that made equipment for video recording and motion pictures filming. Marie and I began telephoning each other, and I made some trips to New Hartford."

They exchanged vows in 1974, when Kristin was about five years old. According to Peter, all four of the kids were a "lively group," but she was the bubbly one. The twins, Robin and Rick, and even little Stephanie, were relatively quiet. Kristin had a gregarious personality, liked people, and loved to laugh. When she began attending school, said Peter, "she did reasonably well but could have done better. She was very social, and her peer groups were more important to her than her grades. Not that she did poorly. She was just very lively."

Peter took his new family to a home in Bolton, Massachusetts, located in the suburbs of Boston. "It was a small town, maybe five thousand people, and great for kids, with good neighbors. Everyone had two or three acres of land, giving plenty of space for children." Kristin's congenial personality made it easy to meet and befriend other families.

An expert skier, Peter also taught the sport. "I got them

involved in skiing, and Kristin took it up with wild enthusiasm. In my job as ski instructor, at a place near Leominster, I could get them on the slopes for free. When you teach young kids, they take it up easily because they have no fear. Kristin was one of the better ones, absolutely fearless. She loved going straight down the hill, objecting to making any turns. The faster she went, the more thrilled she was. The other three kids were a little more cautious. Remember, she was just a young tyke, six or seven. I still laugh when I recall one of her antics. I taught ski racing, and Kristin loved that. She noticed people on the Poma lift, a device to pull people up the hill. You straddle a bar that is attached to a moving cable, and lean back against a small platter, which rests against the back of your thighs. Kristin thought the spacing of people on the Poma lift looked like gates on a slalom course. She got up to the top, and started skiing down, zigzagging between them, ducking under the cable. Of course, the ski patrol spotted her, and they kicked her out for the day. She hadn't hit anyone, but they didn't appreciate her scaring the bejesus out of people going up the lift. Yeah, she was very exuberant."

Peter Means ensconced himself in the hearts of his new brood of kids. Robin still spoke of her second stepfather with a special reverence in her voice. "Peter Means was the one who raised us and was the only man in my life I consider my father. My birth name was Arlington, but I have never talked about it. We were so attached to Peter. He was our dad. We needed some normalcy, and he gave it to us. All of us kids took his name. He treated us like his own, but he related really well with Kristin."

Rick, Robin's twin brother, in reminiscing about those childhood years, said, "I was really close to Kristin, even though she was three years younger. Sometimes, though, like most brother-sister bonds, it would be like a love-hate relationship. We were totally best friends or we were pissed off at each other."

In 1978, Peter's employer offered him a promotion by moving to the West Coast. He realized that Marie and her children had lived a nomadic existence and wanted to put an end to their frequent relocations. Peter bought a home in one of the most attractive and affluent residential sites in Southern California, packed his family into a vehicle, and headed to the "Golden State."

Speaking of the trip to the West Coast, Rick recalled, "Kristin and I were not allowed to sit next to each other because we had too much fun. It was like, 'Hey you guys back there, be quiet!'"

Westlake Village is located at the westernmost edge of Los Angeles County and overlaps into neighboring Ventura County. It is separated from Malibu Beach by only a dozen miles across the Santa Monica Mountains. Nestled against picturesque hills, the tree-laden community surrounds a man-made lake. Personal boat harbors lie within a few steps of waterside homes, and a luxurious golf course is nearby. The quiet, spacious ambience lured numerous celebrities from the world of sports, entertainment, and business. Legendary football star Joe Montana, Los Angeles Dodgers' announcer Vin Scully, and former wrestler Hulk Hogan bought homes there, as did film stars Robert Young, Martin Lawrence, George C. Scott, and Mariel Hemingway, among many others.

The new two-story, five-bedroom house acquired by Means occupied the Ventura County side. Diagonally across the street lived a girl born just a few weeks sooner than Kristin. Jennifer Gootsan, a native and lifelong resident of Westlake Village, would eventually become almost like another sister to Kristi, but not at first. Recalling their shared childhood, Jennifer said, "When Kristin and I first met, we actually didn't get along at all. It's weird how we became the-best-of-the-best of friends, and extended it later on in our lives. At first she and I clashed over silly, girly things, just teenage stuff. It wasn't about boys. They were not really an issue. It was more about whose hair looked better that day or who had the cuter clothes."

In the upscale neighborhood, the children reveled in their newfound lifestyle. "There were lots of big families. Lots of block parties. At Christmas, we had a piñata," Robin described. "All the neighborhood kids came to our garage. Most of the families in the surrounding area were there, not just one or two kids. Jennifer was friends with Kristin, and her younger brother was friends with my youngest sister. Same with several other families, lots of friends. Several of us ran track and played softball together, and everything was always about the neighbors."

Looking back fondly at those years, Peter Means smiled as he told of Kristin's debut as a "singer." "We went down to San Diego for a vacation and stayed on Harbor Island. In the hotel, they had a karaoke-like event, which turned out to be more of an impromptu talent show. Kristin was about eleven or twelve and decided she wanted to go up and show off her skills. She sang 'Tomorrow,' the big song from the Broadway show *Annie,* and she did it in a very animated way. She brought the house down. I don't know that she was a particularly natural singer, like some of those remarkable people who show up on *American Idol.* She did well, but it was her animation that wowed the audience. And she won the contest. She liked belting out that song. That event followed her around from then on."

In the summer during school holidays, the kids spent as much time as possible at Malibu or Zuma Beach. Kristin fell in love with the ocean and became a dedicated beach bunny. A deep tan became her trademark, and she gradually mastered surfboard skills in the crashing Pacific waves.

Several summers included visits to a relative's farm in Vermont, where Kristin and her siblings learned to ride horses. Always athletic, Kristin adapted to the saddle as easily as she did to skis and a surfboard.

While Robin and her twin, Rick, entered Westlake High School, Kristi and her friend Jennifer enrolled at nearby Triunfo Elementary School. "Jennifer lived close to us," Rick said, "and I used to mow her lawn. I mowed everybody's lawn on that street because I was a real entrepreneur."

With misty eyes, Jennifer recalled, "Kristin and I were classmates and could walk to the school together along paved, tree-shaded paths. I remember her in the fourth, fifth, and sixth grades, and then later in seventh and eighth grades at Colina Middle School, in Thousand Oaks. It's a blue-ribbon school. And then we moved over to Westlake High. By this time, we were great friends. She spent a lot of time with my family too. Like, if Kristi and her mom would get in a little fight or something, she would come over and stay in our guest room. My mom looked at her like another daughter and always sided with Kristi when we had fights. I was the wild one. In high school, I had a boyfriend right away, like when I was fourteen. And I don't remember exactly who she dated, but I know all the guys wanted to go out with her. She was so outgoing. This is one thing I can tell—she was always the life of the party."

Rick acted as big brother and covert protector to Kristin. "I was a senior and she was a freshman. She was cute and a lot of guys liked her, but I let them know that I was there to see that nothing happened to her. I don't think she ever realized that."

If Jennifer took on the role of another sister to Kristin, then her real sibling Robin soon became a de facto mother. It came about as the result of yet another divorce.

Peter recalled the breakup. "Marie and I separated and went our different ways. I moved out and took only what I could carry in my car. All the kids were teenagers at the time. I stayed around the area, of course, and got to see them a fair amount." He resettled in Simi Valley, about fourteen miles northeast of Westlake Village, and eventually took a beautiful new bride named Sue.

Looking back, Robin recalled, "When I turned eighteen, my parents were getting a divorce, so I was sort of the mom for Kristin and my little sister, Stephanie. My mother, newly divorced, went back to work and spent time finding herself. This put me in the motherly mode. It was no problem for me. Instead of being sisters, it was more like a mother-daughter relationship with both Kristin and Stephanie. They needed me and accepted me in the role of mom."

To Rick, the divorce meant fewer restrictions on the kids. "Mom worked at night and usually didn't get home until about three o'clock in the morning. So we pretty much had the run of the house. Our friends discovered this, and a lot of them would come over and hang out. It was like the neighborhood party house. All hell would break loose, especially in the summer when school was out."

At Westlake High School, the camaraderie between Jennifer and Kristin grew even stronger. "We took the bus together. She was an excellent student and was very smart—always pleasant, very witty. It's no exaggeration to say she was always one of the most gregarious and admired kids. In our yearbook, Kristi was singled out as the most popular girl. She had a million friends."

Peter Means also recognized Kristin's esteem among her peers. "It is correct that she was elected as most popular. She was a real social person and friends with everyone, with no fear of people. Kristin would talk to anyone, no matter what social level, rich or poor. She loved working with handicapped kids and volunteered with an Easter Seals group. The kids adored her because she was a lot of fun. Bubbly and outgoing, she could relate to them."

At the time they first moved to Westlake Village, Robin and Kristin were impressed with the knowledge that numerous celebrities lived in the enclave. Robin said, "Of course, growing up there, we had a lot of stars in our lives. Every summer we went to Catalina Island for ten days. We met Arnell Simpson, O.J.'s daughter there. She was a good friend of ours. In our neighborhood, we often saw Heather Locklear and Courteney Cox. Her dad was friends with my dad. We often ran into celebrities. Jayne Mansfield's son grew up in Westlake and was best friends with Vicky, who was my best friend. So we were always interacting with someone who had links to celebrity. We'd go to the Malibu chili cook-off and see Charlie Sheen and his brother Emilio Estevez. That was all part of being raised where we were. We spent a lot of time in the beach area, especially at Malibu. As we got older, we were no longer awed by celebrities. We realized they were just regular people too."

Kristin's exposure to people in show business inspired a growing fantasy. Her bright mind, creative wit, trim stature, and mesmerizing emerald green eyes gave her the potential to fit right into the Hollywood scene. Early on, she appeared to have entertainment skills. Robin spoke of her terrific knack for hearing people's accents and imitating them perfectly. "She made it hilarious. She had a great sense of humor and was always laughing. We can thank our father, Peter, for that. He is a very intelligent man and taught us that humor can get you through hard times. She was always in the spotlight and wanted to be an actress. But she never made any real plans to do anything about it. She just said, maybe someday."

Jennifer agreed. "She did. She told me she wanted to be in movies someday."

All four of Marie's children had been legally adopted by Peter Means, so they all took his surname. Later, though, Kristin would revert to Baldwin for a convenient reason. Peter knew all about it and understood.

Rudyard Kipling wrote, *Never praise a sister to a sister. . . .* If he had lived to know Robin, Kristin, and Stephanie, Kipling might have rescinded his comment. These siblings generously praised one another mutually or to anyone else who would listen. In introducing Kristin to strangers, Robin would proudly say, "This is my sister."

CHAPTER 3

A SAD RIDDLE

Detectives Christopher Fisher and Mike Gilliam, of the San Bernardino County Sheriff's Department (SBCSD), Homicide Unit, sped across the desert and arrived at the body discovery site a little before noon. They realized that the witnesses, Allura McGehay, Robert LaFond, and Christopher DeWitt, had been wilting in the blazing heat too long. After interviewing them briefly and noting vital information, Gilliam released the two men so they could continue to their original destinations.

A tow truck had shown up prior to the detectives' arrival and had pulled Allura's Dodge pickup out of the sandy shoulder trap. She, too, breathed a sigh of relief when they allowed her to leave.

Accompanied by forensic specialists, Fisher and Gilliam inspected the body more closely. Gilliam observed that the decedent not only wore a gold-colored wristwatch, but also a bracelet, ring, and earrings. The presence of jewelry certainly didn't rule out robbery, but it suggested other possible motives for her death and disposal in the desert wash. No purse or identification papers could be found, so she would be categorized as a Jane Doe for the time being.

Scrutinizing the face, almost devoid of flesh, Gilliam thought he could see damage to the skull, especially around the nasal cavity. This injury could possibly be related to the cause of death, perhaps a blunt-force trauma or even a gunshot wound. Of course, it would take a careful autopsy to deal with those issues.

Another interesting fact caught Gilliam's attention. Even though the fingers had been dehydrated, blackened, and shrunken by the sun, the fingernails remained in perfect shape. The neat manicure made a jarring contrast between decayed flesh and the nails still radiating a lifelike glow.

The victim's clothing had been ravaged by weather. What remained appeared to be a tank top and a pink bra, both pushed up high so they encircled the body under her armpits. A pair of shorts, sheer and possibly white, clung to her lower body. Positioning of the pitiful rags could suggest a possible sexual assault.

Detective Fisher took extensive photos of the human remains, the bridge, and the surrounding terrain. Standing on the bridge's shoulder, he tried to decide if the person who had dumped the body had carried it down to the wash or had dropped it from the bridge. Since only the victim's arm protruded from the dark underside, it looked to the detective that someone must have lugged the body down there. Still, Fisher couldn't rule out the possibility that the corpse, perhaps still in rigor mortis, had been dropped the six or eight feet from above, and had tumbled partially under the structure.

Neither investigator could be certain the woman could ever be identified. Yet, the timing of the miraculous discovery, attributable to Allura McGehay's bad luck at getting stuck in the sand, at least left some window of opportunity for identification. In just a few more days of blazing heat, the body and shards of clothing would have been deteriorated beyond any chance of recognition.

Deputy Doug Alexander had already photographed the shoes worn by Robert LaFond and Christopher DeWitt to eliminate footprints they had left near the body. Now the sleuths meticulously searched the perimeter for other prints, cigarette butts, or anything that might be related to the victim's death. Several plastic bottles and aluminum cans were collected, bagged, and tagged. The team sifted sand and gravel, looking for possible bullets or fragments. Nothing useful turned up.

After coroner's technicians loaded the corpse into a van for transportation to the coroner's office, Gilliam knew he couldn't yet rest. Amazingly, two other dead female bodies were found in the vicinity that same weekend.

All three victims of savage depravity were transported to the coroner's office. In the case of the Jane Doe found near Daggett, the possibility of identification through fingerprints at first appeared to be zero. But, despite the terrible condition of her leatherlike flesh, one of the specialists decided to try a recently developed method. The Microsil process involves using a pastelike substance that contains silicone to form a cast. Forensic uses for the procedure include lifting finger-prints from difficult surfaces, preparing a three dimensional replica of a human bite mark in flesh, and to cast prints from fingers that have been subjected to advanced decomposition. Incredibly, it worked. A set of fingerprints, even if imperfect, at least offered a chance for an opening gambit in solving a sad riddle of probable murder.

CHAPTER 4
"I'LL NEVER FORGET THAT DAY"

The mysterious discovery of an unidentified female body in the desert near Daggett would eventually have a profound impact on the lives of two dynamic women in Hollywood. Detective Vicki Bynum and her supervisor, Detective Wendi Berndt, veteran members of the Los Angeles Police Department (LAPD), worked at one of the most well-known police headquarters in the country, the historic Hollywood Station. Vicki Bynum, gentle and soft-spoken with a hint of mirth constantly in her blue eyes, had started as a patrol officer in 1989. Her veteran supervisor, Wendi Berndt, articulate and captivating, would bring to classic film buffs' minds the remarkable actor-director Ida Lupino. Berndt had been in the Hollywood Station twenty-six of her twenty-eight years as a cop. Both of the bright and impressive women maintained their femininity while keeping an equal footing with thick-skinned male colleagues.

* * *

Another former LAPD officer, famed author Joseph Wambaugh, has used the Hollywood Station as a venue for numerous action-packed novels. He also immortalized it with his first true-crime book, *The Onion Field,* in which he chronicled the 1963 murder of Officer Ian Campbell. Visitors to the building cannot fail to notice seven prominent star shapes decorating the entrance pavement. They are cast in the same style as the Hollywood Walk of Fame, which features more than 2,400 pink terrazzo stars embedded in darker-colored sidewalks along the streets of Tinseltown, each one containing the name of a celebrity. The seven stars at the LAPD station memorialize officers who died in the line of duty, including Ian Campbell.

In two of his recent books, *Hollywood Station* and *Hollywood Moon,* Wambaugh acknowledges Vicki Bynum and Wendi Berndt as sources of information. The author expertly weaves real-life places, people, and events into both works of fiction. The title *Hollywood Moon* refers to bizarre events and crimes that occur when a full moon illuminates the entertainment capital.

One of Wambaugh's fictional cops in *Hollywood Moon* describes to his colleagues a hideous double murder that ranked among the weirdest in the station's history. It proved that bloodcurdling events can occur even when the glowing orb above is only half covered by Planet Earth's shadow. The perpetrator, the narrator states, entered the house of a ninety-one-year-old retired screenwriter and "cut the guy's head off" with a meat cleaver. The victim had been a blacklisted screenwriter who coauthored a movie called *Bud Abbott and Lou Costello Meet Frankenstein.* According to Wambaugh's fictional detective, the killer then carried the head to a house next door, broke in, and murdered the occupant: a sixty-nine-year-old retired and recently married doctor.

If readers think this gruesome scenario came from the

author's imagination, they underestimate the sometimes insidious nature of Hollywood. The stunning crime actually occurred in June 2004. And Wambaugh's character does not mention that Vicki Bynum was one of the investigators!

In real life, the murdered screenwriter, Robert Lees, had worked as a minor actor at the beginning of his career. He appeared as a bellboy in the 1932 classic *Grand Hotel,* starring Greta Garbo, John Barrymore, and Joan Crawford. The next year, Lees showed up as a dancer in another Crawford film, *Dancing Lady,* costarring Clark Gable.

Unable to break out as an actor, Lees turned to screenwriting and achieved notable success. Between 1935 and 1952, he helped create scripts for thirty-seven films, including two comedies starring Bud Abbott and Lou Costello. Afterward, he penned scores of television episodes. Unfortunately, Lees faced the House Un-American Activities Committee (HUAC) during the McCarthy era of witch-hunting for Communists in the early 1950s. Lees invoked his Fifth Amendment rights, and found himself on an extensive roster of blacklisted writers. He continued to work under the pen name of J. E. Selby.

Long after his retirement, and the 1982 death of his wife, Lees lived peacefully in his Hollywood bungalow. On the other side of a fence, at the back of his property, lived a retired doctor, Morley Engelson.

In early June 2004, former U.S. Marine Keven Graff, age twenty-seven, wandered aimlessly along Selma Avenue after dark. Dirty, shoulder-length brown hair curled over his ears and forehead, and a three-day growth of beard shadowed his wide jaws. Graff came to Courtney Avenue, crossed over it, and entered Robert Lees's yard. Convicted just a month earlier of gross lewdness in Las Vegas, Nevada, along with petty theft, resisting arrest, and possession of drugs, Graff had been released on bail. He drove his pickup to Hollywood, where he found solace in using methamphetamine and shouting quotes from the Bible to anyone who would listen.

Graff broke into the retired screenwriter's house, snatched a meat cleaver and a butcher knife in the kitchen, and cornered Lees in a bedroom. No one but the killer knows why he carried out the incredibly savage attack. Using the sharp instruments, he beheaded the elderly victim, sliced his penis off, and carved out his heart. Graff grabbed a belt and ran it through the severed head's mouth until the large buckle lodged against the lips and teeth. He looped it through the throat opening, making an improvised carrying strap. Holding his bloody prize, along with the knife and cleaver, Graff exited the house, crossed the backyard, and vaulted over the wooden fence. He landed in Morley Engelson's property.

The retired doctor didn't hear Graff silently climb through an open window. Having telephoned Southwest Airlines to make reservations for a planned trip with his recent bride, Engelson devoted his attention to the conversation. His wife was out at that time.

On the other end of the line, the agent was in the middle of routinely explaining flight arrangements when she heard screaming and the sounds of a scuffle. She immediately called the LAPD (from her Arizona workplace) and Hollywood officers were dispatched to the house. Upon their arrival, they found an open window.

Inside, the officers discovered Engelson's nearly nude body, dressed only in white socks and a gray sweatshirt pulled up to his neck. An attempt had been made to behead and emasculate him too. It would be later theorized that the killer had heard noises outside and left before he could complete the job.

In another bedroom, investigators recoiled at a stunning sight. On the corner of a soft white comforter, neatly covering a king-sized bed, reposed the bloodied head of Robert Lees! A round belt buckle with a raised black-and-red five-point star covered the mouth, while the leather belt extended from the throat and onto the white fabric. One of the eyes had been gouged out. Few people have ever witnessed a more sickening vision. Not even a Quentin Tarantino film would have gone this far.

At about the same time as the excruciating discovery, a woman who had tried unsuccessfully to call Lees showed up at his house and nearly fainted upon seeing his mutilated body.

Every detail of the macabre event had been permanently etched in the mind of Detective Vicki Bynum, even though she has wished she could use a delete key to cleanse her memory.

"I'll never forget that day," she said with a grimace. "I think it was Sunday—a beautiful day. Got the call to come in and meet with Liz, another detective, who now works cold cases. We were briefed by officers, who were really creeped out. At least we had the luxury of knowing they had already gone through the house and made sure no suspect was in there. We learned the victim had been on the phone making reservations with Southwest Airlines. He and his wife were going on a trip. She, thank God, had gone out shopping. All the windows were open, and none of them had screens. The house is a lovely old bungalow type, on the west side of our division. Dr. Engelson had been playing classical music while talking on the phone.

"Fortunately, the airline agent had already taken down his address and phone number. The psycho comes from the house where he had decapitated the first victim, and carried the head with him like a purse. He crawled through Dr. Engelson's window while carrying that head. This poor guy is on the phone, sees this grisly sight, and gets attacked. The Southwest agent hears it and calls the police. Officers respond. There is blood outside. They look through the window and see someone lying on the hardwood floor. I get there and they are explaining this to us. We went in, very gingerly. I remember the first victim, a neighbor, had been mutilated. His penis had been severed and it was lying next to him. The assailant had also used a fireplace poker to stab him. The whole scene was as gruesome as it gets. So, in Engelson's house, Liz and I are going through it and we get to a back bedroom. Officers on the scene hadn't warned us. We are like, 'What is that on the bed?' We get closer and it's the head of the previous victim, with the belt buckle, like a star shape, pulled tight against the mouth." At that moment, Bynum wondered if she really wanted to stick with the job.

Keven Graff had stolen Engelson's car and driven to Hollywood Boulevard, where he abandoned it. Investigators found ample fingerprints at both crime scenes and they expedited computer identification. Within hours they started searching for Graff. LAPD chief William Bratton arranged for the suspect's photo to appear on several local television stations. On Monday afternoon, an alert guard spotted him just outside the famous gate of Paramount Studios and called the police.

It took four years to bring Graff to justice. In April 2008, he pled guilty to double murder and was sentenced to serve life in prison without the possibility of parole. Prosecutors welcomed the plea, concerned that a jury could have believed Graff's attorney, who asserted that his client was "very, very mentally ill."

Vicki Bynum had never even considered a law enforcement career while growing up. She wound up with the LAPD almost by accident.

A native of San Antonio, Texas, she and her two younger brothers traveled extensively as children. Their father, a pilot in the U.S. Air Force, moved approximately every three years, from one military base to another. Vicki regretted being unable to remember their time in Europe, and the birth of her first brother in Paris, but she couldn't be expected to since those events occurred between her third and fifth birthdays.

A third brother arrived after the family landed in Wichita,

Kansas. While he still wore diapers, the next assignment took them to Tampa, Florida. "My parents bought a beautiful home there, close to the beach, for about thirty thousand dollars." She loved it, but hated the absence of her dad while he served in Vietnam. "When he came home, they transferred him to North Dakota. It was horrible. And they made an awful mistake by selling the Florida home." The property's value today would exceed a million dollars.

She attended three years at Red River High School in Grand Forks, and nearly froze to death. Before Vicki's senior year, her father decided to retire from the military and move to Danville, Illinois, the state where he and his wife had been born. "It was basically just a little cow town," says Vicki. "Not much to do except drive around the cornfields and have a drinkfest now and then." She graduated from Danville High School, which had originally opened in 1870 and counted among its alumni actors Gene Hackman, Dick Van Dyke, and Jerry Van Dyke.

Vicki chose Southern Illinois University (SIU) to continue her education. She laughed when she recalled that the sports teams were known as the "Salukis," a name chosen in 1951, after the dog breed that enjoyed royalty status in ancient Egypt. Not yet certain what profession she wanted to enter, Vicki majored in education. "I thought about being a teacher, but spent way too much time having fun in those first two years. I quit school and on a whim went with two friends to Tucson, Arizona, with the intention of completing my education. I had lived there once when my dad was stationed at Davis-Monthan Air Force Base. But my school plans didn't work out."

A few months later, she returned to SIU, changed her major to recreation therapy, and graduated in 1979. "My goal was to work with special populations—handicapped people or veterans. But when applying for jobs, I saw a lot of raised eyebrows, like 'recreation therapy?' There didn't seem to be a huge demand for that specialty."

Not long after receiving her degree, Vicki moved to California. "I had a boyfriend at the time and he came out here to Los Angeles. Like most stupid young girls, I followed my heart and came to L.A. The second I got here, I found that he had already discovered the beach littered with countless beautiful women. He lost interest in this little Saluki. But that was okay. Everything happens for a reason, and I always try to turn a negative into a positive."

With very little money saved, and no friends, Vicki went job hunting. She landed one as a recreation therapist at a downtown Los Angeles senior citizens home, in a building across the street from MacArthur Park, where some of the city's less well-to-do population congregated. "I knew nothing about Los Angeles—had no clue. I worked there about three months and it was an interesting job. I met some fascinating people, including a person who had been in Lawrence Welk's band, a Holocaust survivor, and a former Nazi woman. It didn't take long, though, to realize that this was not my forte; much too depressing. People I became fond of got sick and passed away. That was kind of hard."

Considering a career at the Veterans Administration (VA), Vicki discovered that she would need additional education to become a registered therapist. Instead, she found employment with the city of Hermosa Beach doing clerical work for the police department. "I met another female employee, who owned a duplex right near the sand. Perfect! I am twenty-five, working for the city, living by the beach, working nights and enjoying the surfside atmosphere in the daytime. The duplex owner had a lifelong dream of becoming a police officer and talked about it all the time.

"Some of the guys I worked around seemed pretty dumb to me," Vicki recalled. One of them, though, made her heart flutter. He told Vicki of his floundering marriage, that he had filed for divorce, and then asked her to go out with him. She refused until the divorce would become final. He agreed; and when it came through, Vicki began dating him. At the beginning of their relationship, his participation in a notoriously gory murder case consumed a great deal of time and visibly impacted his psyche. It involved a couple of career criminals, Lawrence Bittaker and Roy Norris, who had met in prison and jointly fantasized about raping and killing teenage girls after getting out. Following their paroles, the pair reunited, and one of them bought a van. In the summer and fall of 1979, they turned the vehicle into an abattoir. The thugs kidnapped six females, five of them ranging from ages thirteen to eighteen.

In the back bed of the van, the savage pair raped and tortured the five teenage victims, using vise grips, pliers, and an ice pick before strangling each of them to death with wire hangers. The only adult woman, age thirty, escaped after they sexually assaulted her.

Criminals often make the error of boasting to cronies about their conquests. One of these "pals" heard details of the horrific murders and called the police. After Bittaker and Norris were arrested, evidence collected from the van included photographs and a hideous audiotape of an eighteen-year-old girl pitifully screaming as she was tortured to death. The adult victim who escaped identified her captors and their vehicle.

Facing potential capital punishment, Roy Norris testified against Lawrence Bittaker, accusing him of the actual killings. Found guilty, Norris received a sentence of forty-five years to life, while Bittaker was sent to San Quentin's death row.

The case, even though solved and adjudicated, resulted in symptoms of post-traumatic stress disorder with nearly everyone involved. The man Vicki dated had worked long hours on it. She wondered if it may have been a factor in the divorce. It certainly induced nightmares for years. (Vicki helped him through the trauma and eventually married him. He passed away in 1987.)

Meanwhile, her friend at the duplex convinced Vicki to accompany her to an LAPD recruitment drive. "We drove up to the academy. They have a program for interested candidates where they work out with you and get you in shape to take the test. I went along only to observe, but someone convinced me to apply. They said that since I had a college degree, I probably wouldn't have to take the written exam, kind of like army recruiters. So, just for the heck of it, I took the physical and passed. The degree did help by eliminating the need for a written test and starting me at a better salary."

Hired in 1981, Vicki Bynum started as a patrol officer in the beach community of Venice, adjacent to Santa Monica. Police work, she said, was like wearing many hats. "Out on the streets, you are not just a cop. You are a teacher, a psychiatrist, and a protector. I became fascinated with it. The job was fun, exciting, and well paid. So I pretty much fell into it by accident."

One of the first training officers assigned to rookie Bynum was Charlie Beck. He would later become LAPD chief in November 2009. This enabled her to say, with that incandescent twinkle in her eyes and a charming smile, "Now I can call him Chief Charlie."

The city of Venice had originally been designed and named to emulate the famous Italian site on the Adriatic Sea. But the canals in California's Venice had long since dried up, turned into receptacles for trash, and were finally paved over. The city's wide stretch of sand and palm trees earned the sobriquet "Muscle Beach" in the 1950s. Over the decades, a series of amusement parks sprang up on oceanfront piers, the last one, in 1958, called Pacific Ocean Park. But they all failed and vanished. Notable musicians, from Lawrence Welk to Spade Cooley and even the Doors, performed for television from local venues. Venice Beach's famed boardwalk, with its eclectic lineup of merchants, still attracts throngs of visitors throughout the year. For the most part, the community is safe, but some of the rougher edges are plagued by crime.

"Venice was an eye-opening experience," Vicki Bynum recalled. "I was assigned the night watch, and stupid me, I rode my bike to work all the way from Hermosa Beach, about ten miles. I was very much in shape at the time. But my training officer scolded me and put a stop to that because he said it was too dangerous."

After three years in the beach area, the brass reassigned Bynum to LAPD's Communications Division downtown. "It was really disappointing to do desk work after being a gunslinger out on the streets. Right before the 1984 Olympics in L.A., they pushed us out because they needed a lot of cops on the street." She found herself working skid row, patrol at first and then vice, from 1984 to 1988. After that came an administration assignment, to ease the strain on the widowed mother. Another patrol job came next in the Hollenbeck Division, which contains some tough areas in East L.A. "I got tired of that because there were big fights every night." Another move took her undercover for five years in the vice squad, in which Bynum participated in the arrest of the notorious Heidi Fleiss, known as the "Hollywood Madam," who allegedly provided prostitutes for the rich and famous.

More undercover work followed in the Rampart Division West, of downtown Los Angeles. "We tackled slumlords, drug dealers and gangs. Jeans and tennis shoes were my uniform."

Finally Bynum took the test to become a detective and aced it. She worked Hollenbeck again, partnered with Tom Herman. He later headed up the investigation of Rebecca Salcedo and her two cousins, Alvaro and Jose Quezada, who conspired to kill Rebecca's husband, Bruce Cleland (*Honeymoon with a Killer,* Kensington, 2009).

Regarding Detective Herman, Bynum laughed. "He was kind of a cowboy type, like George Jones, and always wore his jeans too tight. In one of my last days working with him, a request came for units to assist in a perimeter. Some suspects had been pinpointed in a specific area, and they needed officers to cover different points. Tom and I somehow got separated. A helicopter gave instructions from overhead. I heard its radio saying, 'Female detective, female detective, suspect running your way.' I look around and I'm all alone. The guy came right toward me and almost ran into me. I start chasing him, running. The chopper overhead. I'm thinking, 'What am I doing?' I'm yelling at this guy, 'You had better stop. I don't want to shoot you.' I wasn't going to, but I figured I'd better scare him. In this high, little-girl voice I'm yelling, 'I'm going to shoot you. You better lay down.' I turn around. 'Where's Tom?' I had lost him. For years afterward, I kidded him, and said the reason he wasn't able to keep up was because his jeans were too tight. He couldn't run."

Other team members captured the suspect.

Bynum didn't want to leave Hollenbeck, but her one-year trial period as a detective had expired, necessitating a change of location. "I put in for Hollywood, thinking it would be an exciting place to work. Before the deadline, I came over and introduced myself to the Robbery Detail supervisor, hoping for an opening. I was lucky. I served in the Robbery Unit first, then Gangs, and then to Homicide in 1997."

Maintaining her fine sense of humor and soft-spoken demeanor, Vicki earned the respect of her peers and bosses. At Bynum's desk in the Hollywood Station, just above and to the right of her computer screen, can be seen photos of her two best pals; Bella, her "chubby Chihuahua," and her miniature pinscher, Topaz, both acquired as gifts from her daughter.

Ten years into her tenure as a homicide detective, Vicki Bynum heard the name Kristin Baldwin for the first time.

CHAPTER 5
SHOT IN THE FACE

A confusing chain of communication triggered an investigation in LAPD's Hollywood Station. It began late at night on May 31, 2007—sixteen days before the discovery of an unidentified body in the desert near Daggett.

In Orange County, south of Los Angeles, an enigmatic caller to 911 stated that a murder had taken place in Hollywood on May 27. The receiving agency relayed it to the Orange County Sheriff's Department (OCSD), which forwarded the information to the Los Angeles Police Department. At one of the stations, an officer thought it sounded like a prank call and hung up. The caller persisted and tried again. From LAPD, the report was forwarded by a radio telephone operator (RTO) to the night watch at the Hollywood Station. By this time, the clock had ticked past midnight.

At the desk in Hollywood, in the first half hour of June 1, Officer Tracey Fields received information that an unidentified male caller had said he was a witness to a homicide at a Cole Crest Drive address. The crime had occurred on Sunday, May 27. The informant said that his roommate, David Alan Mahler, shot a woman in the face and later asked for help in disposing of the body. Unwilling to identify himself, the caller left numbers where he could be reached, fell silent, and hung up.

Officer Fields, on temporary duty answering telephones due to her advanced pregnancy, notified her watch commander, who contacted Detective Ray Conboy, on duty as the night watch detective.

Conboy recalled the convoluted sequence. "I called the three numbers I had for the PR (person reporting). There were no answers, but I left voice mail messages on all of them giving numbers for my cellular phone and the Hollywood desk. At 0125 hours, I called my supervisor, Detective Wendi Berndt. She advised me to conduct a follow-up at the residence."

With twenty-eight years of experience behind her, Wendi Berndt not only had achieved admirable success, but had also retained a youthful, attractive appearance. Exceptionally bright, she had worked her way up the ladder from raw recruit to Detective III, in charge of homicide investigations in the Hollywood Station. Originally from Wichita, Kansas, Berndt had married and moved to New York, where she earned a degree in police science. In the small township of Montgomery, New York, Berndt went directly to the police chief and told him she would like to apply for a job. He promised to get back to her and kept his word a few days later. Recalling it with a laugh, Berndt said, "I got two calls. In the first one, he said, 'I'm sorry, but we can't take you on because we don't know how male officers' wives would react to their husbands working with a female.' The second call came after what I imagined to be a discussion with their legal department. This time he said, 'Okay, you know what? We're going to accept you.' I said, 'Great. What do I do?' I was wondering if they would send me to an academy or provide some special training. He said, 'Just go out and get a gun and come to work.'"

Speaking between bursts of laughter, Berndt continued. "Well, I went out and bought a .357 Magnum. And then I'm thinking, 'I don't believe I really want to do this.' The whole Montgomery force at that time was about four people." Berndt postponed her ambitions and focused on keeping a shaky marriage together. It didn't work.

After a painful divorce, she launched a job search in major cities, which included interviews in Los Angeles and Houston, Texas. Just prior to a trip to Kansas City, she received an offer from Houston. "Actually, I really wanted to work for the LAPD, so I turned Houston down. I came here and was accepted. Just like everyone else, I started as a recruit. Unless recruits are fired, they become a police officer and serve a period of probation."

As a patrol officer in Hollywood, Berndt inevitably encountered celebrities. She recalled being dispatched, along with paramedics, to the home of Orson Welles when he died. His amazing obesity has stuck in her mind. "He was up in a second-story bedroom. The man was huge. I've never in my life seen anything like the size of his ankles, like elephant legs. That memory has stayed with me all these years."

Berndt knew right away she wanted to be a detective and began working toward that goal. "For twenty-six of my twenty-eight years, I have been in Hollywood. I was in uniform for nine years before making D-I, the first step as a detective." She worked cases from 1990 to 1995, and then accepted a promotion to supervisor in 1996.

In the early-morning hours of Saturday, June 2, 2007, from her bedroom at home, Wendi Berndt spoke by telephone to Detective Conboy. He had a remarkably odd case on his hands. An anonymous report had been telephoned from another county. The unknown informant had spoken of a woman being shot by someone named David Mahler several days earlier. However, no unexplained reports had been received of a dead body or a wounded victim.

Retrospectively discussing the case, Wendi Berndt said, "Ray called me and told me that a call had come in about a murder up at a house in the hills. He got the address and said that a suspect known to the caller had done it. I realized we didn't have enough information to go out and kick in the door, but certainly could go there and knock. I asked Ray, 'Can you get some more information?'"

Conboy went into action. He recalled, "At 0145 hours, I received notification on my cellular phone that the PR's call was transferred to the Communications Division by the Orange County Communications Center. He reported that a man killed a lady and came to his door and wanted help to dispose of the body. At 0200 hours, the Hollywood Desk called to say the PR had called the station and was on hold. I advised the desk officer to have the PR call my cellular phone."

At last, four minutes after two o'clock, Conboy spoke to the mysterious informant and learned that his name was Karl Norvik (pseudonym).

Norvik's voice throbbed with stress as he spoke of spending Saturday night, May 26, and Sunday at the house up on Cole Crest Drive. He had heard shouting and screaming coming from the bedroom of David Mahler, the leaseholder and manager. At about six twenty-five, Sunday morning, Norvik said, he had been awakened by the sounds of hard knocking on the door of his studio apartment, two levels below Mahler's quarters. He responded and found Mahler at his door. Mahler had said, "I need to dispose of a dead body."

According to Norvik, Mahler led him upstairs to his bedroom, where he looked in and saw the deceased body of a white female dressed in white pants of a thin material and a halter top. It appeared to Norvik that she had been shot in the face. He left Mahler's room and returned to his own quarters. He said that he did not help Mahler move the dead woman.

Later that day, said Norvik, he left the location and went to a relative's home in Orange County. He wanted the detective to understand that his delay in reporting the crime stemmed from a mortal fear of David Mahler.

Now armed with salient facts, Conboy once again reached Wendi Berndt. She retrospectively said, "Ray contacted me and said he had personally talked to the informant. So I said, 'Go ahead up to the house and knock to see if anyone is there.'"

Berndt also contacted a sergeant in the Hollywood Gang Enforcement Detail and requested some backup for Detective Conboy. Several officers headed up to the scene. "Ray drove up to Cole Crest, did what I asked, and called again. No one was answering the locked front gate. Now, this is all after one thirty in the morning. I said, 'Ray, tell them to kick the door. We need to go in. You've got firsthand information that a murder occurred at that location.'

"As it turned out, we didn't have to kick the gate or the door in. A resident of the building, a man named Jeremy Moudy, came to the front entry, which is a locked gate and opened it up."

Jeremy Moudy had occupied the studio apartment, just below Mahler's rooms, for a couple of years. Sometimes his girlfriend stayed overnight. A construction worker, Moudy stood well over six feet tall, with a muscular build. Handsome and youthful in appearance, at age thirty, he kept a dark mustache and short beard neatly trimmed.

Courteous and calm, Jeremy invited the officers inside. He explained that he lived downstairs in a studio apartment. The leaseholder and manager, a man named David Mahler, occupied the upper floors. Just below Jeremy's bedroom, in a subdivided unit, lived a guy named Karl Norvik. Conboy recognized that name as the mysterious caller's. Another guy, said Jeremy, lived in the bottom apartment. While Mahler, Norvik, and the other tenant all interconnected socially, Moudy said, he kept his privacy and seldom even spoke to the other three. He did observe "a lot of women" coming and going in the upper floors occupied by Mahler. On numerous occasions, he had heard sounds of arguing upstairs, with women's voices shrieking their anger. He had also noticed a green-and-white minivan parked in front of the garage many times.

Explaining that a report had been received of a possible homicide at this address, the police asked Jeremy Moudy's permission to have a look around. He offered no objections.

As they filed into the short corridor, one of the uniformed cops, Bill Wilson, noticed a door to his left standing open. To be certain no suspect might be hiding in there, or any bodies were stowed, he aimed his flashlight beam into the area and saw that it was a garage in which two, sleek, dark-colored vehicles were parked. As he moved the circle of light back and forth, Wilson saw something else. On the floor, he spotted several stains of what appeared to be blood. He informed Sergeant Aikens and Detective Conboy.

Following routine protocol, they initiated a "protective sweep" of the entire residence to see if any "victims down" might need physical or medical help. As they explored the living room, stairs, and master bedroom, more stains that looked like blood appeared.

Bill Wilson and another officer descended a switchback staircase into a lower level, in which they found no one, and then into Moudy's rooms. Jeremy had told them of his girlfriend still asleep in his bedroom. The cops courteously knocked and allowed her a few minutes to get dressed before continuing the "sweep."

Entering a large, deep walk-in closet inside the bedroom, Wilson observed a makeshift shelf that had been built four feet above the floor to store a pile of clothing, boxes, blankets, and a suitcase. He shined his flashlight at the stack of clothing and thought he saw something move. Reaching into the clutter, Wilson pushed some of the material aside and looked into the stricken face of a man crouched in a fetal position.

The foiled evader's skin turned pale and then reddened in embarrassment as he climbed down to the floor. He admitted to the officer that he was David Mahler, resident of the upper apartment.

Bill Wilson and his companion officer escorted Mahler upstairs into the office and kept an eye on him, pending orders from a supervisor.

At the bottom of the exterior stairs, still a few minutes before three o'clock, another pair of cops knocked on a door until they heard someone stirring inside. Donnie Van Develde opened it, stood there with saucer eyes, and almost shouted, "I know why you are here! David killed that girl. Her name was Kristi. I never saw the body, but I saw it wrapped in a blanket, and I think I saw her arm. This is bad! I didn't have anything to do with it. David was tweaking." The cops understood that "tweaking," in street lexicon, meant using methamphetamine.

Detective Conboy made another telephone call to his supervisor. "Wendi," he said, "we've got blood at this location. And guess what? We also have David Mahler, the guy our informant named. He was hiding in one of the other occupants' closet. And that's not all. We have another renter, a guy named Donnie Van Develde, a witness who might have seen the body."

"Transport them to the station," Berndt ordered. She also directed some of the officers to stay at the location, secure it, and wait for a search warrant to continue the probe. Officers escorted David Mahler and Donald "Donnie" Van Develde to a pair of patrol cars and transported them separately to the Hollywood Station. Jeremy Moudy agreed also to be interviewed at the headquarters. Wendi Berndt allowed him to drive his own car so he could leave after giving his statement.

Everything so far pointed toward a probable killing.

Berndt decided to call in two of the best detectives ever to work the Hollywood Homicide Unit.

With the sun still at least three hours below the eastern horizon, Detective Vicki Bynum answered her phone and instinctively jumped out of bed. Thirty miles away, her partner on this case, Detective Tom Small, didn't think twice about being summoned in predawn darkness. It came with the territory.

Now and then, detectives find it a little inconvenient to be called out.

In real life, as well as in whodunit movies or novels, humor becomes an essential element of psychological survival for homicide detectives. They believe the old axiom that laughter is the best medicine. Often, in recalling grim events, they lighten it up with hilarious asides. Wendi Berndt, Vicki Bynum, and Tom Small were no exceptions. Discussing the opening stages of the David Mahler case and the early-morning call-outs, they couldn't resist telling a story about one of their colleagues.

Berndt started it by saying, "As a supervisor, I've heard every excuse in the world for not coming to work today. One time when I was in a grocery store, my phone rings. I was too busy to pick up and it went to voice mail. A little later I listened to it, and one of my detectives didn't want to come to work. The voice mail message said, in a pitifully croaky voice, 'Hey, I'm really sick. Gotta stay in bed. I'm just really, really sick.'

"A little bit later, my phone rang again and I accessed this second call. He had accidentally done something to have his phone redial after the first call. And he didn't know it. So what I hear is a recording of him having a wild romp with his girlfriend, 'Yahoo, oohhh, ohhh.'

Laughing so hard she could hardly talk, Bynum added, "We heard someone say, 'Spank the monkey.'"

Also chuckling, Small tossed in, "You can tell he is running all through the house."

Berndt said, "So the next day, everybody is gathered around, and the three of us are asking him, 'Are you feeling better?' I said, 'Just after I heard from you, I got another message and I can't figure out who made the call.' I played the second message. We are all circled around my cell phone and he is listening carefully. And when he heard 'spank the monkey,' he knew he was busted."

Small said, "We have this binder we call 'The Stupid Book.' It is a record of all the dumb things detectives have done, all the way back to the 1980s. So I ask him to explain 'spank the monkey.' He came up with the biggest BS story I've ever heard. He told us, 'Well, I was at my girlfriend's and we just got this brand-new TV set. She's got a kid and we call him 'the monkey.' And I was playing with him—like, 'Come here, I'm going to spank the monkey.'"

Small made certain this explanation landed in The Stupid Book.

Neither Detectives Vicki Bynum nor Tom Small claimed to be sick when Berndt summoned them to Hollywood long before dawn on that June morning.

Night watch Detective Conboy's shift would soon be ending, so Berndt dispatched Detective Larry Cameron, another member of her Homicide Unit, to relieve him. Berndt also left the station to join Cameron at the scene. To her, it was important to supervise an investigation in person, not from a desk. As soon as the expedited search warrant was approved, the hunt intensified.

As Cameron and other officers looked for a possible murder victim and any associated evidence, Berndt not only observed and directed—she also participated. Later speaking of it, she said, "There was no noticeable odor. If a body had been there since Sunday, we should have been able to detect a smell."

Something else struck Berndt about David Mahler's living quarters. "There was trash, dirty food, and unwashed dishes. It was not a clean place. So when we saw quite a few bottles of detergents and cleaning fluids, we knew something was weird. The obvious came to mind. It looked like someone was trying to clean up a bloody crime scene."

Chapter 6
Strange Patterns

A location in the Hollywood Hills' western edge became the epicenter for a remarkable synchronicity of events and dates involving the sons of two world-famous entertainers, a kid from the USSR, and, eventually, a man named David Mahler. One celebrity son was kidnapped and the other one murdered. Fate would draw all of these individuals from widely divergent geographical locations to a tight circle of real estate within Los Angeles's world of movies and mayhem. To Vicki Bynum and her partner, Detective Tom Small, one of the men would become a source of deep consternation.

On December 8, 1963, while the nation still grieved over President John F. Kennedy's assassination and reeled in shock at the televised murder of Lee Harvey Oswald, a different crime unfolded in California. It victimized Frank Sinatra's only son, Frank Jr. Coincidentally, the iconic singer-actor had sought to establish a social relationship with Kennedy.

Two men, pretending to deliver a package at a Lake Tahoe, Nevada, hotel room, kidnapped nineteen-year-old Frank Sinatra Jr. Driving through a heavy snowstorm, they transported him south to a house in Canoga Park, Los Angeles County. Via several telephone calls to Sinatra Senior, they arranged for a ransom of $240,000 to be dropped near a gas station on Sunset Boulevard. As one of the kidnappers retrieved the money, a third conspirator drove young Sinatra along the I-405, known locally as the San Diego Freeway, into the Hollywood Hills and dropped him off under the Mulholland Drive overpass. Close to midnight, the relieved hostage walked several miles to safety.

Clumsy mistakes by the trio soon led to their capture and trial. Even though they would actually serve only a little more than three years, a judge sentenced two of the men, on March 6, 1964, to life imprisonment.

On the very next day after that hearing, a woman in Flushing, Queens, New York, gave birth to a son and named him David.

Exactly fifteen years after the kidnapping date, another birth took place in Ukraine, USSR, on December 8, 1978. The mother immigrated to the United States with her young son, Mikhail Markhasev. He grew up in Orange County and drifted into a life of crime.

In mid-January 1997, nearly an hour after midnight, Markhasev and a few of his criminal associates stopped at a remote park-and-ride lot to use a pay phone for calling a drug dealer. This took place within short walking distance from the site where Sinatra Jr. had been released.

A few minutes earlier, Ennis Cosby, twenty-seven-year-old son of actor-comedian Bill Cosby, while driving north along the I-405, near Mulholland Drive, felt the thumping of a flat tire on his Mercedes. He exited on Skirball Center Drive, passed the park-and-ride lot, and pulled over to the shoulder next to a hillside cliff. Cosby telephoned a female friend who drove immediately to the site to aid him by aiming her headlights at his car while he changed the tire. She kept her engine running.

Shortly after her arrival, Markhasev strolled away from his companions, approached the woman's car, and demanded money from her. Startled, she inadvertently jammed her accelerator down and barely missed Cosby's Mercedes as she surged up the street away from danger. Markhasev moved instantly over to Cosby and repeated his order to hand over all of his cash. Evidently dissatisfied with the response, he executed Cosby with a gunshot to the head.

The female friend later helped a police artist prepare a drawing of the man she saw. The killer is serving a life sentence in prison.

The strange linkage of events continued. Just a few years later, the boy born in New York and named David Mahler would move to the Hollywood Hills. He would occupy a home on Cole Crest Drive, less than five miles from the site where Ennis Cosby died and where Frank Sinatra Jr. was released. That hillside residence eventually became the site of yet another tragic murder.

David "Dave" A. Mahler, the first of three children delivered by his mother, grew up in comfortable circumstances, first in New York's Long Island and later in New Jersey. His father, a dedicated workaholic, accrued considerable wealth as a stockbroker and commodities trader, which enabled him to provide everything his wife, son, and two daughters could want. But underlying tensions resulted in familial strain. Arguments flared between the parents, as well as between father and son. Eventually the marriage ended in divorce, and David's father soon remarried.

A popular website of horoscopes makes some interesting observations about David Mahler based on his birthplace, date, and time. It suggests that he is full of self-confidence and likes to dominate. He overcomes difficulties through sheer willpower. A taciturn person, he would have few close friends due to a reserved nature. Perhaps loved insufficiently by his parents, he would never get carried away by love for others. Irascible, he likes to criticize and contradict. His arguments are noisy and animated. A key weakness, the horoscope notes, is an immoderate taste for the pleasures of life, gambling, entertainment, and luxury. In relationships he likes amorous adventures, and, "of course," is unfaithful if he has a serious relationship: *He boils over, and is easily exasperated, with difficulty in controlling himself.* Influenced by the opposing positions of Pluto and Mars at the time of birth, *He is violent, brutal, and irascible. He succeeds in crushing others without giving it a thought.*

It would turn out to be remarkably on target.

Nothing extraordinary marked David's childhood. He accepted his parents' Jewish heritage, but followed the tenets marginally. The family lived in Long Island, until David turned thirteen, then moved to Bergen County, New Jersey, just below the New York border.

In elementary and high school, he earned better than average grades; even though, according to a personal admission he made years later, he enjoyed using cocaine before graduating the twelfth grade. "It was a bad vice, but I liked coke."

David decided to leave home for his college education, but he didn't venture too far. Fairfield University, in Fairfield, Connecticut, is an approximate thirty-mile drive from his parental home.

The respected institution boasts a pastoral campus offering scenic views and all the amenities of a major, comprehensive university in a setting of rolling hills, sprawling lawns, picturesque ponds, and bucolic wooded areas. One former associate of Mahler's expressed the opinion that David's influential grandfather helped ease the way for admission and finances.

David's selection of studies might have been influenced not only by his father's success in business, but by notable alumni of Fairfield. These have included E. Gerald Corrigan, the seventh president of the Federal Reserve Bank of New York, Joseph DiMenna, a pioneer in hedge fund management, and William P. Egan, a venture capital leader.

Or, he may have followed the legal profession path set by Fairfield alumni Raymond J. Dearie, chief judge of the U.S. District Court, Eastern New York District; Joseph P. Flynn and William Lavery, chief judges of the Connecticut Court of Appeals; or Joseph Russoniello, two-term U.S. attorney for the Northern District of California.

The latter group possibly carried more weight with David, since he moved next to New York University of Law, on NYU's Greenwich Village campus. Established in 1835, this prestigious model of academia produced a long list of notable graduates. Among them were former New York City mayors Fiorello LaGuardia, Ed Koch, and Rudy Giuliani, as well as sportscaster Howard Cosell and John F. Kennedy Jr. Other legal eagles from the famed university later flew west to Hollywood. They included former chairman of Paramount Pictures Jonathan Dolgen, Hollywood and Broadway producer Marc E. Platt, and producer/former chairman and CEO of Sony Pictures Entertainment Peter Guber. David certainly found no shortage of role models while earning his degree, which he took in 1991.

By this time in his life, at age twenty-seven, Mahler had developed into a sturdy, solidly built man. Standing one inch over six feet, he weighed about 190 pounds. With dark brown hair, brown eyes, and a smooth, oval face, under a high, wide forehead, his features would appeal to many women. Adopting a serious demeanor in both personal and business dealings, he sometimes gave the impression of being overbearing or threatening. He didn't smile often. When he did, he compressed his lips, giving them a brittle look. Now and then,

Mahler allowed his temper to leap out of control. Still, he could be charming and gallant with his dates.

After passing bar exams for both New York and New Jersey, Mahler set up a private practice. He rented an apartment in Hackensack, New Jersey, across the street from a residential co-op, where his grandmother lived. Using a room in his living quarters as an office, Mahler began representing clients in divorce cases, civil suits, and an occasional criminal defense. As his business grew, he also defended narcotics and prostitution cases and then branched into Wall Street civil suits.

As David Mahler's workload increased, so did his bank account. Following the pattern set by his father, he dabbled in Wall Street investments, and provided financial advice to his clients.

According to a longtime friend, David also enjoyed associating with alleged underworld characters. He sometimes patronized nightclubs favored by these people and occasionally accepted invitations to attend their social functions. At these times, David would caution his companion, "If I introduce myself as 'Anthony,' just go along with it." But he wouldn't explain why he wanted to use a phony name. Nor would he acknowledge any monetary transactions involving the so-called Mafia connections.

With an ever-expanding network of clients and cases, Mahler's practice required traveling to other states. In the final days of the 1980s, he jetted to Southern California and met someone who would share the next twenty years of his life, on and off.

Two women who would play crucial roles in David Mahler's future chose to spend segments of their lives in Newport Beach, an affluent, picturesque Pacific Coastal city in Orange County. Blessed with a scenic bay, populated islands, and magnificent residential sites, the city harbors a fleet of yachts and overflows with garish mansions. John Wayne occupied a home in Newport for many years and moored his 136-foot pleasure boat, *The Wild Goose,* within a few steps of his bayfront estate. He could often be seen patronizing, in both food and drink, a nearby restaurant known as the Arches. One of the most popular beaches in Southern California graces Newport's shoreline. The pier and the white sand attract thousands of visitors year-round.

A diminutive blonde, with a knockout figure and blue-green eyes, lived near the beach in the late 1980s. Stacy Tipton had been born and raised in Visalia, about 220 miles north of Newport, in 1963. After high school, and a short tenure at the local College of the Sequoias, she had accompanied a girlfriend south to attend Orange Coast College. She earned an Associate of Arts degree and continued her studies at Cal State, Long Beach. Sharing quarters with her pals, Stacy worked first as a receptionist for an advertising firm, then later for a boat sales agency. She characterized her time in the bay community as "living the good life in Newport with the other beach bums."

While Stacy enjoyed a few drinks with some friends one evening in the Cannery Restaurant, right next to the bay, she made the acquaintance of a man with a New Jersey accent. "I met David Mahler when he was visiting from New York. He was at the restaurant with a mutual friend. He asked for my phone number and he gave me his. I think this was about 1988."

The brief encounter might have ended there, but an odd coincidence kept it alive. "The following week, I was with a girlfriend and we stopped by another friend's house. And David was there! My friend didn't know that we had already met. It was really strange. At first, David and I were just sort of like pals with friendly flirtations, but grew fonder of each other through phone calls. Then, when he got busy in New York, I didn't hear from him for quite a while. But one night, while I was still living in Newport, I got a call really late and it was him. He said he was going through his old phone messages and found one from me. After that, we corresponded regularly. He sent me a ticket to New York, and that began a series of visits. I would fly back and forth, and wound up living with him in the East."

Asked if she had been attracted to David Mahler from the very beginning, Stacy replied, "Well, it was really hard not to be. He was very charismatic. I made the trip back and forth at least ten times, and we fell head over heels in love."

Stacy moved in with Mahler, despite reservations by her mother in Visalia. "She was very hesitant about it because I would be so far away. David assured her that she need not worry and that he would take good care of her little Stacy."

In the apartment they shared, Stacy helped him with his legal work, performing mostly clerical and typing duties. But they also found time for entertainment. "We had so many wonderful times. We went to Atlantic City, the Hamptons, to New York City, just all kinds of fun stuff. One of my favorite times was when we went over to the city and we caught a hansom cab for a ride around Central Park. It was absolutely beautiful. He explained he was trying to get me to marry him. I wouldn't say yes, so he said, 'Let's just do the whole ride again.' It was so much fun. I think he knew that even if I agreed, he could deny the whole thing—as an attorney—and say he was just drunk."

Mahler, Stacy said, had been quite generous with her. "We used to go get our hair styled together. I would get a five-hundred-dollar styling and we'd have our nails done. It was so nice having a guy you could run around with and do things like that."

His generosity went a little too far with one gift David presented to Stacy. She laughed with embarrassment when speaking of it. "He decided he wanted to get me this certain toy. It was before Rudy Giuliani put a crackdown on all this stuff, and David bought this 'machinery.' I didn't want anything to do with it. I didn't want it, so he decided to take it back to the store. Picture him, getting on the subway with it. He didn't wrap it. Everybody could see, and he didn't care. The store was closed at first, and he had to carry it all over town. He finally goes there, handed it over, and said, 'She wore it out.' Talk about making me blush."

A more pleasant recollection Stacy chose to talk about regarded another remarkable coincidence. "One time we went to the top of the Empire State Building when he was showing me all of the sights. You go up elevators to a certain point and then get in line for another ride to the top. We were in line and struck up a conversation with another couple. They were tourists and we asked where they were visiting from. One of them said, 'Oh, a little place in California you've never heard of, I'm sure.' I said, 'Well, try me.' They said, 'Visalia.' I couldn't believe it. He worked for someone I went to high school with. So that was kind of fun."

When the first Christmas drew near, David took Stacy to spend the holiday with her parents. "That was the first time he met them. He and my dad got along handsomely. The next year, we spent Thanksgiving with them. We would alternate being with his parents for one holiday and with mine the next holiday, and then reverse them the following year. His mother was a wonderful woman, and his dad is extremely strong-willed. I really liked his stepmother too, who is a very nice woman."

One particular aspect of Stacy's relationship with David's father, an expert in commodity trading, delighted her. "He would do all this analyzing of stocks, and then I would pick one at random, and mine almost always outperformed his."

Relationships between Stacy and David's family also extended to his sisters. "Beth was wonderful. Alice, I didn't know that well." Asked if Mahler had conflicts with them, Stacy could only grimace and say, "Isn't there always issues between siblings?"

Even if David at first seemed "charismatic" to Stacy, she could see a few conflicting characteristics. "He had a good sense of humor, but sometimes it didn't show. You would say something off the cuff that you thought was funny and he wouldn't crack a smile. He really wasn't much of a joke teller." In trying to identify what Mahler did laugh at, Stacy couldn't think of anything. She rationalized, "Sometimes his idea of comedy would go over other people's heads." She cited an incident in which they were playing Monopoly with some relatives. "The game requires some intelligence and they were playing like yo-yos. David was just running the board and they didn't even get what he was doing. He and I were on the same page and we were just cracking up. In the conversation, the subject of capitalism came up, and they had no idea what we were talking about. That's the whole concept of Monopoly. I guess they took offense. The woman said to me, 'You just wait. I know you are laughing at me, but some-day you will get yours.'" Describing this, Stacy's face turned grim. Obviously reflecting on events that would change her life, she said, "That was terribly ironic."

After Stacy lived with Mahler most of a two-year period, during which misunderstandings and arguments became more frequent, she began visiting her family in Visalia more often, and staying there for longer periods of time. Asked if David lost his temper easily, Stacy hesitated. She thought about it and said, "He used to be an absolutely terrific person."

"Did you see that gradually change?"

"Yes."

To the suggestion that something deep inside David drove him to undergo drastic changes, Stacy said, "We all blame circumstances and different people for stuff in our lives. But then, you just get over it. There were some things he didn't get over, and it breaks my heart. I wish I could have been the person who could help him get through all of that. But it's hard to pinpoint exactly what it was."

A different twist on Mahler's interests in women became apparent to Stacy, something she had not previously recognized. He seemed to be fascinated with strippers. At least he made no attempt to hide it, and even invited Stacy to accompany him to the joints where dancers disrobed. "Back East, I went to a few strip clubs with him. I thought they were kind of funny."

Other cracks in the relationship planted seeds of doubt in Stacy's mind. She recalled, "We went for a drive one time and he showed me their old house from when his parents were still married. When his grandmother passed away, I was there for her wake, and David took that really hard." It puzzled Stacy when she learned the grandmother had lived right across the street from their apartment—yet she had never met the woman.

Regarding Mahler's use of alcohol or other stimulants, Stacy took a noncommittal stance. "I don't partake in any of that." Asked again, she replied, "I saw a lot of things."

Another incident set a pattern that Mahler would repeat too often. "I went to the city with David to attend the wedding of one of his friends. Both of us dressed formally. I wore a long black gown, with gloves up past the elbows, and had my hair done up perfectly. It was a beautiful ceremony. But at a gathering afterward, he took me to a joint with a band, and the place was filled with cigarette smoke. I can't stand that vile smell and we got into an argument. He said some hurtful things and then abandoned me. There I was in New York City, in midwinter, with very little money and no warm clothing. I had planned to go to Visalia afterward and had my plane ticket, but no transportation to the airport. I finally talked a cabdriver, who was from India or Iran or somewhere like that, into giving me a ride to the airport."

The tendency for Mahler to take Stacy somewhere and abandon her after a dispute became a recurring theme. "He took me to New Jersey and Manhattan other times and just stranded me." The last time he deserted her nearly ended the relationship.

It happened in 2000, on what should have been a romantic, festive vacation in Hawaii. Before departure from New York, a nasty argument between David and Stacy erupted. He contacted the airline and changed the name on her reservations, giving it to one of his male pals, who lived in Hermosa Beach, California. As usual, he and Stacy were able to patch up their differences, and he bought another ticket for her. In Hawaii, they checked in at a luxury hotel, where the buddy also stayed. Another furious quarrel ensued, and Mahler departed with his friend, leaving Stacy stranded with no return ticket. "I had to wire my dad for money so I could go home. All I know is this was not the romantic Hawaii trip we had planned."

While she continued to spend time with David Mahler, Stacy no longer lived with him in New Jersey. Instead, she resumed the original pattern of flying back and forth from California to the East Coast, spending some time with him, then returning home. Their arguments increased in frequency and volatility. If friends and relatives wondered why she didn't just end the relationship, they didn't understand the power love holds for a woman.

Ruminating about that period in her life, Stacy tried to pinpoint the causes of their fights. Was he jealous? "That was one of the problems. He was jealous because he thought I was seeing other guys, but I really wasn't. We couldn't seem to talk anything out and try to understand. I didn't approve of a lot of things, so I would just wind up saying, 'Well, just forget about it.'"

By 2001, Mahler's life in New Jersey had grown difficult. Rumors abounded of connections with Mob money, of shady deals, and indebtedness to the wrong people. He felt restless and discontented.

A law enforcement investigator would later say, "He needed to get away from New Jersey because he was on the run. An investigation was under way for some major frauds. A buddy of his was hooked into the Gambino crime family. He was the treasurer of an alleged corporation and owed them some money. I talked to some of the people involved, but they weren't willing to say very much. New York cops investigated and uncovered more than four hundred grand in fraud. The so-called corporation probably was in debt for more. I think Mahler was in it pretty deep. But there is no solid evidence."

Looking to leave town, Mahler began thinking of a move to the Golden State. Why not give Hollywood a try? Wouldn't it be great to live among filmdom's glitterati, maybe in the pattern of *Playboy* magnate Hugh Hefner? How much fun would it be to have beautiful starlets surrounding you, and maybe even dabble in film production?

Even though women would probably be plentiful in the freewheeling Hollywood social scene, the move would also make it easier to see Stacy more often. Instead of making an expensive five-hour plane trip, she could drive from Visalia in about three hours and stay overnight or even a few days. Perhaps they could even live together again.

At last, a couple of years into the new millennium, David Mahler made the decision to go West. He didn't know it yet, but in California, he would eventually meet the other woman who had lived in Newport Beach, and who would have a profound impact on his life.

CHAPTER 7

FROM PARADISE TO PORNOGRAPHY

Kristin Baldwin, still known then as Kristin Means, graduated from Westlake Village High School in 1987. She had reached her full height, five-five, and weighed about 115 pounds. With blond hair and green eyes, she easily attracted the attention of men, but she wasn't ready yet for any serious entanglements.

Eager to sprout wings and fly on her own, she moved from the home her stepfather had provided and migrated about eighty miles south to Orange County. With a couple of girl-friends, Kristin found an apartment in Newport Beach. And just as Stacy Tipton had done, Kristin enrolled at Orange Coast College in neighboring Costa Mesa. They may even have crossed paths on campus. Instead of trying to obtain a car, Kristin used a bicycle, pedaling to classes at school, to the beach, and to work.

Peter Means later spoke of it. "She moved down there because she loved the beach. The girls she lived with, who seemed to rotate quite frequently, were there just to enjoy the party life. Six or eight girls piled into a four-bedroom place. They supported themselves as waitresses in the numerous restaurants that line the harbor. Kristin worked too, took classes, and spent as much time as she could sunning on the sand. It was a typical lifestyle for fun-loving young women, eighteen or twenty years old."

If Kristin had thought of breaking into the entertainment industry, as her sister Robin and Jennifer Gootsan mentioned, Peter Means didn't think she ever set earnest goals in that direction. "She never really indicated a serious desire to get into show business. But like most girls, she thought it looked glamorous and easy. If you hit it right and become a star, you can make a lot of money. But as we know, it's a tough business to break into, and if you don't know people who can help, success isn't very likely. It is nepotism and who you know. I think she liked the idea, but never really attempted it. She was in a couple of high-school plays, but never did any serious acting. For her, it was more of a dream than a real goal."

After about eighteen months, Kristin dropped out of college, preferring to work full-time. With her good looks and gregarious personality, tips from restaurant patrons came easily and generously. The money, surfing, tanning, and social activities didn't allow enough time for stuffy classrooms. She kept in contact with her three siblings, Robin, Rick, and Stephanie. Robin had stayed in the San Fernando Valley area to work, while Stephanie continued her education. Rick had found a niche in the food-service business, specializing as a banquet captain. In January 1991, he moved to Hawaii, the Big Island, and worked steadily in hotel dining rooms.

"I'm the one," Rick later stated, "who convinced Kristin to move over there. I was talking to her on the phone and said, 'You would love it. Come on over. You will really dig it. With your experience, you can get a job in a restaurant.'" Kristin followed Rick's advice in the spring of 1991. She first stayed with Julie Henson, a woman who would become their sister-in-law when her brother married Robin. Julie had been a classmate of Rick and Robin's at Westlake High School.

Kristin decided that the island of Maui offered the best opportunities to earn a living. In the popular tourist city of Lahaina, she found a roommate and a job serving tables at one of the busy restaurants. According to Rick, newcomers who settle in the Islands don't find it easy in the beginning. "It's kind of hard at first because you don't know anyone and you don't have many friends. In Lahaina, apartments are really expensive, so most of the people who work there can't live in town. You share apartments and do whatever you have to do to survive. And Kristin went through that period, living in the next village, Kahana. She made it, though, and just like I told her, really loved the atmosphere."

Even though Kristin enjoyed soaking up sun, swimming, and surfing, she never avoided work. Peter Means respected her industrious efforts. "In addition to serving tables in restaurants, she supplemented her income as a salesclerk in a few of those little gift shops, where they sell puka shell jewelry and other tourist trinkets. In waitress's lives, they get good shifts and bad shifts, where the tips are smaller. She did well at that, but was also willing to work in the gift shops, which certainly did not pay high wages. Hawaii is not a cheap place to live."

It didn't take long for the "aloha" spirit of conviviality, and the "hang loose" attitude of many locals, to possess Kristin. She found those qualities even more prevalent "up country." Maui residents give that sobriquet to higher elevations and small villages along roads leading up to Haleakala, a towering volcano dominating Maui's eastern end.

New friends spoke to Kristin of a small town called Makawao, about sixteen miles upslope from the airport at Kahului. She trekked up there several times and decided it would be the perfect place to live and work. To *malihinis* (strangers), Makawao appeared to be a place of supreme tranquility, but young locals knew that super parties could be found behind the serene mask.

One of the best-known restaurants on Maui, Polli's Mexican Cantina, hired Kristin, and she would stay there nearly eight years. Having lived in California, she knew all about burritos, tacos, nachos, chimichangas, and Polli's specialty, margaritas. Coincidentally, the eatery is located on Makawao Avenue and *Baldwin* Avenue. Baldwin had been Kristin's surname during her mother's second marriage, and would be the name she would eventually use again. "Polli's is one of the most popular places around there," said Rick.

Speaking of Makawao, he noted, "That's where they have a rodeo every year. The *paneolos* (Hawaiian cowboys) participate, and they have a parade. Kristin rode a horse in the parade one year. It belonged to one of her friends. She knew how to ride at a very young age from our visits to the farm in Vermont."

In Peter Means's memory, Kristin seemed quite happy with her life in Maui. She could walk from her first residence to the beach, and carried her board over there almost every day. "She did a lot of surfing and spent a lot of time on the beach. She would be out there on her board at the crack of dawn, before work. She was in love with the ocean."

On one occasion, her love affair with rolling waves nearly ended. Kristin had paddled out about forty yards, and sat waiting for the next breaker. A sudden, different kind of motion rippling the water underneath startled her, and she saw fish scattering in panic. Robin laughingly told of Kristin's fright. "She just knew there was a huge tiger shark in the water right below her board. That girl paddled back to dry land like she had an outboard motor. She was shaking and scared to death. I know because she called me and her voice was still trembling. She was like, 'I'll never go back in the water.' I told her, 'Oh, you have to go back, but go to a place where a lot of people are swimming.' Of course, she did and forgot all about the possibility of sharks."

Her devoted stepfather kept in contact with Kristin during the entire ten years she lived on Maui. After he remarried, Peter and his wife, Sue, visited there on more than one occasion. When Kristin moved up country, she needed a car. Peter came to the rescue by shipping his Acura to her.

Although Rick and Kristin, due to living on different islands, weren't able to spend a lot of time together, they still managed to exchange visits periodically. He recalled, "She came over to see me on the Big Island once and spent three days staying in my house. We went to the beach and hung out. It was great being with her. Another time I went over there for Halloween. That event is a big thing in Lahaina. They close off the streets and everybody dresses up in costumes. They walk up and down the town and have contests about the best outfit and makeup. I flew over there with my roommates, and the whole plane was full of people in costume who had rushed to the airport at the last minute."

Kristin spent most of her time working or on the beach, but she still managed an active social life. She never had trouble attracting men who wanted to date her, and even though an abundance of pretty women can be found in Hawaii, she seldom found herself sitting at home alone. None of the guys, though, lodged themselves in her heart.

This pattern ended when Kristin met Mike Luna (pseudonym) and immediately felt a powerful attraction. Mike's friends and acquaintances called him "Keoke." Describing him, Rick said, "He was a couple of inches taller than I am, about six feet, slim, with short dark hair and a great tan. Nice-looking and a nice guy." Asked if he appeared to be of Hawaiian or Islander descent, Rick replied, "Not when you first saw him. You would say no, but the minute he started to talk, you would say yes. He used that noticeable pidgin English."

Nearly everyone in local Hawaiian social circles has a color-ful nickname. Rick laughed as he spoke of it. "Mike was 'Keoke' and Kristin became 'Chickie.'" No one could explain why. She was just "Chickie." Everybody knew her and thought she and Keoke made a handsome couple.

Keoke's private pilot's license allowed him to fly a small plane frequently between the Islands. It nearly cost him his life. He crashed in a remote section of Molokai, the island once known for its leper colony. Rick recalled it. "If he hadn't had a cell phone with him, Keoke probably wouldn't have sur-vived. I believe he called Kristin from the wreckage. She re-layed it to emergency responders, who arrived on the scene and transported Keoke for medical help. She spent a lot of time with him in the hospital helping him to recover. They really seemed to love each other a lot."

As with most love relationships, problems developed. Kristin's fun-loving behavior perhaps grated on Keoke's nerves. Said Rick, "Keoke didn't like Kristin partying. He wasn't into that kind of activity. He was really a good guy, and would have a few beers with his buddies, but wasn't a hell-raiser. He grew up in Maui, and a lot of guys who are from the island are not big drinkers." A smile lit Rick's face as he made these observations, and he added, "But a lot of them smoke quite a bit." He explained that there is a lively trade of locally grown marijuana available. It was once known as "Maui Wowie."

Before Peter gave Kristin a car, Rick offered to provide her with a vehicle. He recalled, "Cars change hands over there, sometimes as gifts. A guy might have a car worth only a few hundred bucks, and when he decides to leave the Islands, sometimes it's easier to just give it to a buddy rather than try to sell it." It happened to Rick. "My neighbor had a little mini–station wagon. In his job as golf pro, he used to drive Michael Jordan around in that car so the famous basketball player could remain incognito. He said he couldn't get the passenger seat back far enough and Jordan had to jam his knees against the dashboard. When that guy was getting ready to leave, he asked me if I wanted the car. I told him I didn't have any money. So he said, 'Aw, just take it,' and he signed it over to me. That's part of the aloha spirit over there."

In 1994, Rick left the Islands for California, then lived in Tampa, Florida, for a while, moved to Puerto Rico, and returned to Hawaii in 1997. A friend had offered him a job on the pineapple island, Lanai.

By this time, Kristin had moved into a plantation-type house owned by Keoke. Rick liked the place. "The floor was about three or four feet above the ground for airflow ventilation, like a plantation house. Kristin had a room there for some time before she and Keoke began living together. I went over there for Kristin's twenty-ninth birthday in May 1998 and stayed a couple of nights. It was roomy and quite comfortable."

Robin, Kristin's sister, also succumbed to the lure of the Islands and moved to Maui. She brought her two children, ages one and two, and lived in Kahana at the Island's western shore. While her husband did construction work, Robin followed Kristin's pattern and found employment in a restaurant. Rick, Robin, and Kristin, although widely separated by water and mountains, managed periodic visits with each other. Robin's stay lasted only six months, and she returned to California.

As the decade of the 1990s drew to a close, circumstances for Kristin began to fall apart. She had moved in with Keoke, but strong differences of opinion tore at their feelings. Said Robin, "When they split up, it was probably for the best, for both of them. But in their hearts, they knew they would be together again, sometime in the future."

To make matters worse, Kristin lost her job at Polli's. Peter Means didn't know the exact cause, but later guessed, "It may have been related to an argument with a customer, since

Kristin was a person with very strong opinions. I believe it went from the customer to her boss, and in cases like that, the boss always wins."

More bad luck surrounded Kristin. She totaled the car Peter had given her in an auto accident. Looking back at that time frame, Peter Means's face grew somber. "In 2001, after she lost her job, things spiraled down for a period of time and she called me. She said, 'I think I need to come home for a while.' She flew back to California and stayed with us a couple of months in our Simi Valley home. But she wasn't thrilled with the dry, rocky area where I lived. It is not the beach. This is a conservative town, not much for parties and such."

The next few years flew by for Kristin with several moves. She spent a good portion of that period in various San Fernando Valley locations. Through mutual friends, she met a woman named Tara Rush, who invited Kristin to be a roommate in her spacious Canoga Park apartment. Kristin stayed with Tara several months. Even after she moved out, they kept in touch at least weekly and often visited one another.

Peter Means recalled that Kristin went through a couple of relationships, but the guys turned out to be less than admirable, and one of them physically abused her. She worked at several restaurants, but never again found a place that gave her the feeling of contentment she had experienced at Polli's.

Kristin's mother, Marie, had moved to Mesa, Arizona, just outside the capital city, Phoenix. Kristin joined her for more than a year, but she missed being near the Pacific surf. Arizona, she joked, had huge stretches of beach, but no ocean. By 2005, Kristin moved back to Southern California. Between jobs, when she ran short of cash, Peter always came to her rescue. Even though she loved him, Kristin changed her surname to Baldwin. Robin explained why: "Kristin was in Orange County driving an old car and ran into a big pink Cadillac. It was her fault and she was going to lose her driver's license. A lawyer friend advised her to apply for a license in the surname of a close relative. He said the Department of Motor Vehicles did not have computer hookups across the nation and wouldn't be able to check it out. Women do it a lot, using maiden names, and married names. So Kristin followed his suggestion and reverted to Baldwin, the name of our first stepfather."

Back in the San Fernando Valley, Kristin stayed for a while with Robin. A particularly pleasant memory of that period has lingered in the sister's memory. On Sunday mornings, Kristin would get up and make pancakes for the kids. The aroma of warm pancakes and syrup filled the rooms, and seemed to make everyone happy. "There was a lot of silly stuff too," said Robin. "I have four daughters, and when Kristin was there, it was like a girly house. My kids were quite young and they would be so enthralled watching her get ready to go out, putting on makeup, doing her hair, and getting dressed. They would do their best to imitate every step, [and] pretend they were going out. Those were precious times."

Something not quite so precious occurred when Kristin drove north to Ventura one weekend. She partied with a few friends, then headed back to the valley. Flashing red lights behind her wrecked the whole experience. The traffic officer smelled alcohol on Kristin's breath, administered a test, and arrested her for driving under the influence. Booked, photographed, and fingerprinted, she spent a few hours in jail before Peter Means bailed her out.

Even if Kristin experienced a few bumps in the road of life, she still maintained loving relations with her family. In 2005, she joined them for a reunion in Vermont to celebrate the seventy-fifth birthday of her maternal grandmother, Frances O'Neill. A special bond existed between Kristin and Grandma, who later said, "She has always been very special to me. No matter where she lived, Kristin always kept in touch sending me cards and notes for every occasion. She was the only one that ever sent me a Grandmother's Day card. And she always provided pictures with them."

Still searching for herself and seeking some sort of permanence, Kristin also lived for a period of time with her best friend from school days, Jennifer Gootsan. Reminiscing about it, Jennifer said, "Kristin was so cute. I had stepped out of the house for a few minutes and she was in there with my little boy. He was about eighteen months old, loved Kristin, and called her 'Uncle Kwisty.' He was a little confused about aunts and uncles. She used to decorate her face to entertain him—make a mask by painting her skin all green or white with circles around her eyes. I got back in just in time to see him sitting on the bed as she stepped out of the bathroom with her goofy mask. She goes, 'Hi, Anthony.' He looked at her and said, 'Uncle Kwisty, your face is cwacking.' He meant 'cracking,' and we just broke up laughing."

According to Jennifer and Robin, Kristin had a couple of unusual obsessions. First, she always needed to be clean. Second, she didn't want anyone ever touching her feet. If someone sat next to her and accidentally made contact with her foot, she would instantly pull away. No one understood either of these characteristics, but just accepted them as part of Kristin's makeup. Jennifer later spoke of a remarkable exception. "One evening she came in, obviously very tired. She seemed sort of needy and vulnerable. I had a bunch of nail polishes out and I was doing my toenails. I poured a glass of wine for each of us. And it really amazed me when she slipped her shoes off, put her feet up, and said in this sweet little girl's voice, 'Do my toes.' So she laid there and I painted her toenails. She fell asleep while I was doing it. She was so comfortable and her face was angelic. That was the last time she was ever at my house."

Once again working in a restaurant, Kristin met a man who told her he had been in several movies. He first introduced himself as Damien Michaels, but quickly confessed that his real name was Michael Conoscenti and "Damien" was his screen name. While growing up, Kristin had brushed shoulders with numerous celebrities, so this man's claim to fame didn't impress her. But his relaxed, friendly attitude did. At five-eight, and weighing a slim 145 pounds, Conoscenti looked much younger than his fifty-four years of age. His brown eyes retained a youthful sparkle, and very little gray showed in his full mane of brown hair. In their conversation, she mentioned having trouble with her car. Conoscenti suggested that he might know someone who could help her get it fixed. Kristin agreed to a subsequent meeting.

A few days later, in the fall of 2006, Conoscenti took her to a large, gated Calabasas residence in the San Fernando Valley, about twelve miles east of Westlake Village. He explained that he lived in a guest room there. The place belonged to Sheldon Weinberg (pseudonym), who had made his fortune in the film and finance industries. Inside, Kristin met Weinberg, a frail, gray-haired man only ten years older than Conoscenti, but appearing to be of more advanced age. He said he had lived in Calabasas for many years.

Decades ago, Calabasas drew visitors interested in the history of California. It had once been a stagecoach wayfarer's stop on the original El Camino Real linking the Spanish Missions. One of the oldest adobe buildings in the county still stands there. Tourists, after viewing the Old Town structures, often associate the town with cowboy days, as seen in countless B movies. Silent-movie directors found it great for background shots. From the 1920s to modern day, the lower slopes of the Santa Monica Hills on the south edge of Calabasas drew celebrities who wanted to live outside the hubbub of Hollywood. Entertainers from the Lone Ranger (actor Clayton Moore) to Lady Gaga have lived there. Loretta Swit, who played "Hotlips" Margaret Houlihan in the long-running M*A*S*H television series, owned a home only about ten miles from the remote, mountainous site where exterior scenes were filmed for both the movie and the series. Legions of actors, directors, and sports stars have found Calabasas a comfortable place to live.

One prominent resident of Calabasas, Jose Menendez, later moved to Beverly Hills. The name became world famous in 1989 when Jose's two sons, Lyle and Erik, used shotguns to slay him and their mother. Convicted of first-degree murder, both are now serving life sentences in prison.

While living in Calabasas, Menendez had allegedly been connected to the pornographic film business. Their neighbors had pressured the family to leave the community, not because of the pornography issues, but as a result of suspicions that Lyle and Erik had been burglarizing their homes. The boys had later rationalized that Jose, despite his fabulous wealth, had refused to provide them with an allowance, preferring that they learn to work for their money. They chose the wrong line of work.

No evidence exists to connect Jose Menendez with porn producer Sheldon Weinberg. The multibillion-dollar industry is well known to have long tentacles throughout the San Fernando Valley, and business relationships can be somewhat secretive.

Neither Weinberg nor Conoscenti bothered to mention to Kristin that the films they participated in were pornographic. Having performed in a long line of triple X-rated films as Damien Michaels or sometimes just "Damien," Conoscenti knew the business intimately. Now in the twilight of a career that requires unfailing libido among male stars, Conoscenti had entered into a partnership with Weinberg to produce the "adults only" movies.

Whether or not Kristin learned that her new acquaintances worked in pornography, she appeared to be content with the friendship. She and Conoscenti enjoyed just hanging out once in a while over a period of several months.

Through her new friend, she met a man named David Mahler.

CHAPTER 8
A TANGLED WEB OF WOMEN

When David Mahler finally decided to leave the East Coast and make Hollywood his new base of operations, he wanted to find the perfect residence, one that suited his fantasies and personal needs. Stacy Tipton later spoke of his reasons for the move and his search for an ideal home. "I think he just got tired of living in the East. Maybe he was attracted by the glitz and glamour of Hollywood and the show business lifestyle. But I think he just wanted some new challenges. Later, he would look up at that big Hollywood sign on the hill and say, 'It should be Mahlerwood.' He took pride in that.

"He told me that when he first came out here, he stayed in a hotel. It took him forever to find what he was looking for, and the house he finally chose fit his needs perfectly."

The search for a residence took Mahler into the Heights overlooking Sunset Boulevard, and stretching over a series of ridges, in which an eclectic variety of dwellings, from cabins to castles, perch on hillsides, canyons, and mountaintops. A daunting maze of narrow, twisting, crooked lanes provides harrowing access. First-time visitors are amazed at how crowded the region is. Instead of rural, spacious lots, the houses are jammed together on every possible site conceivable for supporting a structure.

Only Mahler knows the exact reasons for his selection of a seven-level cliffside house on a short cul-de-sac called Cole Crest Drive. Viewed from the street, it gave a deceptive appearance of a modest two-story home. Further examination revealed five additional lower levels sloping down a steep canyon wall. Three outdoor decks jutting from rear doors offered spectacular panoramas, including the distant HOLLYWOOD sign.

From the Sunset Strip, Laurel Canyon Boulevard is the most common route into the hills. It begins at an intersection with Sunset Boulevard, climbs a northwesterly, serpentine path through the canyon, and, after a little less than five miles, drops down into the San Fernando Valley. The mountainous region resonates with colorful entertainment history and personalities. Among notable former denizens of Laurel Canyon (named for the abundant laurel vines observed by early settlers) were Mary Astor, Liberace, Anne Baxter, Lupe Vélez, Natalie Wood, Orson Welles, and David Niven. More recent luminaries still occupy lavish mansions in the Heights.

Tourists in search of sites where legendary film and music stars lived, or still reside, often regret turning west onto residential streets such as Kirkwood Drive or Lookout Mountain Avenue. Adventurous drivers invariably find themselves lost or desperate to escape the narrow, twisting, curbless, ascending, or plummeting lanes, where an oncoming vehicle is a breathtaking adventure. Some of the streets, if they can be called that, are no wider than sidewalks in other neighborhoods. They change names without warning and often lead frustratingly to dead ends. The most common utterance from strangers is "Why in hell would anyone want to live up here?"

Yet, thousands of residents love the colorful atmosphere of

fame and spectacular city views below. The lure is addictive, almost as much as drugs that have made their way into the Hollywood Hills culture for generations. The "shocking" arrest of Robert Mitchum for using marijuana at a tiny bungalow on Ridpath Drive, shortly after midnight on September 1, 1948, focused the spotlight on substance use and abuse during an innocent era. From Mahler's back balcony, the historic site of Mitchum's misadventure can be seen.

Later, in the flower power 1960s, everything from pot to cocaine to meth flowed abundantly throughout the hills.

It could be that drug-induced euphoria among the Canyon denizens helped inspire a revolution in music. According to author Michael Walker, in his riveting 2006 book *Laurel Canyon,* a new musical genre evolved in the Kirkwood Drive home of Chris Hillman. Jim McGuinn, aka Roger, Gene Clark, David Crosby, Michael Clarke, and Chris Hillman united to call themselves the Byrds. In 1965, they recorded a song written by Bob Dylan called "Mr. Tambourine Man," which shot to number one on the charts and changed the music industry. Walker describes this introduction of folk-rock as "a milestone of twentieth-century popular culture." Four years later, Crosby joined Stephen Stills and Graham Nash at Joni Mitchell's home on Lookout Mountain and sang together for the first time, before becoming world famous as Crosby, Stills and Nash.

Other Hollywood Hills dwellers, such as Joni Mitchell, Frank Zappa, and "Mama" Cass, helped the new sound sweep the nation for the next decade. Nearly every top name in the music industry spent some time in the Laurel Canyon peaks and valleys during that period. Several of them focused their lyrics on local life. Joni Mitchell wrote and sang "Ladies of the Canyon," painting a fanciful picture of "Trina, Annie, and Estrella" as flower children residents who wear wampum beads and gypsy shawls while baking brownies (presumably spiced with cannabis) and pouring music down the canyon. "Love

Street" by the Doors tells of a wise and wonderful female canyon dweller and mentions a store "where creatures meet."

This store may be a paean to the real-life Canyon Country Store, situated on the east side of Laurel Canyon Boulevard at the intersection with Kirkwood Drive. First established in 1919, the same year the historic Musso and Frank Grill opened on Hollywood Boulevard, the store offers crowded shelves of groceries and a deli, all in small Midwestern-town ambience. If Laurel Canyon is the essential artery of the Hollywood Hills, then Canyon Country Store and the restaurant below it are the heart. Celebrities, such as Sophia Loren or George Clooney, are commonplace in the narrow aisles. Jim Morrison lived a few steps away at one time, and silent film star Lupe Vélez died tragically in her home a block down the hill. During the era of music revolution, everyone knew that a variety of drugs could be found just by hanging out in the parking lot outside the Canyon Country Store.

The music and music makers, along with their money and easy access to drugs, acted as a magnet to young, adventurous women. Author Walker described it: *In the canyon, grinding indulgence was replacing the frothy high-spirits. . . . A house on the backside of Lookout Mountain hosted weekend sex parties, the rooms crammed with bunks proffering straight and gay sex, bowls of Quaaludes and poppers, and scores of naked bodies groping, snorting, licking. . . .* Walker told of a female journalist who not only wrote of the wild activities, but experienced them as well. In a magazine story, she noted, *A lot of these parties ended up in orgies.*

David Mahler found his ideal home on Cole Crest Drive.

Before Mahler's arrival in the Hollywood Hills, the Cole Crest home had been leased, occupied, and managed by Karl Norvik for six years. An intelligent, articulate bachelor in his late forties, with high cheekbones, blue eyes, and shaved head, Norvik had achieved success in his profession as artistic technician, mostly in the motion picture industry. His high IQ and adept use of language had often led people to say, "You should have been a lawyer." He lived in the upper two split-level floors and rented out the lower floors as studio apartments.

The house occupied a narrow lot on a short cul-de-sac street, Cole Crest Drive, near the dead end. Six homes, with only a few feet separating them, occupied the street's north side—all were perched at the top of a steep slope. An eight-foot concrete wall had been erected on the south edge of the narrow street to buttress another rise in the terrain topped by a row of towering eucalyptus trees. A huge modern mansion occupied the hilltop above, and two more luxury homes neighbored them to the west.

Mahler's residence featured a two-car garage at street level. On the right side of the garage, a steel gate blocked the main entrance. Visitors could press a button that would activate an intercom, allowing the occupant to remotely unlock the gate. Opening it would lead into a short corridor. To the left, a door provided access to the garage. A few more steps straight ahead ended at the main entry. The right side was open air, with a view of a long staircase of fifty-four steps descending the steep slope and leading to the bottom-level studio apartment.

Just inside the front portal, a landing at the top of a short stairway provided access to the interior rooms. Two more stair-steps down led to the living room and guest bath. A sharp left turn offered a second flight down to the office and a master bedroom. Another interior staircase, this one offering a series of landings and switchbacks, gave entry to a studio apartment.

Access to the next apartment in descending order could also be made by a continuation of the stairwell. The lowest-level apartment could be entered from the long exterior staircase, which required a certain amount of athleticism to navigate, down or up. A pair of landings provided rest stops.

For a short period after David Mahler moved in, Karl Norvik continued to function as landlord, but the new tenant took over the lease and became, in Karl's words, "the master leaseholder." In this role, Mahler also acted as manager. Mahler took over the garage, kitchen, and den above the garage, living room, and master bedroom. Karl moved his possessions into a bedroom and bath below him. By mutual agreement, Karl Norvik could also use the den and kitchen. To David Mahler, the place was the ultimate "bachelor pad."

Mahler furnished his space in a masculine fashion, with black leather couches on light gray wall-to-wall carpeting gracing the living room. In the office, a converted bedroom complete with bath and toilet, he conducted business from a cherrywood desk illuminated by a torchiere featuring a black reflecting bowl. A high-back, black-cushioned rolling chair became his throne, while guests could sit in a pair of sleek, modern office chairs. Wall-mounted shelves above Mahler's head held his books, and a globe of the world stood in one corner.

His master bedroom, carpeted in dark red, contained a king-sized bed, plus a walnut wood dresser and chest of drawers. An imposing black marble fireplace filled one corner at a 45-degree angle. The roomy walk-in closet provided ample space for the expensive suits that Mahler brought with him from New Jersey.

The master bathroom, with black marble counter and giant mirrors, contained an oversized combination spa and bathtub. A bachelor intending to entertain women in his home might have been expected to hang a painting or photo of a beautiful woman in the wall space at one end of the tub. Mahler oddly chose a different image. He hung a framed poster of Al Pacino in the role of Tony Montana, a brutal cocaine dealer and killer in the 1983 film *Scarface*. Mahler's odd taste in bathroom decoration would later raise considerable speculation that it reflected the way he saw himself.

Despite David Mahler's takeover of Cole Crest, he and Karl Norvik worked out an amicable relationship and became close friends. The staircase from Norvik's rooms allowed him free access to the common office space, den, and kitchen they shared.

As soon as Mahler felt comfortably ensconced, Stacy began making trips from Visalia to Cole Crest. "I would stay anywhere from an hour to a few nights. Sometimes we went to Newport Beach and visited my friends. My job in sales gave me a territory all the way from Merced to Bakersfield, which made it convenient for us to meet. Sometimes he would come up to Bakersfield for a rendezvous." Describing this, Stacy laughed. "What a rendezvous place. Bakersfield is not exactly the entertainment capital of California. We did that several times."

Of course, spending time at Cole Crest meant that Stacy came to know Karl Norvik. She had mixed feelings about him. "He seemed kind of remote to me at times. They had a baby grand piano in there. David and I would be getting ready to go out and he would be in there playing the piano. It was strange. You're up there in the hills being serenaded by this concert pianist, but he was absolutely great in playing it. I can't explain it. I just had this weird feeling about him."

At one point in time, said Stacy, Mahler considered forcing Norvik to move out. She explained, "His room was the one with a hardwood floor and David wanted to get him out of there so he could turn it into an art studio for me. I was going to attend art classes at UCLA, but it never happened."

Even social occasions with Karl Norvik bothered Stacy. "Karl had a girlfriend and we four were all going out to dinner one night. She had a male roommate, and when we went to her place, that guy had a dress on. Every time we would go anywhere with them, it would get more weird. His girlfriend finally left him and went back to her husband."

While Stacy thought the house was beautiful, she hated the narrow, tortuous streets. "You couldn't get me to even try to drive up there on those crazy, winding roads. Sometimes, to avoid them, I would take the train to Los Angeles and get him to come pick me up at Union Station." She made the trip, either by car or train, numerous times. "I would go every chance I got and spend time with him—but I never lived in that house with him; I just commuted back and forth." Stacy eventually discovered she was not the only woman who spent prodigious time at Cole Crest.

David Mahler reportedly tried twice to pass the bar exam in California, but he failed. Unlicensed to practice law in the state, he became a "commodities trader" who also dispensed legal advice. It didn't take him long to establish a network of clients and associates and to find profitability in his business. For his own reasons, he used aliases in some of the transactions. In these trades and with his income, he acquired a BMW and two Jaguars, one brand-new and one three years old. Mahler registered two of the vehicles in fictitious names.

Karl Norvik, still living in the Cole Crest house, trusted Mahler with his savings, as well as the estate of a close relative. Somehow, Mahler became a majority co-owner of an expensive home and car belonging to Karl and his kin.

Mahler's relationship with Stacy Tipton continued to careen along its rocky path, sometimes fun and sometimes nerve-racking. Stacy enjoyed going out to nightspots where celebrities also flocked. "We ran into Jennifer Aniston one night at a club and saw several other stars over the years." After one evening of entertainment along the Sunset Strip, Stacy and Mahler stopped at a popular nightclub for a late supper. Finding it full, even at midnight, they waited outside and watched a film crew at work on a motion picture. "I'm a real film buff," said Stacy, "with the ability to spot actors, and

I saw Dabney Coleman there. I pointed him out to David, and he went over and started talking to him between shots. David said, 'We're having a party' and invited Coleman to come. I'm sure that he wondered, 'Who the heck is this guy?' But David introduced the actor to me like they had been friends forever. We finally go inside and get a table. David is trying to be Mr. Big Shot. I seriously doubted that Dabney Coleman knew him. He certainly never showed up at the party."

Mahler's audacity probably worked well for him. His aggressive sociability resulted in a growing network of clients for his commodities trading business. But one new business contact came about as the result of a weird coincidence.

Midway through 2005, porn actor Michael Conoscenti had been arrested on a narcotics charge. He needed a lawyer and told a good pal about his problems. The buddy, known as "Captain Bob," said he had a very good friend who might be able to help, and he gave him the telephone number of a man named Dave. Conoscenti called and spoke to Dave, but he could only get informal advice from him, since Dave had no license to provide legal representation in the state. But the two men chatted about Michael's problems. This led to more telephone conversations over the next twelve months, but no face-to-face meeting.

Michael happened to have a friend who lived on Cole Crest Drive in the Hollywood Hills. In mid-2006, he stayed with his buddy a few nights and heard mention of a lawyer who lived next door named Dave. The two men strolled over to Dave's place and were invited inside. In the ensuing conversation, Michael learned this was the same Dave he had been talking to by telephone over the past year. The timing could not have been more propitious for David Mahler.

With his underlying ambitions to find a wedge into the world of celebrity and film, plus a long-standing interest in strippers, fate had stepped in to lend a hand. Through Michael Conoscenti, Mahler met Sheldon Weinberg, and he could see a golden opportunity. This guy had the power to open doors that many men, and more than a few women, could do nothing but fantasize about. He knew countless wannabe actresses willing to do anything for a chance to be in movies. He could provide access to being on-site in houses where porn stars performed for the cameras. On top of that, acquaintance with Weinberg might lead to lucrative financial deals. This all appealed to David Mahler.

The new friendship also struck Weinberg as fortunate. He had long been interested in expanding his investments, and considered Mahler's knowledge of stock, commodities, and financial dealings worthwhile. The two men immediately bonded.

The companionship with Sheldon Weinberg and Michael Conoscenti led to entanglements for David Mahler with two women who liked showing it all. One of them would become his "fiancée."

Conoscenti, as Mahler's new buddy, escorted him to a strip club in the San Fernando Valley. His interest focused on a performer who fit Mahler's preference for diminutive blue-eyed blondes. He couldn't take his eyes off Cheryl "Cherry" Lane (pseudonym) who stood five-four, weighed one hundred pounds, and hadn't yet reached her twentieth birthday. She described herself as an "exotic dancer." Mahler engaged her in conversations between performances, and perhaps, although there is no evidence to prove it, paid for a private lap dance. She agreed to a subsequent date.

Later speaking of David, Cheryl said the initial relationship was "professional," meaning he provided her with legal services. But it quickly developed into something closer and more intimate. By early summer 2006, she moved into the Cole Crest house with him.

Mahler's horoscope had suggested he would have an immoderate taste for the pleasures of life, be domineering, unfaithful in love, violent, brutal, and irascible. Cheryl wouldn't argue with those predictions. She got her first hints of it when he began showing up in the club where she worked and provoking loud arguments with her, which resulted in the management firing her. During the ten months she shared bed and body with Mahler, Cheryl fell into some legal trouble. He provided money for her bail, facilitating her release from jail while awaiting trial. She later asserted that she paid him back in full, but he claimed she still owed him $7,000. The disputed debt became an ongoing contention between them.

As the live-in relationship deteriorated, Cheryl complained, David's anger turned physical.

His fury erupted not only against Cheryl, but also at Stacy, who had not given up on Mahler despite his philandering. She came down from Visalia on February 2, 2007. Not surprisingly, a dispute flared up. Stacy reached for the phone, but David grabbed it away from her. He threw it across the room and then violently pushed her into the bathroom. As she collapsed, her head struck the sink, and she landed on the marble bathtub, which inflicted a deep bruise on her lower back.

Appalled, Stacy used her cell phone to call the police. David Mahler was arrested and charged with domestic violence.

Stacy went back to Visalia, and David seemed determined to take out his wrath on Cheryl. During arguments he would push her around. In March, while they yelled at each other, she placed her hand on his open laptop computer. He slammed it into a partially closed position, trapping her fingers and causing a deep laceration. It would leave a noticeable scar. She did not notify the police, but she moved out soon afterward.

If the loss of Cheryl Lane hurt David Mahler's feelings, he didn't grieve very long. Michael Conoscenti had met a curvaceous young woman, Kitty Carter (pseudonym), introduced her into acting in porn films, and brought her to Calabasas to live with him. As Mahler's interactions with Weinberg increased, he met Kitty and was immediately enchanted. It helped when Kitty and Michael had a violent argument, in which he bit her on the wrist. Any remaining conjugal relationship between them came to an explosive end. David grabbed the opportunity. He would eventually say, "I was really in love with Kitty, other than being that porn star stuff. I met her through my client, Mr. Weinberg. He was having these film shoots in his house. She came over for that, and became my paramour."

Referring to Kitty as his "wife," Mahler acknowledged that no marriage had taken place but said he bought her an engagement ring. "You know, we talked about getting married. I said, 'Will you quit the profession?' And she just—she couldn't. And then the whole thing got to be too much for me."

Stacy Tipton knew of the affairs with Cheryl and Kitty, plus numerous dalliances with other women, but she did not allow his skirt chasing to sever their ties. "He told me about them. Sometimes I would call him, and a party would be going on, and I knew there were hookers there. I would ask, 'Is that another one?' I think he had so many that he didn't even know most of their names."

Without admitting any jealousy, Stacy said, "I didn't like a lot of the stuff that went on. I knew all about the stripper and the porn actress." With a disgusted expression on her face, Stacy added, "I met them. I'd walk into his place and they would be there. Oh, heck yeah. The pictures I have in my mind about that are not pleasant ones."

Sex between Stacy and David became increasingly problematical. "He could be a little kinky at times." Some of his desires repulsed her, but she tried to accommodate him as much as her personal values would allow. She later complained, "I'm more of a romantic. Lovemaking is personal, and I didn't like all of that other stuff."

Silently pondering those recollections, Stacy spoke up again and divulged more. "One time he and I went to the porn industry's convention in Las Vegas. I think it was called the Pornfest. Those women, Kitty and Cheryl, along with one of their boyfriends, were actually staying in our room with us! I thought,

'This is really weird.'" Stacy's expression made it clear that the memory disgusted her. She quickly dropped the subject.

The stripper's youthfulness seemed to bother Stacy more than the girl's cohabitation with Mahler. "Cheryl, she was the young one, only about eighteen or nineteen. Oh, my God! She was born about the time I graduated from high school! I have seen pictures of her online, too—stuff she later sent me by e-mail. I didn't really like her. One time I kicked her out of the Cole Crest house. Not really kicked, but just told her, 'Get out of here.' I was visiting and couldn't believe she would be there at the same time."

Another element of Mahler's declining existence didn't escape Stacy's attention. At the mention of a need for cocaine, she snapped, "Oh yeah, that was him."

The convoluted affairs and fractured relationships with Stacy, Cheryl, and Kitty were not David Mahler's only source of female companionship, some of which he chose to pay for directly.

In his tangled network of contacts, he enjoyed a long-term acquaintance with Atticus King (pseudonym), who described himself as an independent contractor–taxi driver. Others called him a pimp. A rotund African American, King stood five-nine and weighed in excess of 250 pounds. Whether unable to find conventional clothing that would fit his rounded body, or just by preference, King's garish apparel drew attention like a flashing neon sign. His uniform of choice generally consisted of jumpsuits, either brilliant white or glowing red.

Speaking in colorful terms that any self-respecting rapper would envy, King's vocabulary and creative expressions entertained everyone who knew him.

He and Mahler met in 2002, and they formed a bond of professional convenience, along with a personal friendship.

If anyone asked King, he would deny providing prostitutes to Mahler. In his version, Mahler would contact the women, and then call King to go pick them up in his dark green-and-white minivan, emblazoned with a TAXI sign, and bring them to Cole Crest or to a hotel. This took place "many times," and the driver would usually hang around until Mahler and his "date" completed their liaison.

Atticus also insisted that he didn't have anything to do with drugs, but he observed that his cohort Mahler used methamphetamine and cocaine liberally. It worried Atticus when he saw this pattern substantially increase in the first few months of 2007. In addition to the narcotics, David Mahler appeared to be consuming a great deal of alcohol.

According to other people in Mahler's social circle, he was not a pleasant drunk. Some men turn romantic under the influence of drugs and booze; others are hilarious; some turn angry and belligerent. For David, getting high seemed to light a fire of fury inside him, and a tendency to turn violent.

Still, David Mahler could exercise the same charm Stacy Tipton had seen in the early years of their relationship. And when Michael Conoscenti introduced him to yet another woman, Kristin Baldwin, he put on his best face.

The meeting took place before 2006 ended, and prior to an upheaval among Conoscenti, Weinberg, and Mahler.

Kristin happened to be visiting Conoscenti in Calabasas at the same time Mahler showed up for a business conference with Sheldon Weinberg. Conoscenti handled the introductions. David Mahler made the usual flirtatious comments, standard fare when meeting an attractive woman. Kristi Baldwin, gregarious as always, smiled and returned the banter. Neither of them made any overtures for a future hookup.

CHAPTER 9

"ARE YOU MY FRIEND?"

Kristin Baldwin's periodic presence in Sheldon Weinberg's home, while visiting Michael Conoscenti over several months, kept her in David Mahler's field of vision. Eventually a traffic ticket she received emboldened Mahler to invite Kristin on a date. She complained about the citation in the presence of the group at Weinberg's Calabasas home. Mahler overheard, and offered to help her out with the problem.

His timing couldn't have been better. Kristin's relationship with an abusive man had ended earlier; so with no regular male partner in her life, she was open to companionship. Grateful for Mahler's offer of help, she saw no harm in dating him. He drove a new indigo blue Jaguar convertible, wore expensive clothing, seemed to have plenty of money, and behaved pleasantly enough in her presence. She accepted his offer to join him for dinner.

While their friendship grew closer, the roots of business dealings between David Mahler and Sheldon Weinberg also increased in strength. But those same roots undermined and cracked the sidewalk Michael Conoscenti treaded in connection to his film partnership with Weinberg. In Conoscenti's view, Mahler, Weinberg, and the actress known as Kitty had been gradually levering him from the business. He couldn't help but believe they had formed a conspiracy to ease him out and take it over completely. Infuriated, he confronted Weinberg, spelled out his suspicions in explicit terms, and moved out of the Calabasas quarters.

At about the same time, Sheldon Weinberg invited Kristin Baldwin to move in. She had been helping out with a few chores while visiting with Michael. Weinberg not only appreciated Kristin's skills, but he liked her upbeat personality. He offered her free living quarters, plus a modest salary, in exchange for doing a few clerical duties, helping to keep the place neat, and perhaps cooking a few meals. Kristin agreed and brought her things to the guest room in the first week of March.

The initial dinner session with David had been pleasant enough for Kristin and she saw him more in the next few weeks. A couple of his tenants at Cole Crest would later say they thought she spent a few nights with Mahler, but no one could be certain. It is doubtful that Kristin felt any serious attachment to him, but, as many women might, she probably liked the two Jaguars he kept in the Cole Crest garage, his money, and the glamorous ambience of his lifestyle.

With both Kristin and Kitty living in the Calabasas estate, they began having conversations. Inevitably the subject of David Mahler came up. At that point, Kitty still considered herself his fiancée. But when she learned that he had been dating Kristin, all hell broke loose for David.

An insider to the ongoing saga of Mahler's love affairs revealed that he and Kitty "routinely engaged each other in vicious physical fights that continued after the dating relationship ended." In David Mahler's estimation, the romance tapered off to a deep, enduring friendship. Kitty moved out of the Calabasas residence. Her friendship with Kristin remained intact. In April, when Kristin sometimes grew bored with the environment at the Weinberg house, she would spend a few nights with Kitty in an apartment about eight miles from Calabasas.

Romantic turbulence and business problems increasingly led to stress for David Mahler, and he amped up his dependence on chemical stimulants. If Kristin knew about David's growing drug usage, it did not prevent her from socializing with him. She had known countless people in Westlake Village, Newport Beach, and in Hawaii who felt no compunctions about smoking, snorting, or injecting everything from pot to meth. Thus Kristin drew no judgmental conclusions about people who enjoyed getting high. To her, Mahler was just a guy who could afford expensive entertainment. Several other people close to him grew worried about his expanding drug and alcohol consumption. Sheldon Weinberg would say that Mahler was "definitely" a drug user, "meth or coke, I think." Drugs may have caused an explosive incident that came in April.

Michael Conoscenti had moved to a home with a gated entrance. Still on amicable terms with David Mahler, he had even arranged yet another meeting for him with a different porn actress. Mahler drove to Conoscenti's address at a prearranged time, and waited outside the gate for her to appear. Never a patient man, he drummed his fingers and clenched his jaws for much longer than he thought a reasonable amount of time, and he grew angrier by the minute. When the woman still failed to appear, Mahler turned his vehicle around, put it in reverse, jammed his foot down on the accelerator, and rammed the gate. The collision did no damage to the car's bumper, but it virtually destroyed the gate.

The noise brought Conoscenti out, shouting at Mahler.

They exchanged vitriolic threats before Mahler peeled out of the driveway and vanished. Conoscenti would later tell police officers that he recognized a black woman who had been in the car with Mahler as someone he knew named Crystal. Why she would have accompanied him, Conoscenti had no idea. Her presence may have been only in his angry imagination.

The episode sparked an ongoing conflict between the two men. Michael Conoscenti repeatedly demanded that David Mahler either have the gate repaired, or cough up the money to have it done. Mahler finally agreed to send someone over to fix it. A few days later, a heavyset Hispanic man calling himself "Edmund" showed up. He poked around at the damaged gate and ineffectively attempted to bend a few metal bars back in place. Within the next two weeks, Edmund made several more appearances, sometimes accompanied by another overweight fellow in greasy overalls. They hammered, banged, and scraped at the gate, but made little visible impact. Conoscenti shook his head in disgust, and finally evicted the "repairmen." The damage stayed.

Frustrated and angry, Michael called David again to demand a proper repair job. Mahler said he would send a handyman over named Donnie.

Donald "Donnie" Van Develde and his wife, Joni, had been renting the lower studio apartment in the Cole Crest home for about a year. In recent months, the self-proclaimed "rock star" had been enduring some lean times and even had difficulty paying his monthly rent or even buying groceries. David Mahler doled out odd jobs to him, with promises of compensation, but according to Donnie, David failed to pay up.

No one could dispute the idea that Donnie looked the part of a rock star. His lean five-ten frame, blue eyes, unkempt, shoulder-length dark hair, with greasy strings over his eyes, and numerous tattoos all enhanced the image, especially when he didn't shave for a few days. Anyone who judged him as a pretentious dreamer, though, would be badly mistaken. Van Develde had been an onstage performer for the better part of two decades.

In 1984, Van Develde organized a rock band in Illinois and called it Enough Z'Nuff, which evolved to Enuff Z'Nuff. Achieving moderate success over the next few years, with Donnie writing, producing, and singing, the group's best known tracks were "Fly High Michelle" and "New Thing." In his own words on a myspace.com page, Van Develde later wrote, "I'll start by saying my name is Donnie. . . .You most likely would remember me as the red-haired, lipstick [wearing], big mouthed, drugged up pretty boy that sings like the Beatles . . . on MTV videos back in 1989-1990." He liked comparing his talents not only to the Fab Four, but also to Aerosmith, Led Zeppelin, Rolling Stones, and Elvis Costello.

He had met Joni on the road while performing. "We were in Ohio, opening for a band called Poison, and I met her at one of the concerts. We had some moderate success, but also a lot of very tough breaks. We had a couple of MTV hits for a while there, and I was signed with some top promoters." He added, "We got in the middle of some political things, an internal thing with one of the labels, and were just in the wrong place, at the wrong time. We were being built up to be this next super band, but it all fell apart."

By 2002, Donnie decided to try a solo career. It fared adequately for a while, and like so many musicians preceding him, he succumbed to the irresistible draw of the Hollywood Hills and illegal stimulants. His career began a precipitous slide. Asked if David Mahler ever provided him with drugs, he replied, "I did one line of meth with him. He really doesn't share his drugs." He added, "I got arrested once for crystal meth." By 2007, he had gone through a rehab program. On medications he found himself struggling and doing menial labor in order to pay the rent.

Kristin's occasional visits to Cole Crest resulted in her meeting Donnie. One time, according to him, Kristin Baldwin drove her own car, but she came only as far as the Canyon Country Store on Laurel Canyon Boulevard. From there she called David Mahler to come down, meet her, and lead the way back up to his house. "Her car, I guess, barely made it to the top, so Mahler called me and asked if I would take a look at it. He was at the point of asking me to do every little thing in the way of odd jobs. So I cleaned her spark plugs and did a few adjustments. She was supposed to pay me twenty dollars for the repairs, but never did."

Van Develde had grown accustomed to seeing women come and go, often staying overnight in Mahler's upper floors of Cole Crest. "I have never socialized or hung out with David or anything like that. But there would always be this green taxi minivan sitting outside all night, sometimes for two or three days. And if any of us who lived there saw David, he would be all loopy. You'd see a black girl and this big, overweight black guy, and they would finally leave in that taxi. Sometimes that guy would sleep in the van out in front of the house."

The few times Donnie was allowed inside David's quarters, primarily the office, he observed drug usage. "He had this top drawer of a chest he kept opening up and pulling out some kind of pipe and smoking it, and putting it back in the drawer." Donnie also observed business transactions. "What he does mainly for his income is . . . he plays the stocks. He sits at his computer and watches it like a hawk, like he has to react in seconds. He showed me once that he had made a million bucks in one night."

To Van Develde, Mahler's "clients" seemed strange. "I think he's doing some shady deals . . . maybe for drugs or something like that." The drugs Mahler acquired, though, said

Donnie, probably came from elsewhere. "He usually goes somewhere to get them." It would be speculated that the desert community around Daggett could have been Mahler's source.

Trips to Las Vegas, several with Stacy Tipton, familiarized Mahler with the long drive intersecting the Mojave Desert. He knew of the "Y" intersection at Barstow, where Interstate 40 splits off from I-15. He might very well have also known that some of the desert communities have a reputation for covert methamphetamine labs, and a thriving market for the illicit product. It certainly wouldn't be unreasonable to suggest that Mahler, through his contacts with drug users, might have learned some specific addresses where he could buy meth. With David Mahler's need for drugs, not only for himself, but to warm the hearts of his numerous female guests, he could conceivably have made other trips out to areas surrounding the tiny burgh of Daggett. If so, he certainly would have also recognized the area's potential for disposing of anything an individual would wish never to be found.

Even though David had promised to send a handyman named Donnie to repair Michael Conoscenti's gate, it never happened. It would be Conoscenti's problem to have it fixed.

Most broken love affairs wind up with the man and woman curtailing future contacts with each other. David Mahler, choosing to take a different course, seemed to enjoy continued visits and correspondence with his women. In the middle of May, Kitty's telephone answering service relayed a message to her from Mahler. He asked Kitty and her current boyfriend to join him for a trip to Hawaii, and indicated that Kristin was accompanying him. Kitty laughed it off.

On Wednesday, May 23, Mahler invited Kristin to accompany him to a business meeting in Newport Beach. She still had friends in the bayside community from the time she had lived there after high school. Delighted at the opportunity to perhaps visit old pals, and to eat at any one of the great restaurants she remembered, Kristin accepted David's offer.

In the late evening of that Wednesday, Mahler and Kristin drove fifty miles to Newport Beach in his newer Jaguar convertible. After a business stop for several hours at a Marriott Hotel, they drove to an upscale shopping mall called Fashion Island and pulled into the entry port of the luxurious Island Hotel.

If Kristin had been concerned that he planned to take her to some "quickie" cheap motel, her doubts instantly vanished. The twenty-story Island Hotel offered refined elegance. An expansive check-in area featured dozens of light earth-toned couches and chairs enhanced with inviting pillows. A long walk through the lobby led to a man-made lagoon—a cross-shaped swimming pool offering a fireplace for evening ambience and plenty of loungers. Most of the upper-story rooms, including a lavish luxury suite, provided picturesque views over the city and the ocean beyond, all the way to Santa Catalina Island.

Later discussing the incident, David skirted the issue of whether or not he had told Kristin he planned to stay a couple of nights. A security camera in the lobby captured David and Kristin, along with a man Mahler called his client, at the check-in desk. They could be seen taking an elevator to their room after midnight.

In his version of events, Mahler recalled arguing with Kristin, blaming her for instigating it. He said she refused to leave the room at checkout time; so he departed alone. Hotel records show that Mahler checked out on Friday. A manager revealed that the occupant and his guest had been asked to leave because of the disturbance they created.

In his explanation, Mahler didn't mention his previous pattern of exploding in anger and abandoning his longtime girlfriend, Stacy Tipton, several times in New York and in Hawaii.

Instead, he painted himself in much gentler terms. "I didn't mean to be a —please don't get me wrong. I'm a gentleman."

Other people expressed conflicting understandings of what had happened. Their consensus suggested that Kristin had been abandoned at the hotel after an argument with Mahler. To make matters worse, she had been left without any money or transportation back to Calabasas. She called, or tried to call, a few friends in the Newport area and in the San Fernando Valley without success. Peter Means later stated, "I had a phone message from her. She called from Newport Beach, where she was with Mahler. When I returned the call, she was no longer in the room." Means tried to connect with Kristin on her cell phone, but he couldn't reach her.

A male friend of Kitty's, who also knew Kristin, told Kitty that he had received a call from Kristin, sobbing that she had been abandoned in Newport Beach by David. A few days later, Kitty called David and asked him how the trip to Newport with Kristin had turned out. He refused to give any details, but he acknowledged that "there had been trouble."

Tara Rush, with whom Kristin had lived two years earlier, recalled a chilling message on her cell phone. "It was so odd. I just saw her about ten days before that. She called from Newport Beach and said she went there with some lawyer guy she had been dating. They had a fight and he left her there. Her voice was scary, like she was screaming for her life." When Tara tried to call back, she was unable to make contact with her friend.

Eventually Kristin made her way back to Calabasas, but how she did it has remained obscured in a cloud of mystery. If Mahler knows, he hasn't divulged it. It has been suggested that she talked a cabdriver into taking her the sixty miles, on the promise that she would pay, or that someone in Calabasas would come up with the money. Peter Means doubted that.

"She never carried enough money to pay for such an exorbitant taxi fare, and she didn't have a credit card." Her stepfather felt it would have been difficult for her to pay the fare on her own.

A hotel employee observed her with an unidentified man in the lobby after she left the room. A security officer said he saw her leave in a taxi.

If one of Kristin's friends, either in Newport Beach or the San Fernando Valley, provided either a ride or the cash to pay for commercial transportation, they haven't yet come forward. The facts may never be known.

Enraged and livid over the desertion by Mahler leaving her stranded, Kristin telephoned him the next day.

In David's sanitized version, he explained, "She called me on Saturday asking if she could have some piece to [her] car." He explained that she had removed something from her car in Calabasas so no one could use the vehicle, and had left the component in Mahler's garage. "I said, 'Fine, come on up.'" He didn't bother to clarify how or when Kristin had left the "piece of her car" inside his garage.

Tara Rush later described a different scenario. She said, "I saw her after she got back. It was on Saturday. She took a cab over to my place in Canoga Park." Rush said that Kristin called the guy who had left her in Newport. They had apparently made up, because he drove over and picked her up in front of a liquor store on DeSoto and Nordhoff.

Another woman had planned to spend that weekend at Cole Crest. Stacy Tipton recalled, "I had just got this neat car, a Jeep Cherokee. But my dad didn't want me to drive it down there until some work it needed was done. When they completed it on Saturday and I was ready to go, I called David three times and he didn't return any of them. I was supposed to be there. I could go on and on about that, but I don't want to." She wondered if her presence might have changed everything.

Kristin, David claimed, had arrived at Cole Crest late Saturday at the same time as a man named Edmund, who drove a green flatbed pickup truck. "He's a Mexican fellow, about five-eight, or maybe five-ten, overweight, about two hundred twenty pounds." David acknowledged that he had seen Edmund before, but with Michael Conoscenti, never with Kristin. This man, said Mahler, was a drug dealer. "But he fancied himself a little more than that. He likes to think he is a ladies' man. He would ask me, 'Oh, you need girls tonight?'"

This time, though, said Mahler, there was no offer of women. Instead, Kristin "started indicating that she wanted drugs."

Continuing with his fanciful recollection of that Saturday evening in his home, Mahler said, "There was a little bit of an altercation, which made me uncomfortable—slapping, that kind of thing." He stated that Edmund had started slapping Kristin. It had taken place in his bedroom.

Shocked—perhaps like Claude Rains in the classic film *Casablanca* was "shocked" to see gambling in Humphrey Bogart's nightclub—Mahler said he had telephoned a couple of his friends to ask advice: Karl Norvik and Donnie Van Develde. "This is a problem. What do you think I should do? You know, I got a guy slapping a girl here. Do I get involved?"

The situation, in Mahler's tale, became too much for him. He decided to leave the premises. But first, he gave Edmund a warning to be out of there before he returned. He also ordered Kristi to take whatever property she had there and leave. Mahler made one other call before exiting the house. When Atticus King answered, Mahler yelled into the phone, "I have an emergency. Are you my friend? Go to the Beverly Wilshire Hotel and meet me there!"

King replied, "I ain't goin' to the Beverly Wilshire, man. That's too far. How 'bout the Marriott by the airport?"

Mahler uncharacteristically agreed without argument. Recalling it, he said, "I left and checked in at the Marriott

Hotel at the Los Angeles International Airport, early Sunday morning."

A few of David Mahler's assertions would prove to be true. He did check in at the LAX Marriott not long after dawn on that Sunday. Among the calls he made was one to Atticus King. And Mahler's story about telephoning Donnie and Karl, both of whom were in their apartments below Mahler's, also proved factual. But the subject of their conversations turned out to be far more loathsome than the duplicitous yarn about Edmund slapping Kristin.

CHAPTER 10

"I NEED TO DISPOSE OF A DEAD BODY"

En route to the Marriott, David Mahler left his Cole Crest residence at six twenty-one Sunday morning. He drove down, zigzagging Sunset Plaza Drive, narrowly missing rows of trash cans placed near driveways. At a nearly indiscernible intersection, he passed within a few paces of the home owned by singer Johnny Mathis. Near the bottom of the hills, he drove by a high hedge that hid the former estate of screen star Anne Baxter. Reaching the first traffic signal, at Sunset Boulevard, Mahler turned west. The quickest route for his destination would have been to make his way through Beverly Hills, enter the I-405 Freeway, and head south. About twelve miles later, he exited on Century Boulevard, where it empties into LAX, and then drove a few blocks west to the Marriott Hotel.

After letting a valet park his 2007 indigo blue Jaguar at seven o'clock that morning, he made his rendezvous with his taxi driver buddy, Atticus King. At the registration desk, Mahler checked in with a special request not to be listed under his true name. The hotel, respecting their guests' privacy, put into effect their "code blue" protocol to keep his identity confidential. Both men went up to a room on the fourth floor.

King would later express the opinion that Mahler seemed terribly upset and agitated. Perhaps to quiet his frayed nerves, Mahler contacted room service and had a $120 bottle of Rémy Martin fine champagne cognac delivered, along with food, costing in excess of $200, to which he added a generous tip.

A little later, a young woman with long, dark hair joined the two men. Her method of transportation to the Marriott would be disputed. An employee of the hotel thought Atticus King had left and returned with her in tow. A police report stated, *Atticus King brought the girl to him.* King denied it, while admitting that he often "picked up and delivered" girls at Mahler's request. In this case, though, he insisted that she arrived on her own. The woman told Mahler her price was $2,000 for the full night.

With that, the party began. Booze flowed freely, several lines of cocaine went up noses, and a meth pipe also had prodigious use.

During the course of that Sunday, May 27, all day and well into the night, hotel security staff personnel visited Mahler's room more than once. They observed the occupants—Mahler, a woman, and a rotund African-American man—appeared to be engaged in a "brawl." The security people twice requested that the trio please reduce the noise level. But it continued. At one point, when Mahler woke up after a sex-induced nap, and the woman asked for her $2,000, Mahler exploded. He began trashing the room and attacking her. King intervened and calmed the situation down by pulling them apart. He promised the hooker that Mahler would pay her later.

Mahler reluctantly handed his bank card to King and instructed him to find an ATM, withdraw $700, and bring it back.

During the tempestuous day and night, Mahler made frequent calls from his cell phone. His whispered conversations puzzled King. After several attempts, Mahler reached Stacy Tipton in Visalia, told her that he had a serious problem, and asked if she could come to Hollywood and meet him.

When they checked out just before noon on Monday, Mahler used a credit card to pay a bill for over $3,706! During the wild night, the occupants had destroyed an expensive plasma television set. He gave the angry prostitute $700, and promised to pay her the balance later. She and King left together.

Mahler headed back to Sunset Boulevard and the Standard Hotel, where Stacy waited for him. Of course, during their two-night stay, they argued frequently. Mahler accused Stacy of standing him up on Saturday, and ignored her explanations about having work done on her new car, and that she had repeatedly tried to contact him. His nervous, erratic behavior, much more intense than usual, shocked her.

On that same Monday, they paid a brief visit to the house on Cole Crest. Later discussing it, Stacy said she did not go inside with him. In Mahler's recollection, he contradicted her. "We stopped at my house on Monday, for all of about two minutes because I needed to grab my computer. Things looked normal inside, other than there was some blood. That freaked me out, but Stacy freaked out more than me. I said, 'Stacy, we'll deal with this later.' The blood was in my bedroom, where Edmund was slapping Kristi."

Back at the Standard Hotel, said Mahler, Stacy was still upset and absolutely refused to go back to the house. She departed on Wednesday for Visalia.

By Thursday, May 31, Memorial Day, Mahler returned to his home. The presence of detergents and cleansers in

Mahler's bedroom suggested that he attempted to clean up the blood from the crime scene.

In neighboring Orange County, Karl Norvik also thought about the blood in Mahler's house. He had agonized over a decision, crushed by fear and anguish every minute of the last four days and nights. Unable to eat, sleep, or even think clearly, he had lost weight from his slim five-nine frame. *Should I call the police? Will I endanger my own life or the lives of people I love? Will this man I've regarded as a close friend take violent revenge?*

The final week of May 2007 had not been particularly warm in Southern California, but Norvik found himself soaked with perspiration brought on by anxiety. His stomach had wrenched itself into painful knots. *Damn! What to do?*

In his work and his social life, Karl had found serenity, something he valued above everything else. Had that all crashed? Norvik couldn't believe the stunning events that had turned his life upside down. Would he ever be able to resume working among the glitterati of Hollywood? For more than twenty years, he had been involved in production, sound mixing, and even film editing for what he preferred to call "top industry names." Now, a man he had trusted completely had potentially destroyed everything. How could he ever have regarded David Mahler as his best friend?

Since the early-morning hours of Sunday, May 27, Karl had avoided returning to the house on Cole Crest Drive. For several years while he had managed the home built on a sloping canyon wall, the upper floor had been his domain; while renters lived in the lower levels. But David Mahler had changed all of that when he took over.

For six years, they had enjoyed a friendly coexistence. Norvik had even trusted Mahler with investing his money, and a relative's life savings. They shared personal insights, and enjoyed the ambience of residing atop an elevated ridge among neighbors from all levels of the entertainment industry. The wannabe actors, struggling screenwriters, musicians, camera operators, artists, all the way to studio executives, lived in every conceivable type of structure from cabins to castles speckling the Hollywood Hills.

In recognition of Karl's intelligence, David had said to him more than once, "You have a mind like a steel trap. If you had chosen to become a lawyer, I wouldn't ever want to oppose you in court."

During these last five days of living hell, Karl Norvik had endured the most troubling period of his life while staying with a relative fifty miles from Cole Crest Drive. He could only ask himself, "What was I thinking?"

The incident seemed at first like some goofy misinterpretation. Piecing events together in his mind, Norvik still couldn't believe he might be personally involved in a murder. The whole thing sounded to him like a film noir script or a complex murder novel.

It began after a Saturday evening business meeting with a colleague in the upper-floor office that Mahler and Norvik sometimes shared. At one point, while Karl and his guest studied data on two computers, David had walked in, accompanied by another man whom Norvik had never before seen. The duo lingered only a few minutes and then vanished into a separate part of the house. After another half hour, and conclusion of their transactions, Karl's guest said good night and left. Karl descended an interior staircase to his bedroom, treated himself to a couple of drinks, and took off the clothing he had adopted almost as a uniform; slim-fit black slacks and a black T-shirt. He collapsed on his bed at about eleven thirty that night and fell asleep.

Sometime in the early-morning hours of Sunday, shrill,

piercing voices snapped him into full consciousness. He later described it as "loud, screaming profanities, which basically escalated to a much more vitriolic and heated level. I heard a woman screaming and Mahler's very recognizable loud voice." Reluctant to repeat the exact language, Norvik described it as including "the *B* word, the *C* word, and the *F* word . . . just a string of very, very hateful profanities." At first, Karl wondered if the stranger he had seen with Mahler was involved, but finally decided that only two people were yelling at each other. Most of the shouted invectives, he realized, came from David Mahler. He could not recognize the woman's voice.

This scenario had been played out more than once in recent months. "I had heard, in past occasions, when a woman had been over at the house in the company of Mahler, very heated arguments and it almost seemed as if 'here we go again,' to put it bluntly."

Even though Norvik attempted to block out the annoying clamor by hugging a pillow over his head, he clearly heard another noise interrupt the barrage of yelling and cursing. He interpreted it as a loud thump. "It first sounded like a heavy piece of furniture had been thrown." With his own bedroom situated below Mahler's sleeping quarters, the sound came from overhead. He visualized either someone jumping on someone else, or perhaps a chest of drawers toppled to the floor.

A welcome period of calm followed, almost allowing Karl to exhale and go back to sleep. But before ten minutes elapsed, another audible thud resonated from the floor above. This one, he later recalled, "sounded more like a body thump . . . something that weighed well over one hundred pounds." It seemed to emanate from near a fireplace in the bedroom above.

Another brief period of quiet ended with something that brought to Karl's mind images of movement. "I heard a dragging noise, as if furniture, or possibly a body, was being pulled across the floor." It came intermittently, "Like a pull and a stop, another dragging, and stop."

This noise, too, came to an end. At last, Karl thought, *It's all over*. Never in his life had he been more mistaken. Just as he closed his eyes, a thunderous pounding on his door tensed every muscle in his body. "It was very, very insistent and non-stop banging." He leaped out of bed and slipped into his trousers and shirt. Glancing at his cell phone display, he noted the time: 6:25 A.M. Nerves taut, he opened the door a crack and peered out onto the stairway landing. David Mahler stood there, dressed in a dark suit.

"What's going on?" Karl asked, trying to sound impatient but managing only a nervous whisper.

David bellowed, "I have a major emergency!"

"What is it?"

With no hesitation, David Mahler spit the words out in a loud slur: "I need to dispose of a dead body."

Norvik felt himself start to tremble. Not from the chill morning air, but from shock. To him, Mahler's indistinct speech, dilated pupils, and face drained of color made him appear to be drunk. "Even his eyes looked gray rather than their usual brown."

By now, Karl Norvik's mind had developed a scenario. The thump he had heard overhead must have been the woman who had been screaming at Mahler. If there was a dead body up there, it had to be her. From his years of friendship with Mahler, Norvik knew that drugs were commonly used when female visitors came, so the possibility of a drug-induced death flitted through his mind. He asked Mahler, point-blank, "Did she overdose?"

Mahler's mute answer came only in the negative shaking of his head.

Stepping over to a staircase, Karl asked, "What happened?"

Both men moved tentatively up a couple of steps. Before

they reached the entry to David's rooms, Mahler announced, "I shot her near the balcony."

Staggered by the frank admission, Norvik felt like he couldn't breathe. Later speaking of it, he explained, "I was just floored, shocked, in awe beyond consciousness. I walked up about three or four more stairs so I could take a seat on the landing. I needed to sit down and speak with him." But no conversation took place. Instead, Norvik glanced into the open doorway leading into Mahler's bedroom, and felt sick. "I saw a corpse with a big bullet hole in the left side of her face, lying diagonally to the corner of his bed."

The image would stay with Karl Norvik forever. The woman lay on her back, with arms stretched out, palms up, and long blond hair extending from her head as if she had been dragged. He didn't think he had ever seen her before, but couldn't be certain. "It was rather hard to tell, especially when someone has been shot in the face. The hole was about the size of a quarter. Some of the blood had coagulated and there were streaks of it [that] had run over the nose to the other cheek. But it wasn't flowing out. She wore what looked to be like a gold halter top, very small and skimpy, and it was kinda hiked up." The garment's odd position further convinced Karl Norvik that she had been dragged across the floor. "It looked like she was wearing some kind of white thin cotton pants, and I could see a panty line because they were that sheer."

Mahler interrupted Norvik's observation. "So, are you going to help me?" he demanded rather than inquired.

The world seemed to revolve faster for Norvik, in a dizzy spin. Recalling it, he said, "At that moment, I was just so shocked. The feeling of your-whole-life-passing-before-your-eyes kind of thing, and thinking about my family and personal safety and not knowing what to think. I have known this man for years and years—a longtime dear friend. And it was just a lot to absorb in a moment, emotionally impacted."

Despite his mental chaos, Karl Norvik managed a one word answer: "No!"

Without even looking at Mahler, he lurched back down the stairway and entered his own room again. Just before he closed the door, he heard Mahler bark, "Well, don't tell anyone."

Without pause, Karl kneeled in the bathroom and threw up. Thinking he had regained his composure, Norvik stood, but he had to drop down again, twice more, to heave out his guts.

The advice, or demand, to keep his mouth shut had kept Norvik silent for four full days of terror and worry. He would later confide good reasons for his fear. Months earlier, during a driving trip to Las Vegas with Mahler, it had shocked him to learn that David was sending text-messaged death threats to Cheryl Lane. Also, said Norvik, David had "engaged some people" to plant drugs on her so she would be sent to prison.

Worse yet, according to Norvik's recollection, Edmund, who had been supplying meth to Mahler, had secretly informed him that Mahler had offered $100,000 to kill both Donnie and Karl. Edmund had rejected it. Whether or not it had been true, or a threat designed to ensure their silence, could never be proven.

When he could stand it no longer, at about midnight on Thursday, May 31, Norvik made a tough decision. Driven by moral, legal, and ethical motives, he decided that he must do the right thing. First, though, he felt honor bound to notify Donnie Van Develde. Karl knew that Donnie also had knowledge of the shooting and had seen the victim's body. He telephoned the other tenant and advised him, "Donnie, I'm going to call the police and report this. You might want to get out of the house."

In every Hollywood screenplay, a key character must make a life-changing choice, often a heroic action that brings about resolution and redemption. Karl Norvik took on that role.

By dialing 911, Norvik set in motion the confusing chain of communication that relayed through the Orange County Sheriff's Department, the Los Angeles Police Department, to a radio telephone operator, and finally to the night watch at the Hollywood Station. Before 1:00 A.M., Friday, June 1, information that someone named David Alan Mahler had shot a woman in the face reached night watch detective Ray Conboy. He notified Homicide Unit supervisor Wendi Berndt at her home, and she called out two top detectives, Vicki Bynum and Tom Small.

CHAPTER 11

"THAT'S WHAT KEEPS IT INTERESTING"

In Hollywood, art often imitates life. Detective Tom Small, who would partner with Vicki Bynum as lead investigators in the David Mahler case, had actually participated in the making of a movie. It happened when Paul Newman, James Garner, and Gene Hackman shot several scenes from their 1998 movie *Twilight* inside the Hollywood Station. Small not only met them, but he also had a short appearance in the film. Recalling the whole experience, he said, "Paul Newman seemed a little remote and intent on learning his part. But James Garner was very friendly and down-to-earth. I talked to him quite a bit." During the filming, Small befriended the late actor John Spencer. They had coffee together frequently and shared experiences in lively conversations. "He was a great guy who could relate well to us because he had a police officer in his family, and a firefighter, both in New York."

Working with James Garner brought back memories for Small from a previous meeting with the star. "I had met him before when I was in Rampart Division. My boss there, Ron Dina, was a lieutenant who had been Garner's bodyguard. One day he summoned me and my partner to Cedars-Sinai Hospital. We were thinking, 'What did we do wrong?' A little nervous, we arrived at the designated floor. Ron told us with kind of a stern look on his face to go into the coffee room and wait—just to stand by.

"We thought we were really in trouble. A couple of minutes later, he walked in, followed by James Garner. Garner had undergone heart surgery recently, was recovering, and wanted to meet us. He even had an LAPD hat on. Dina had told him about an event my partner and I did—delivering a baby in the front seat of a car. That impressed Garner so much, he wanted to meet us. And then, years later, when they made that movie at the Hollywood Station, he remembered me. I thought he was really a friendly, decent man."

Other movies had been filmed inside the Hollywood Station. Small said, "One, in 2003, was called *Hollywood Homicide,* with Harrison Ford and Josh Hartnett. We met with those guys for lunch and they picked our brains regarding homicide investigations."

According to the IMDb (Internet Movie Database), Harrison Ford's role as Sergeant Joe Gavilan is based on Robert Souza, who was a homicide detective in the LAPD Hollywood Division and moonlighted as a real estate broker in his final ten years on the job. The scene where a handcuffed crook steals the gun from a patrol officer's belt and starts shooting it off in the parking lot actually happened during Souza's tenure.

Small added, "Other actors have dropped by occasionally to research roles in police procedural films. They ride with us, see how we behave, how we dress, our mannerisms, and how we talk to people. Vicki actually does more of that than I do."

The personal history of Tom Small would fit a screenwriter's concept of the perfect homicide detective. A native of

Racine, Wisconsin, his father ran an electrical fixtures and contracting business, while his mother worked as a bank teller. With an older brother, a younger sister, and a kid brother, Tom admits to being a "little rascal" who wasn't a bad kid, but he enjoyed mischief. "We would hide underneath our house and plink people with a BB gun—shoot 'em in the butt, nonsense like that. We would go down and hop slow-moving freight trains. I almost got skinned alive when my parents found out about that. I guess they had spies everywhere."

As an athlete in Catholic school, Tom excelled in football—from the fourth through twelfth grades, and during a year of college—playing fullback and linebacker. Sometimes sports took precedence over classrooms, in which he earned a B average, fully aware of his capability to get A's, with a bit more studying. During his teen years, he admired his cousin, a captain in the Racine Police Department with the Homicide Unit. "He hoped I might get into law enforcement, and always said the two best places to go would be the FBI or Los Angeles Police Department, which are the premier agencies in the country. So I had that in mind for a long time."

In 1972, the military draft system still existed and Small's number came up that August. Instead, he chose to enlist in the U.S. Marines and follow a long family tradition. Nine relatives served in the Corps from pre-World War II to the Gulf War. After basic training, Small landed in Okinawa and crossed paths with his older brother, who was en route home at the end of his hitch.

Looking back, Tom Small said, "When I got out in 1974, I joined a USMC reserve outfit in Milwaukee and enrolled at the University of Wisconsin. I had continued my football tradition in the marines and played some more in college." As a marine reservist, he attended Officer Candidate School (OCS) at Quantico, Virginia, and earned second lieutenant bars. Graduation from college came in 1978, with a sociology major emphasizing law enforcement. "But what I really wanted to be was a football coach." Instead, he served three more years in the U.S. Marine Corps as an officer.

"When I got out the second time, I started looking for a job with all kinds of police agencies. I tested and passed for New York PD, but had always wanted to join the FBI or LAPD, so declined on New York. I tested for the FBI successfully, but was placed on a waiting list. I finally joined the Racine PD and worked there about eighteen months while coaching high-school football in my off-duty hours."

One of his longtime goals came up in 1983. "An offer came from the LAPD and I grabbed it. After the academy, I went to Seventy-seventh Street Division. I was doing fine, and then the FBI contacted me and gave me ten days to respond. I was in a real quandary because I really liked working for the LAPD. But I thought, 'Hey, this is the FBI.' So I accepted."

Small soon found himself in Washington, D.C., and once again at Quantico. In a voice registering disillusionment, he said, "When I got into the Bureau, it was quite a bit different from working as a police officer. You don't have the exhilaration of the job. You don't have all the good stuff, which I really enjoyed. It was more the corporate type of law enforcement."

The FBI sent him to Omaha, Nebraska, and then to Cedar Rapids, Iowa. Sorely disappointed, Small made a life-changing decision. "I reapplied with the LAPD, came back on July 1, 1985, and I've been here ever since." He wore the uniform in tours at Harbor and Rampart Divisions, served in Narcotics and Fugitives Details, and earned his detective's shield in 1993 with the Hollywood Division.

Some people might think working in the Hollywood Division would be all glamour and glitz. Not so, said Small. "The community has a dark underbelly. You do see some famous people now and then, and some of them are arrested. When I first arrived here, they had huge vice problems, some of which still exists. On the west side, you had competition among the prostitutes for street corners. On the east side, you have the transgender people and cross-dressers doing the same thing—males dressed as women. In the lower east side, gang problems exist. So Hollywood has a little bit of everything. You've got skaters, drugs, pornography business, and regular show business, a potpourri of people—the high end and the low end. But that's what keeps it interesting."

Responding to Wendi Berndt's early call, before three o'clock that hectic Friday morning, Tom Small arrived at the Hollywood Station within forty-five minutes, and Vicki Bynum arrived at about the same time. Their boss, Wendi Berndt, contacted them by cell phone from Cole Crest. She and Detective Larry Cameron, Berndt said, would continue activities at the Cole Crest house. Meanwhile, she wanted Bynum and Small to interview Donnie Van Develde, Jeremy Moudy, and David Mahler at the station.

Donnie had been waiting nervously upstairs in the roll call room. He couldn't believe he had been pulled into this horrific mess, and he worried that he might be charged with some crime for failing to report what he had seen.

At 4:45 A.M., a uniformed officer escorted Donnie into a small interview room on the main floor. He offered coffee, but Donnie said he would prefer plain water. Always loquacious, apparently eager to speak out and perhaps thinking the officer would be conducting the interview, Donnie said, "I'm cooperating one hundred percent."

"Yeah, you should," the cop replied.

"I have absolutely no problem doing that. Did Karl talk to an attorney?"

"What?"

Words spilled from Donnie's mouth like a ruptured water pipe. "Karl talked to an attorney to find out exactly what to do about this situation, and he called me [last night] to tell me exactly what's up and that—what exactly we have to do, and he said he would be calling me around eleven thirty or twelve, and so that's why I stayed home 'cause I figured you guys would be coming once he did."

Bemused, the officer asked, "Karl?"

"Yeah, he told me he would make the call. On our behalf, you know? I never—I never dealt with anything like this in my life. This is—had me in a—had me in shock. The first person I went to when I—made aware of this situation was actually David. The guy that did this actually called me on the phone and told me to go up and look in his room. I mean, like he's a very sick guy."

Nodding his head in the affirmative, the officer listened.

Donnie kept the fountain flowing. "And I—I just seen—I seen a hand sticking out from under the blanket. I went to Karl's room and told him what's going on. . . ."

At that moment, Vicki Bynum and Tom Small entered the diminutive room, where Donnie had remained standing during his rattled recitation, ignoring the three vacant chairs. Bynum said, "All right, thank you, Officer. We appreciate it."

With a smile as he exited, the uniformed cop replied, "Sure, no problem."

Pointing to one of the chairs that had a tiny bit more padding than the others, Bynum said, "You could sit there in the good one, if you like."

As if he hadn't heard, Donnie resumed his spiel. "I assumed you guys would be coming tonight or whatever, but—that's why I stayed home, but I didn't know you'd be coming the way you did."

In her usual sweet, calm, melodic voice, Bynum asked, "You assumed we were coming? Why is that?"

At full pressure again, and spraying in all directions, Donnie said, "Well, Karl, my upstairs—the guy that lives up in—we're—my wife and I are tenants and the bottom floor is our apartment. We pay rent. We don't have any access to the upstairs house or anything like that. Karl is . . . a tenant or a roommate of David Mahler, who owns the house, and Jeremy is another roommate up there. They rent rooms in David's house so they have, like you know, maybe run of the house, you know, and everything like that. We don't. But . . . should I just tell you what I know just from—just from the beginning?"

Gesturing for the witness to sit, Tom Small said, "Yeah, why don't we do that? You are . . . ?"

Slumping into a chair, Donnie gave his full name. Small nodded, and stated the date and time, 4:45 A.M., for the recording machine. Both detectives gave Donnie their names; to which he courteously said, "Nice to meet you." He asked them to call him Donnie.

Bynum repeated his surname, Van Develde, and inquired, "Is it a Dutch name?"

"Actually," said Donnie, "I'm Italian. That was my step-father's name."

The uniformed officer interrupted to tell both detectives that Jeremy Moudy had arrived. Realizing that it would probably take several hours to complete hearing Van Develde, and that interviewing Moudy could very likely be finished in a few minutes, they asked Donnie to stand by for a little while. He patiently agreed.

In the adjacent interview room, identical to the one in which they left Donnie, Tom Small and Vicki Bynum spoke with Jeremy Moudy. They learned that he and his girlfriend had arrived at their Cole Crest apartment late Sunday afternoon, on May 27, after a weekend trip to Bakersfield. Nothing, he said, seemed to be out of the ordinary. Both of them knew David Mahler to be the resident manager, not the owner. They did not see him that day, nor had they heard any unusual noises. Jeremy stated that he did not maintain a close relationship with David, but that the guy treated him okay. In passing,

Moudy had met some of Mahler's girlfriends. "He had lots of women in his life," Jeremy said while shaking his head.

Speaking in calm, clear terms, Jeremy told the detectives of being awakened in the early hours of that same Friday, June 1, at about one forty-five by the sound of his cell phone buzzing, indicating a low battery. As soon as he shut down the noise, Moudy heard what sounded like someone trying to open his bedroom door, where he and his girlfriend had been sleeping. He asked who the hell was there. Mahler's voice replied, "The police are here. I need to get out."

Puzzled, Moudy said, he had unlocked and opened the door. Mahler stood there in "an agitated state." He had descended the interior stairwell, normally unused, into Moudy's quarters. Fighting off a sense of anger at the intrusion, Jeremy stepped out and carefully closed the bedroom door to block David from seeing his sleeping girlfriend.

He told the detectives that he initially suspected that some woman in Mahler's life had possibly brought some male help to beat him up. Perhaps they announced themselves as police to catch him unaware. "He asked me to go up and see what the police wanted." Mahler told Moudy that he feared the possibility of some people being outside, thugs who might try to harm him over some bad financial deals. He had heard the commotion outside his front gate, and voices claiming to be police officers, but he had no way of verifying they were indeed from the LAPD.

"At first, I had the impression that he had come down the interior stairwell, through my apartment, planning to escape through the side door that goes outside to the exterior stairs. But then, he asked me if I would go up there and see who was at the door.

"It all seemed really strange, but because he was so scared, I couldn't turn him down." Jeremy said he agreed to see what he could do. "I told him he couldn't go into my bedroom because my girlfriend was still asleep in there. So I climbed the stairwell, thinking that he was following behind me. But he dropped out of sight and I didn't know where he was. This whole thing had taken about five minutes, so I opened the front gate at about one fifty A.M. I saw several uniformed cops out there and opened the front gate and door to let them inside."

One of the officers, Moudy said, asked where David Mahler was. "I didn't know exactly, so I told them I didn't know. It was only partly true, because he was still somewhere in the building." The little white lie had worried Jeremy, he admitted, and it came as a relief when the cops found Mahler hiding in the closet downstairs.

"They had told me to wait in the living room. I was sitting there when a couple of officers brought him in. They took him outside right away. When I found out they captured him in my closet, I was not very happy that he had gone in there."

Asked if he had noticed red stains on the floor of David's quarters, Jeremy said he had seen them both on the carpeting and in the garage. He had made these observations last Sunday evening when they arrived home from the weekend trip. He hadn't even thought of the stains as blood, and he certainly didn't associate them with a crime. Jeremy stated that he had heard some vicious fights between David and his female visitors on prior occasions, although none had been brought to his attention recently.

Before leaving, Moudy volunteered information about seeing a heavyset African-American guy bring women to Cole Crest in a green-and-white taxi minivan, and sometimes stay for quite a while. In regard to Mahler's profession, Moudy said he understood the landlord was an attorney who mostly dealt in stock trading.

Bynum and Small thanked Jeremy Moudy, allowed him to leave, and returned to resume the interview with Donnie Van Develde.

CHAPTER 12

"I Could Kill Somebody Right Now"

Still in rapid spurts, Donnie Van Develde told Bynum and Small that he and his wife had lived in the Cole Crest house "about a year and a half." He described the narrow, winding, impossible roads that must be navigated for access to the property, and complained that pizza delivery guys could never find it.

"Who else lives at that address, besides you two?"

"Well, there's Karl. I don't know his last name. There's Jeremy. I think his starts with an *M*, or something." Almost as an afterthought, Donnie mentioned that David Mahler also lived there.

"Is he single or does he have a partner living there?"

"He doesn't have any regular girlfriend that I know of. He just has hookers and call girls and stuff like that almost every night. Parties—and all I've seen is him—just a crazed lunatic doing mass amounts of drugs and hookers and— whatever. So many women coming around, like I've never seen."

Tom Small wondered aloud about David Mahler not having a regular girlfriend. Donnie explained, "I don't think the guy would be capable of having one. He's—he's just the most difficult person to—to know and deal with. I mean, every month, when we don't have the rent exactly on the day it is due, we're threatened with eviction, like the very next day. So the last couple of months—I'm in the music business and so I make records. And I get money in little spurts, here and there." Donnie elaborated about his ongoing financial difficulties, noting that he hadn't even been able to buy food in recent days. "He doesn't understand or care about any of that. He's impossible to get along with."

To Small's inquiry about Mahler's drug usage, Donnie said, "He's a cocaine addict. As far as I can see, he does nonstop cocaine, crystal meth, Xanax, and alcohol."

Pointing out that he had never "hung out" with David, Donnie spoke of doing odd jobs for him. "He was supposed to pay me for the work, but never did. He just spends it all on women. They come by and the next thing you know he's— he acts like he's in love with them and he takes off and they go to Hawaii, or some hotel."

Mahler had seldom allowed Donnie inside his quarters, until a few days ago, said Donnie.

"What did you see last Sunday?" Small asked.

Grimacing and gesturing with his hands, Donnie replied with a preamble about his wife planning to attend a special annual party in Ohio. "She wasn't even around when all this stuff happened. Last Sunday, he called me up to his room and I thought he wanted to pay me the money he owed for some work I had done, and I was glad because my wife had gone to Ohio and I didn't even know how I was going to survive or feed the cat and have a few bucks while she was gone."

Hoping that Donnie would focus a little tighter, Tom Small asked, "Did he tell you he did something?"

"Yeah, on Saturday, before this awful thing, he told me he

had taken a girl to a hotel somewhere near the beach. He came back without her and said she pissed him off, so he left her there without any money or anything, and he said he was going to see this other girl. He was sort of asking my advice about women and he said, 'You know a lot about these things with girls, you know—you're in the music—you're the rock star, in the music business.' I told him that, personally, I thought he was above using the kind of women he was hanging out with, not to be falling in love with hookers."

The detective worked patiently to keep Donnie on track. He asked what had happened on Sunday morning.

Squirming, fidgeting, and perspiring, Donnie said, "He called me on the phone about eight thirty on Sunday morning (May 27) and told me to come upstairs to his bedroom. I thought he was going to pay me." According to Donnie, he knocked on the entry gate. A woman he knew only as Kristi buzzed him in, then opened the bedroom door. Mahler was nowhere in sight. "She said he would be right back."

"Had you met her before?"

"I think she had been there only a few times, and we had just said 'Hi' to each other. When I worked on the spark plugs of her car, we just talked for a minute or two."

"How long did you talk to her this time?"

"No more than a couple of minutes, and then he came in. I didn't see him because I was facing Kristi and he was behind me. I was asking her what happened at the beach." Mahler, Donnie said, "stormed in, screaming, in a violent rage."

Donnie's delivery accelerated, and Detective Small asked him to slow down. He tried, but turbocharged by fear, Donnie had difficulty controlling the speed and volume of his words. Donnie said, "He goes, 'There is nothing personal here, but I'm so pissed off. . . . I could kill somebody right now. This is life and death. Could you excuse us for a little while? I need to talk to her.'" The request sounded more like a belligerent demand than a courteous request.

David's demeanor had frightened Donnie and he headed for the door. "He was talking tough and said, 'I'll call you when I'm done talking to her.' I left and went back downstairs to my apartment."

In Donnie's recollection, the summons came about ten minutes later. "He said, 'Come back up here and do it now!' I still hoped he would hand over the money, so I climbed back up those stairs and went into his bedroom. He had changed into a white bathrobe, which was wide open, showing that he was naked. He was out of his mind, like nobody I have ever seen, and hitting a freebase pipe and smoking crystal meth. He would put one down and pick up the other one. I saw a bunch of Xanax sitting on the dresser, and I know he had been eating a lot of those and they make him crazy. Besides that, he was drinking from a bottle of wine."

"What about the girl?"

"She was in a pair of flimsy white shorts and I think a tank top, or maybe a halter top, sort of gold colored. She was sitting on the floor by the fireplace, with all her bags and stuff, and, like, looking pretty afraid because he is running hot and cold. He would flop down on the bed, and jump up again. As soon as I went in there, I asked him about the money and he freaked me out. I can't remember his exact words, but he would spurt out anything. Anything I said would be wrong."

Small asked, "Did it appear to you that Kristi was going through her bags trying to get out of there?"

"Yeah, she definitely wanted out. She was crying and asking him to please take her home. He just ignored her. She asked me, 'Do you think you could give me a ride home?' I told her that I didn't have a car. But I said that if David would let me use his, I would be glad to take her to her place. I knew that she really needed to get out of there."

This exchange apparently made Mahler even angrier.

"This time he started waving a gun around, like threatening her and threatening me, and he's, like, clicking it at my head with no bullets in it. He was scaring the hell out of both of us—talking about somebody else was coming over and he was going to kill—I don't know exactly what he was saying. I just know it was a scary situation. And he would get all crazy and he'd get up off the bed and start screaming about some situation they'd had."

Donnie's voice sounded on the verge of panic to Tom Small. To prevent him from hyperventilating, the detective said, "Slow down, slow down. You are doing a good job, and I know it's traumatic. But take a deep breath and try to remember as many details as you can."

"Okay," Donnie gasped.

"Do you have any idea why he was threatening you?"

"Yeah, because—as if to imply some kind of jealous thing between me and her. You know, like telling her he thought she was going to be with me, or something like that."

"What kind of a gun was it?"

"It looked like a—I don't know. I'm not too familiar with guns."

"Do you know the difference between a semiautomatic pistol and a revolver?"

"It's a revolver. It's the kind that's got a little . . ."

"It has a cylinder?"

"Yeah, it's got that little thing that spins. It was, like, blackish, dark, wooden handle. He set it down on the bed for a moment and I went to pick it up because I was going to, you know—because he was out of his mind, waving it and pointing at me, pointing it at her."

"Did you see where he got the gun from, or did he have it in his hand when you came up there the second time?"

"I don't remember exactly—he might have walked into the closet and grabbed it. I don't think he had it in his hand immediately when I walked in the room."

"Did you know he had guns in the house?"

Donnie's forehead wrinkled and the tattoos on his arms seemed to move like animated cartoons. "One time he showed me a gun before he went to Las Vegas. It freaked me out. I said, 'This is bad news. This guy should not have a gun,' and I told my wife he had that gun, and she was like, 'Oh, my God!'"

"Why do you think he showed it to you?"

"Because he's a big shot—just to tell me or show me how scary he is, and just to intimidate me."

"That was weeks earlier?"

"Yeah, yeah, when he was going through this whole Cheryl thing and he was seeing the people and hearing the voices 'cause he wasn't sleeping. He was doing drugs, and he got this gun to protect himself, or whatever. He was even talking about sending a bounty hunter to take care of Cheryl—wreaking havoc on her life and scaring her to death."

Once again trying to keep Donnie on a logical path and sequence of events, Detective Small said, "Okay, let's get back to Sunday. At some point, he puts the gun on the bed, and you made an attempt to pick it up. What were you going to do with it?"

Donnie's reply brought to mind a person running in all directions at once. "If he turned his back or if he lost attention with it—'cause he would—he had set it down and he lunged at her and he, like, almost attacked her, and he got up in her face and he's screaming at her. And I was like, like this is—I don't know what to do. This guy's a scary guy, and I see the gun sitting, and I go to pick up the gun. I was going to do whatever—to hide it. You know, put it—and hopefully, you know, he don't remember where he set it, but as soon as I go to grab it, he instantly grabbed my hand and he stopped me from picking it up."

"And then what did he do?"

"He started clicking it at her. And clicking it at me, pulling the trigger, and the hammer is slamming down—click, click. He kept doing that, over and over. There was no bullet in it, supposedly."

Mahler soon remedied that omission, said Donnie. Frowning and shaking his head in disbelief, the musician continued talking. "He went to this little closet and pulled out a single bullet. He put it in the gun and did one of those, like, Russian roulette things where he spun it and then let it click. And then he pointed it at Kristi, and pulled the trigger. The gun clicked. He turned and pointed it at me, and clicked it again."

Donnie's eyes blazed with indignation. In his furious view, Mahler had crossed a forbidden barrier. "I said, 'That's it, I'm out of here, David.' I said, you know, good-bye."

Taking in every important detail of Donnie's harrowing account, Small asked, "He aimed it at your head?"

"He pointed it right at my face."

In the minds of both detectives, the next comment from Donnie established a crucial turning point in the case.

He said, "I rushed out of there. As I was shutting the door, I heard the gun go off."

"Did you go back in the room?"

"No. I just assumed that he was shooting in the air or whatever to intimidate her or scare her. At first, I thought I heard voices in there, like they were still arguing. But I just hightailed. He wouldn't even buzz me out of that front gate, so I turned and went into the garage. I got a rake and put the rake against the buzzer so it would open the gate long enough for me to grab it and get out. I ran down the steps to my apartment."

Inside his own room, Donnie tried to ignore the ring tone of his cell phone. "He tried to call four times in the next fifteen or twenty minutes. And he tried texting me too, but I don't know how to do text messages. I didn't answer any of them because I'd had enough of him. I didn't want to go back up there. I just wanted to lock my door and hide."

Despite his resolve to ignore the phone, Donnie said, he finally answered David's call. "I asked him what was going on, and he said he wasn't in the house anymore, that he had gone somewhere else. I said, 'Where are you?' And he started talking about how 'she attacked me with a knife. She came at me with a knife, and it was self-defense.' I go, 'What do you mean, self-defense?'"

Detective Small double-checked to make certain the video recorder was capturing every word of Donnie's remarkable tale, and signaled him to continue. Mahler repeated the claim, said Donnie, about Kristin trying to stab him. "I really thought he was still upstairs just messing with me, you know? So he says, 'Go up and check.' I said, 'Oh sure. Yeah, right.' He told me he was over at someone's house and had just paid two hundred thousand dollars for protection. I told him, 'I don't even understand what the hell you are talking about.' And I hung up."

"What time was this taking place?"

"About nine thirty."

"So all of this took place in about a forty-five-minute time span?"

"Yes, sir."

"So, did you find out if he was upstairs or had really gone somewhere?"

"At first, I wasn't sure. I called him again about ten minutes later and asked him if he had actually left. He said he had. I asked him, 'Are you serious? You shot her and then you just ran away?' He started twisting things around, like accusing me of arguing with her, trying to imply, like you know, pinning it on me."

Now, Donnie said, he was really confused. "So what I did is go upstairs and—I was freaking out. I didn't know what—I had to see what was going on. I got up there and rang the bell, wondering again if he was actually at his own place. But nobody answers. So I went around—you can go around the side where the garbage cans are and it's his garage window. I can go over the railing and the window was open, and I can step from the railing up through that window. When I got into the garage, I could see one of his Jaguars was gone, and I started thinking he told me the truth."

Inside the house, said Donnie, he made his way to the bedroom door. "I knocked and waited, but nobody answered. After I did it again, and heard nothing, I opened the door to his room. I didn't see anybody. The lights were off. Then I looked down and seen the bedspread laying on the floor. At first, I didn't think much about it, but I took a closer look. And, wow, it looked like something was under there.

"I didn't actually go in the room, but leaned over a little farther, and at the very top, I could see her hand. There was her hand sticking out. And—oh, my God, I got sick to my stomach. I just—I just—stood there about thirty seconds, and the hand wasn't moving, never moved. The bedspread was over the rest of her body. I knew right then that he really did kill her."

Vicki Bynum had listened carefully to the part about David Mahler suggesting that Kristin had attacked him with a knife. She asked Donnie, "Did you see any knife in the room?"

"No."

"Did you see a knife anywhere near her hand?"

"No, there was no knife."

"When you were talking to her earlier, was there any knife in sight, anywhere in the room?"

"No, no. There was no knife. That was a lie. I just didn't—didn't believe him when he said the girl attacked him with a knife and it was self-defense."

Tom Small inquired, "Did you pull the bedspread back and look at her?"

A horrified expression creased Donnie's face. "No, absolutely not. I . . . no way I could do that. I didn't. I got sick to my stomach. I was in shock."

Donnie's wife returned home late Sunday night, he said, and he couldn't bring himself to tell her what had happened. "I've been in shock for the last few days. My wife doesn't even know what's wrong with me. She knows something is up, but I haven't told her, just for her own safety. I don't know what to do."

"So what did you do when you left that bedroom?"

"I went back to my own apartment to have a cigarette and I heard Karl go out on his balcony above me. I go out on my balcony and I can see him up there. I go, 'Karl, Karl,' and he comes and looks over his railing down at me. I go, 'Listen, man, something terrible has happened. David has just shot and killed a girl.' I'm saying it quietly. He's like, 'What?' I go, 'He shot and killed a girl in his room.' He goes, 'All right, come on up.'"

Donnie spoke of joining Karl in his room. They shared some vodka to ease their ragged nerves while Donnie told Norvik the details of what he had seen and suggested they call the police. "He goes, 'I've known this guy a long time and he's scary. Considering the way he does things, going to the police is not the thing to do.' So I asked him, 'Then what are we going to do? There's a dead body, you know.' He started trying to make out some story to keep us out of it. I go back downstairs 'cause he was drinking and maybe not thinking straight. But pretty soon, he starts kicking on the floor above me, and asked me to come back up there."

Back in his neighbor's room, said Donnie, Norvik admitted already knowing about the killing. "Karl said, 'He shot her in the face.' I go, 'What? You knew?' He said, "Yeah, I already knew, before you did.'" According to Donnie, David Mahler had telephoned Norvik immediately after the shooting and admitted doing it. Norvik had gone up to Donnie's bedroom door and actually looked at the corpse.

Tom Small and Vicki Bynum wanted clarification, and Donnie Van Develde did his best. From his statements, it appeared that Karl Norvik had been summoned upstairs within a couple of minutes after Donnie heard the gunshot, and had seen Kristin's body before it was covered up. The shroud, placed after Norvik returned to his room, had left only a hand exposed, the one Donnie had seen.

Donnie repeated Norvik's words: "I saw the corpse shot right through the face. Shot in cold blood. Dead."

Donnie described his own reaction to that admission. "I just threw up. I threw my guts up."

Asked by the detectives what he did next, Donnie said he ran back to his apartment and tried to telephone his wife to prevent her from coming home and getting involved in the horror, and to protect her. "I'm scared for my life. I'm scared for my wife's life."

CHAPTER 13
BLOOD—BUT NO BODY

While Detectives Bynum and Small conducted the interviews, other officers and technicians, under the direction of Supervisor Wendi Berndt, intensified the investigation.

The sun still hadn't peeked over the eastern summit of the Hollywood Hills on June 1 when Berndt contacted the Los Angeles County Coroner's Office to ask if any unidentified bodies—Jane Does—had been discovered in the last few days. A lieutenant checked the log and replied that no extant bodies bore the slightest resemblance to the information Berndt had given.

She made more calls to the LAPD and Los Angeles County Sheriff's Department (LASD) Missing Persons Units, but no reports turned up in correlation to this incident.

At the house on Cole Crest Drive, forensic experts meticulously examined every room in search of evidence related to the alleged shooting of a woman. Wendi Berndt later recalled, "We went through the entire house in search of a hidden body. I wondered if it might be buried down in the canyon somewhere. So we brought in a cadaver dog, but it didn't help. That was the important thing, to find out whether or not the victim was still there."

Bill Wilson, one of the officers among the team that had first arrived and had been invited inside by Jeremy Moudy, had spotted what appeared to be bloodstains leading to and inside the garage.

Other investigators had noted an assortment of cleaning fluids, along with sponges and scrubbing pads, in the master bedroom, on the fireplace mantel, and on the floor. It didn't take a Sherlock Holmes to deduce that someone had been trying desperately to clean the place, probably in an effort to eradicate blood.

LAPD criminalist Wubayehu Tsega answered Berndt's summons to help with the investigation. Tsega's colleagues had trouble pronouncing the Ethiopian native's name, but he took it with good humor. His eight years of experience on the job had earned respect from peers and the brass as well. Along with another criminalist, Raphael Garcia, he arrived at Cole Crest shortly after noon and began collecting samples of "biological fluids." According to Tsega, this could include saliva, semen, perspiration, urine, or any other fluid from the human body—but in this case, it meant primarily blood.

Beginning in the garage, Tsega inspected the areas around two Jaguar convertibles. One of them, a new 2007 XK model, indigo blue, was parked on the far side. Detective Cameron had already checked the Department of Motor Vehicles (DMV) records for both cars. The XK had been registered in the name of David Mahler. The other, a black 1999 XK8, sat close to the door leading into the house. It surprised the detective to learn that it was registered to David Gold, not Mahler. This would later be cleared up by Mahler's sister, who explained that he sometimes conducted business under the "David Gold" alias. But she didn't say why.

Tsega had been advised of blood spots on the garage floor and on the 1999 Jaguar. He traced the sanguine trail all the way from the master bedroom, up two short landings of stairs, and into the garage. The droplets ended within a few feet of the side entry door.

Checking reports of blood on the Jaguar's rear bumper and trunk lid, Tsega meticulously used cotton swabs, similar to Q-tips, to moisten the stains and lift samples. He opened the trunk lid and found more stains that appeared to be blood. In addition to collecting those samples, he made tape lifts of the trunk carpeting and the car's interior to collect any possible hair or other clues of a body having been transported.

To the investigators, it appeared that a body had been carried and dragged from the bedroom, up the short staircases, and into the garage. Because the trail stopped just inside the side entry door, it looked like the Jaguar may have been backed into the garage and the body loaded into the trunk. It may have been wrapped in the bedspread shroud to prevent leaving hair or secretions in the trunk.

Carefully packaging and marking the collected specimens, Tsega placed the evidence in an ice chest for transportation to the LAPD Scientific Investigation Division (SID).

In Mahler's bedroom, the bright red wall-to-wall carpeting at first just appeared to be dirty, as if it hadn't been vacuumed in a long time. But closer inspection by Tsega and Garcia revealed that an amazing volume of blood had soaked the carpet. They cut sections of it, peeled them back, and revealed signs of soaking all the way through to the padding underneath. If someone had suffered a gunshot wound in that room, as two witnesses had reported, the victim must have completely bled out. The logical inference would lead the investigators to believe the body must have been on that floor for many hours.

Wendi Berndt remained at the house to supervise and assure nothing would be overlooked. Following Berndt's instructions, one member of the team began photographing the scene and each item of potential evidence. He took a shot of Wubayehu Tsega inspecting the 1999 Jaguar's rear bumper and the blood spot on it. In the bedroom, the photographer captured images of the unmade bed, cluttered floor, various bottles of cleaning liquids near the fireplace, discolorations on the red carpet, and the sliced-up sections that revealed massive bloodstains.

Later commenting on the search inside Cole Crest, Berndt said, "Once I walked through, I had no doubt this was a crime scene. Based on the blood and the initial witness statements, I was convinced we had a murder. Karl Norvik had said he saw a body and knew that David Mahler shot her. Also, Norvik and Donnie Develde had spoken of Mahler wanting help to get rid of a body. The blood evidence backed it all up. In my mind, a woman had been murdered. I just didn't know where the body was. I believed we had to handle it as a worst-case scenario."

Another team of search dogs showed up, requested by Berndt. A cadaver dog from the coroner's office had found nothing. This pair, from the downtown L.A. Metro Division, handled by Officers Miller and Almarez, sniffed through the entire house, looking for guns. They had no better luck than the earlier four-legged detective.

Shortly after lunch, Wendi Berndt stepped outside, in front of the garage door, and glanced over at the neighboring house on the west side. She spotted something that could have important repercussions. Berndt later said, "Up in that area, with a lot of the higher-end houses of the Hollywood Hills, many homes have security video cameras mounted outside. They enable the resident to see what's going on without going out to personally check. That's one of the things we always look for. And this camera was right under the overhanging eave, in plain sight."

Along with one of the detectives, Berndt pushed the neighbor's doorbell button. The occupant spoke to them over a speaker system. "The guy wouldn't let anybody in. We explained to him that we were investigating a crime, and needed to know if his security video camera had recorded any activity at the Mahler house." The neighbor acknowledged that his system operated 24-7, and that he would make the tapes available to the police. But he insisted that he would have his own technician upload them from a central computer.

Berndt later commented, "He was very secretive. I almost think he had a sex thing going on there. He wouldn't let us come in or look at anything. We didn't have a warrant, so we had to go along with his wishes. He did come through, though. His technician came out at about two o'clock that afternoon. He even gave us the hard drive." Berndt sent the apparatus to the crime scene investigation (CSI) lab to see if anything useful had been recorded.

CHAPTER 14

"I BELIEVED I WAS A DEAD MAN"

Inside the tiny interview room, still an hour before dawn, Vicki Bynum and Tom Small listened as Donnie Van Develde provided more frenetic answers to their questions. Still shaking and spurting his words, he said, "David scared the hell out of me. From what I've seen—and the characters he associates with—and him telling me things like—like that he hired this guy to kidnap—to grab this Cheryl out of her work and—like a bounty hunter or some crap like that—and he was just a psycho over this other chick."

Once again trying to drag an orderly statement from Donnie, Small asked, "After you talked with Karl Norvik, did you remain in the house?"

"Yeah, yeah. I didn't know what else to do." Donnie said the presence of his wife intensified the problems. "I said to her, 'I can't explain, but there's some bad, bad, bad things going on.' And she just assumed that I had got myself mixed up in something stupid, you know—because she always thinks I'm—she thinks I'm an idiot. She started screaming at me and yelling at me that she and her girlfriend were going out. And I just needed to stay there, 'cause Karl had told me to sit tight."

"Karl advised you to stay there?"

"Oh yeah—don't do anything. I said, 'Don't we got to call the police? David said it was self-defense.' But then I seen after another day or two goes by, there's no police coming, that obviously that's not what—you know? And I knew that (self-defense) was a bullshit story, anyway. Obviously, he's an attorney and knew how to handle it in a different way."

Small asked, "Okay, so you remain in the house and your wife comes home. Did you tell her anything at all about what you saw?"

"No. No, no. All I told her was that Dave is off the handle, and I'm really worried about—"

"You didn't tell her about seeing a dead girl up in Mahler's room?"

"No, no. I couldn't tell her that. I ended up having a screaming fight with her. She knew something was up and kept at me about it. 'Are you guys partying?' I said, 'No, I'm not partying with him. I'm just trying . . .' That's my relationship with my wife. It's really stressful. She's just constantly on me, but in any case we were having a scream- ing match, 'cause she just wouldn't stop. I kept telling her maybe she should just go stay with her girlfriend because David was off the deep end."

To the detectives, it didn't make sense that Van Develde wouldn't tell his wife what had happened. It might convince her of the potential danger to both of them. Small put the question to him.

Donnie tried to explain. "I—if you knew her, nothing ugly like this has ever been in her life. You know? I'm the ugliest thing that she's ever known. I don't want her to be—she would just instantly freak out. She'd be scared to death. I've been a wreck all week."

Still skeptical, Small inquired again why Van Develde

neither told his wife nor called the police. Donnie, clearly embarrassed, replied, "It's just—this is the most screwed-up thing I've ever been dealt in my whole life. I wanted to protect my wife. I know David. From what I've seen, and from what Karl told me, I would think David would think nothing of eliminating any witness or anything like that."

"Why did you remain in the house the whole time?"

"I have nowhere else to go. I don't really have much family anymore. I don't have any friends I can stay with. The only people I know out here have wives, and stuff like that. They live in little places. I don't have anywhere else to go."

"And your wife still doesn't know what happened?"

"All she knows is that something bad is up. Just before she went out tonight, Karl called me and said, 'Listen, we got to call the police. I'm going to call them.' I asked him if he was sure. He said, like, yes, absolutely. He had talked to a lawyer. And he said David had called him to say he was leaving—that he was moving out. He's going to be taking off."

"Is that all he said?"

"No. He said, 'If I was you, I'd vamoose. I'd get the hell out [of] there because shit's going to be going down. I'm calling the police tonight.'"

"Have you seen David at all after the event up there in his room?"

"No, I have not seen him since then."

"Have you talked to him?"

"He called me the next day and asked me, 'What's up? How is she doing?' I said, 'David, what the fuck, man?' Excuse my language. I asked him where he was and what he was going to do. But he put some other guy on the phone for a few seconds. He just said, 'Hi, Donnie' in a real weird voice."

In hesitant, sputtering, disjointed words, Van Develde expressed the opinion that David Mahler intended, by putting someone else on the phone, to send a warning, a mortal threat not to speak of the event, or to call the police. "The actual words weren't said, but I know he meant that if I said anything, I was a dead man—that he had hired someone to protect him and to take care of anyone who threatened him."

"All right," said Small. "Now, the whole time, from Sunday until this morning, as far as you know, that body had been lying up there? Or is that body out of there?"

"No. I have no idea. I assumed that David had handled it, or something. Karl implied something about him having it taken care of, or whatever. It's been freaking me out. I didn't smell anything and—oh God! It's really the most unbelievable—I can't even believe it's real."

Answering a few more questions, Van Develde launched another rambling account of meeting someone David had brought to the house several days before the shooting. The individual had been introduced as "the cleaner." This had confused Donnie. "A cleaner? What the hell is a 'cleaner'? I'm a cleaner too. I'm cleaning the walls and railings, you know? That's really been messing with my mind." He had finally decided that this person must be a hit man.

On that theme, Donnie wondered, "Did David plan to kill somebody? Maybe there was someone else he needed to get rid of. David told me he had guns, and that scared me. He said he had three of them, including a rifle. I never seen any of them, except the one he was waving in my face."

"You say Mahler told you he was a lawyer?"

"Yeah. He told me the other day that he represented a guy that ran over someone with his car, then backed over him again and killed him, and then robbed him. David said he got the guy off with only three days in jail. And that made me sick too."

"When he was up there, waving that gun around and pointing it at you and the woman, you said he was wearing a bathrobe?"

"Yes."

"What color was it?"

"White, and it had monograms on it. Like the kind you see at hotels."

Spinning off again on a tangent, and unaware that Mahler occupied a cell on another floor of the Hollywood Station, Van Develde said, "This isn't right. David shouldn't be walking around the streets. I don't think he is at all remorseful. I think he's out getting high and staying in nice hotels, getting girls."

Pulling him back to answer specific questions, Small heard Donnie speak of Atticus King, the green-and-white taxi, and King's frequent visits to Cole Crest, in which he brought prostitutes.

Nearly ready to conclude the interview, Bynum needed to inquire about one more subject. "I need to ask you something. Don't be offended. Please be honest. Have you ever been arrested?"

"Yeah, a couple of times for little minor things."

"Like what?"

"Well, I got arrested for crystal meth."

"Okay. So, do you still use drugs?"

"Not regularly. I got off methadone this year. I'm on medication called Suboxone."

"Did you ever get high with David?"

"I did one line of crystal meth with him, once. He really didn't share his drugs."

Bynum explained, "We know this is traumatic for you, but we're just trying to understand why you never called the police about a murder. If you were getting high with him, and that made you feel a certain loyalty, you need to be honest with us about it."

"No, that's not it at all. I have no—no loyalty or anything to David. I'm just purely afraid of him. I'm not his friend. He's not my friend, you know."

Bynum probed another sensitive area. "Are you afraid your

wife is going to leave you? Were you trying to avoid that by placating her and not telling what you were doing with David?"

Wildly shaking his head in the negative, Donnie Van Develde said, "No. It is getting pretty rough—our relationship, with me being in the music business and not making a lot of money right now. And she's not very happy. But I just didn't want her to know about what David did, so she wouldn't be afraid."

"How long have you been married?"

"Six years. I met her on the road when my group was opening for a band called Poison. We had some moderate success, but we've also had a lot of tough breaks."

"How long have you lived in David's place?"

"About a year and a half."

The two detectives thanked Van Develde for his cooperation and started to rise. He felt the need to explain his reluctance to notify anyone after the shooting. "I mean—I swear to God, I would have come—I would have called the police right away, immediately, except for the fact that I've been under the impression that I'm a dead man if I did that. I thought I was just protecting my wife and myself."

"Did you not have faith in the police helping to protect you?"

"From what I was told by Karl, that wouldn't matter. David would find a way to get revenge."

Bynum sat back down and said, "Hey, Donnie, real quick. Help me describe the female victim better. What length is her hair?"

"Shoulder length."

"Okay," said Bynum sweetly. "Listen—and you won't offend me—I'm five-four. Is she my height, you think?"

Donnie nodded an "uh-huh."

"And I'm not as thin as I used to be. Is she thinner than me?"

"She was very thin. I'd say she weighed maybe one hundred fifteen pounds."

"How about eye color? And her hair was blond?"

"I don't remember the color of her eyes, but her hair was lighter than yours, kinda streaked blond. My wife thought she was really pretty." He said he couldn't remember any jewelry she might have worn.

At last, after spending more than two hours with Donnie Van Develde, Detectives Bynum and Small allowed him to leave.

They called a uniformed officer to bring David Mahler from the tank.

CHAPTER 15

CONFRONTING EVIL

Fuming, pouting, angry, worried, and fidgeting while sitting in the Hollywood Station holding tank, David Mahler couldn't believe he had been arrested. How dare they? He was a lawyer and knew his rights. Sure, they had found him hidden inside a closet at his own home, but this was certainly no crime.

While he still had possession of his cell phone, David had called Stacy up in Visalia. She promised to come right away to be with him during this ordeal.

Vicki Bynum later commented about David Mahler's summoning of Stacy Tipton. "She was afraid of him. When we let him make some phone calls, he reached her, and he was screaming at her, insisting that she come to Hollywood right now. She drove down from Visalia in panic. He is extremely demanding of everybody. Anyone he called, he expected them to help, probably because he had something on them. Everything is an obligatory contract with him."

After enduring several hours of idle stagnation in a cell,

waiting for the inevitable interrogation by detectives, Mahler impatiently wondered what was taking so long.

To make matters worse, a series of sharp spasms made his back feel as if he had suffered a terrible beating. He yelled for someone to help him, complaining of debilitating pain. An officer responded and escorted him to the interview room, which Donnie Van Develde had left just moments earlier. Within a few moments, an emergency medical technician (EMT) checked him out, gave him some aspirin, and left. The Los Angeles Fire Department (LAFD) captain, with the EMT, asked Mahler if he felt better and then asked him to sign a form indicating no further need of medical attention. Mahler said he felt okay and signed it.

Detectives Bynum and Small needed a few minutes to reorganize themselves and regain a sense of order after the cat-herding interview with Donnie Van Develde. He had tried his best to be cooperative and respectful, but his scattergun delivery had required infinite patience to understand and to summarize in a written report.

Now they faced a distinctly contrasting challenge with David Mahler. Both detectives realized the need for an entirely different approach to questioning him. "With Mahler, because he was an attorney, we came up with a game plan of how to approach him," Bynum recalled.

Tom Small explained, "At the beginning of the interview, we figured he would be surveilling us at the same time we would be checking him out. We wanted first to gauge him and find out where his head's at. And to keep it level, we decided to avoid being adversarial, up to a point. We also wanted him to believe that we didn't yet know we had a murder—that we just wanted to talk about a missing girl. Because he was in custody, being handcuffed when brought into the interview room, we took precautions and carefully informed him of Miranda."

Bynum and Small both knew that the interview with David

Mahler would be a challenge. They had already been on the job nearly five hours. His interview would last more than nine exhaustive hours. They were playing a verbal chess game with a self-confident, hubristic man accustomed to dominating everyone around him. They realized it would be a confrontation with intelligence, avarice, and evil.

CHAPTER 16
WEB OF SELF-DESTRUCTION

The long session with David Mahler opened on a note of relaxed informality. Bynum suggested he take the more comfortable chair and offered some water. Dressed in a cotton long-sleeved, pullover black jersey and dark slacks, Mahler accepted the seating arrangement and a drink. In a distinctive, clipped New Jersey accent, he suggested the detectives might need some ID, which he had in his wallet, but complained that it had been taken away from him. "I don't know what this is all about yet, but there may be documentation in my wallet that I can show you." Vicki Bynum replied with a genial smile that it would be taken care of. He kept talking. "I have to say again, and I said it earlier, I understand the process—being a lawyer for eighteen years."

In less than thirty seconds, Mahler had wanted them to understand his importance and ability to deal with people of lower status.

"Right," Bynum replied with deliberate saccharine.

Mahler responded in kind. "Your attitude I must commend. I'm not—at least at this moment—yet charged with anything. I'm not a criminal yet. If that happens and then you take a dislike to a criminal, that's different. But thank you for treating me as a human being until then."

Tom Small, unsmiling, said, "No problem."

Extending an arm across the table, Mahler said, "Now I can shake your hand, I suppose."

"Certainly," said Small. "By the way, I'm Detective Small. This is Detective Bynum. We work the Hollywood Detective Unit. And I've got some information that came to us that we would like to share with you, and also see what your side of it would be." Mahler nodded his understanding. "Being that you are an attorney, you understand the legalities here, right?"

Mahler kept his voice low and calm. "Yes. Please, please understand that it's my profession. If I come—I'm trying to work with you. I'm not usually on this side. If anything I say comes off a little too legalese, or if—"

"If I don't understand it, I'll ask you," Small interrupted.

Sounding a little apologetic, Mahler muttered, "Sometimes I have a tendency to come off a little harsh. That's just my training. . . . I'm going to try to be as humble as possible."

"Okay," said Small. "Well, if you don't get harsh, I don't get harsh. How about that?"

"You have a deal."

"That will be fine, and we can be gentleman to gentleman, or gentleman to lady. That's the way we prefer it. Try to keep it as professional as possible."

Mahler commented that he had the right to a lawyer, since he was under custodial interrogation, under California law, but he volunteered, "I'm waiving it. However, I'd like to keep some notes." Small agreed, and provided him with paper and a pen.

To be absolutely certain of no misunderstandings, Tom Small read the Miranda advisory again to Mahler, to which the suspect expressed full understanding. "With that in mind," Small asked, "are we going to talk?"

Giving an affirmative reply, Mahler noted that if things took "a twist," he could always stop the interview and request legal representation.

Jumping right to the point, Small said that information had been called in regarding a missing person. "She might be known as Kristi. Does that ring a bell?"

"Yeah."

"Okay, what's Kristi's story?"

"I hardly know Kristi, to be honest with you. I don't even know her last name."

"How did you come to meet her?"

"She was introduced to me through a gentleman named Michael Conoscenti last September. I remember that timing because I had just broken up with my fiancée, and Michael felt it would be a good idea. After that, I hadn't seen Kristi for—God, until last week or two weeks ago. How that came about was she moved in with a gentleman named Sheldon Weinberg, one of my clients. He called and needed some documents delivered to me, because I'm helping him with a federal legal case." Kristi, said Mahler, had brought the papers to his home. "At that time, I spent another two or three hours with her."

The detectives had no way of knowing that Mahler had misstated some of the timing and left considerable gaps in the story. He continued, "I was headed down to Newport Beach to meet another client. It was dinnertime. I invited her to go with me. We went down to Newport Beach, stayed there—and I'm sorry if I'm going too fast."

Vicki Bynum assured Mahler that he was doing fine. "What day was it you went to Newport?"

"Last week." He said he couldn't be certain exactly which day, but receipts in his wallet could be checked. "I stayed with her at the Island Hotel. I think it was two nights."

"Did you check in using your name or hers?"

"Under my name." He either lied or forgot the room had

been registered under a different name. Skipping hastily past that point, Mahler said, "I found that it was too quick to ask a girl, you know. At first it was going to be dinner to meet my client . . . then it turned into getting late, so we said we'd stay in the hotel room. Then the next day it was 'Well, we're in Newport. Let's meet a friend.' And things just got dragged out. It wasn't intended to be a two-day sprawl."

Small and Bynum listened with an occasional "uh-huh," took notes, and let Mahler speak.

"And we got into some arguments. When I say arguments, [it reached] a point that I said, 'I'm leaving. Are you coming?' [She] wasn't ready. I said, 'Checkout time is two o'clock.' Security had to go up to the room three times to ask her to please leave. 'Mr. Mahler's not paying for another night.' And I left. I didn't mean to be a—please don't get the wrong idea. I'm a gentleman. I sat outside for an hour after they threw us out of the room, waiting in front with the valet, tipping him a few extra dollars to make sure that he didn't ask that I leave.

"At a certain point, I got a phone call from Mr. Weinberg, whereby she was cursing and screaming that she was going to get another ride. I said, 'Fine. As long as she has another ride, I'm leaving.' And I left. She stayed. I left."

Mahler didn't explain how Kristi had said those things to Weinberg. Presumably, he meant that she had called him.

"Where did you go?"

"I went home. About two days later, Saturday, I got a call from her asking me if she could have—I'm so bad mechanically—some piece of her car she needed that she had left in my garage."

A skeptical expression shadowed Tom Small's face. He asked, "A piece to her car?"

"Yeah, a piece to her car. She had taken it off because when she left from Mr. Weinberg's house, she apparently didn't want some of the kids there to use her car. . . . I said, 'Fine, come on up.' And that's how I knew Kristi."

"So you saw her on Saturday?"

"Yes, I did. Everything seemed okay, until she started in- dicating that she wanted drugs. Which is something that I am—how do I phrase this? I don't consider myself the most conservative guy in the world. I don't want drugs around me or certainly in my home."

Neither Bynum nor Small let it show in their expressions that statements from Norvik, Van Develde, and Moudy had painted a far different picture of drugs in the house. Accord- ing to those men, he used cocaine and meth regularly. Small only uttered, "Uh-huh."

Rushing onward, David Mahler implied that Kristi some- how arranged for a drug dealer to show up. He said, "So she had somebody come to the house. And there was some argu- ment about how she was going to pay for the drugs. And I guess—this is absolute innuendo—so I'm not sure because it wasn't explicitly stated, but I'm a smart guy. It sounded to me like there were sexual favors [offered] in exchange for the drugs. I was in the way, so [they wanted] me to leave."

Another flicker of doubt showed in Tom Small's eyes. "They wanted you to leave your own house?"

"Yes, in my house—making me obviously quite uncom- fortable to the point that I'm asking them both to leave. Make sense?"

It made no sense at all to Small or Bynum, but the time had not yet come for a dispute. Instead, Small simply asked, "Who is this person who suddenly showed up?"

Haltingly, as if he had trouble recalling, Mahler seemed to be searching his memory. It came to him. The guy's name was Edmund.

"Do you know his last name?"

Mahler said he couldn't recall it at the moment, but would be able to supply it later. Acknowledging that he had met

Edmund previously, he described him as an overweight Mexican man who dealt drugs and fancied himself a "ladies' man." Suggesting that Edmund had once offered to bring prostitutes to Cole Crest, Mahler snorted and said, "Needless to say, that wasn't going anywhere with me. It got to the point . . ." Mahler didn't complete the sentence. Instead, he said, "Please forgive me if I'm being a little careful." Citing the absence of legal representation in the room, he apparently thought he was saying too much and cited the old adage "A lawyer that represents himself has a fool for a client."

"I need to be a little careful, but I do want to make sure that I'm open enough that you can get all the facts you need," David remarked.

Tom Small asked for a description of Kristi. Mahler said, "Well, I only spent two days with her, but she was white, about five-six, slender, blondish hair, maybe dyed." Pointing to Bynum, he noted, "Her hair was longer than this young lady's." The compliment about her age didn't impress the detective. Asked about jewelry Kristi might have worn, Mahler couldn't recall any. He was equally vague about her clothing, remembering only that she wore white pants.

"And the last time you saw her was where?" Small inquired.

"At my house, Saturday night." Reconsidering it for a moment, he said, "The last time I saw her was around three, Sunday morning." With that, Mahler began spinning a tale of Edmund slapping Kristi, his own consternation and fear, and making telephone calls to ask for advice. "It was a very strange situation for me. You can imagine. I have so much expensive stuff in my house. Who is this guy? Why does he feel comfortable slapping her in front of an attorney? My licenses are plastered all over the place." (It had all taken place in his bedroom.)

With a hint of suspicion in his voice, Small asked, "In your bedroom?"

Mahler's vacuous answer reflected that his radar had picked up the detective's mistrust. "Obviously, there wouldn't be any, you know. I mean, I'm not going to indicate in any way that I was—let me rephrase that. Since it can't be anything incriminating . . . I'm not going to indicate that I was unaware of his relationship with her."

Small and Bynum exchanged a quick glance, silently agreeing to stick with their game plan to extract as much information as possible from the suspect before challenging his evasion or outright lies. Small simply asked, "Did you leave?"

"I did. Absolutely. I went to another part of the house and spoke to Karl Norvik. I also called Donnie, who lives all the way downstairs." Mahler denied knowing Donnie's surname, stating that he always thought of him as Donnie.

"What did they say?"

"Both of them said that I shouldn't be involved. As a matter of fact, Karl said, 'You want me to take you out of here? We'll both get in the car and leave right now, because I'm also uncomfortable. This is a weird situation.' I didn't want to leave my house with people I didn't know still in there. So I said, 'That would mean locking all the doors, putting valuables away. That takes time.'"

Both detectives knew that Karl Norvik had made the telephone report accusing David Mahler of killing Kristi. Perhaps Norvik had offered to transport Mahler away from Cole Crest on Saturday evening, but probably not in the context of Mahler's self-serving account. Donnie's long interview completely contradicted Mahler's version of getting advice from him. The detectives let him continue weaving a web of self-destruction.

Mahler's narrative took him back to an alleged confrontation with Edmund. "I turned to him and said, 'Listen, I'm leaving. You're going to have Donnie around. You're going to have Karl around. By the time I get back, I expect and anticipate that you [will be gone]. Kristi, you know, it was nice that you came over to pick up your stuff. Time's up. Take whatever you might have in the garage. And good luck.' I said I was really uncomfortable with the talk about drugs. I left and checked into the Marriott Hotel, near LAX, because I know they have good rates. I stayed there Sunday and Monday."

"You left Kristi and Edmund in your house?" It took some Academy Award acting by Tom Small not to betray his contempt. "Were you concerned?"

"Oh yeah, I was very nervous. Wait till you look at the record of my calls. I was calling every hour, thinking maybe somebody would answer the phone. I was calling Donnie, Karl, my phone. I was absolutely flipping out. I finally got Stacy. I said, 'Stacy, this thing's sort of wigging me out. What do you think I should do?' She said, 'David, I'll come be with you.' Stacy lives in Bakersfield. She came and we stopped at my house [briefly] on Monday."

Investigators would soon learn that Stacy lived in Visalia, seventy miles north of Bakersfield. Mahler had either deliberately lied to keep detectives from finding her, or perhaps he had simply misspoken.

Describing the Monday house visit, Mahler said, "We were there for all of two minutes because I needed to grab my computer. Things looked normal other than, you know, there was some blood. I'm not going to lie about that. It freaked me out, but freaked out Stacy even more. I told her we would deal with it later."

Just to see how truthful Mahler would be, Small asked, "Where was the blood?"

"It's in my bedroom, exactly where I left [Kristi and Edmund], exactly where he started slapping her." Forensic technicians would find considerably more blood than could have been caused by slapping someone.

At Small's request, Mahler diagrammed on paper the house interior and indicated where he had seen the blood.

Back to Stacy's presence, Mahler said she refused to stay

in the house that night. To placate her on that Monday, they checked into the Standard Hotel, on Sunset Boulevard.

To make certain he understood Mahler's stated sequence of events, Small asked him to reiterate how long he stayed at the Marriott and how long at the Standard. Mahler said, "Well, if you want to include Saturday night, which was late at night, I was at the Marriott Saturday night and Sunday night."

"I thought you said—"

Mahler interrupted to alter his version. "I checked into the Marriott Sunday morning and checked out on Monday." He knew the hotel records could be examined. He and Stacy had visited Cole Crest briefly on Monday and stayed at the Standard that night. Stacy, he said, returned to her home, up north, on Tuesday. "Before dinner I went back up to the house and tried to clean up some of the blood." He denied finding blood anywhere else except in his bedroom.

"When you were there and saw the guy slapping her, did you see her bleeding?"

"I wouldn't say so far as bleeding, but you could see that, you know, she got smacked."

"Did anyone else see Edmund there in your house?"

"I think Donnie did, but Karl did not." Mahler spun off on another tack, hinting that Edmund had sometimes supplied Donnie with drugs.

Small replied that this was irrelevant to the case. "I don't give a crap where Donnie might have bought anything. We're not dope cops."

"In that case," Mahler declared unequivocally, "Donnie bought his drugs from this guy."

"Is he also a drug connection for you?"

"No. What? For me to get dope? No. No. I don't do dope."

"None at all?"

"None at all."

Both detectives had heard statements by Jeremy Moudy and Donnie Van Develde describing David Mahler's prolific use of drugs. They seemed quite believable, while Mahler's credibility had started to spring serious leaks. Perhaps feeling his boat starting to sink, he tacked in the other direction. "Cocaine? Once in a while. And that's not an admission."

Vicki Bynum remarked, "We don't care." Small agreed.

Ostensibly relieved by their disinterest in his denials, Mahler shifted directions again, to Cheryl Lane. Mentioning that she was his former girlfriend, Mahler said she was due in court today and would be curious why he wasn't there to advise her. He even wondered aloud if the detectives planned to ask if she provided sex to him to be her lawyer. They showed even less interest in that tangent than in his duplicity about narcotics.

Bynum needed clarification on the female relationships. "I'm confused about Stacy. Is she your former fiancée?"

"No, no, that's Kitty, but she's out of this. Stacy is someone I've known for twenty years."

"So she's a very good friend?"

"She's a very good friend. We have consensual sexual contact at times."

"Was she with you at the Marriott and the Standard?"

"No, no, she was not at the Marriott. I was there by myself. Well, not by myself, but not with Stacy." Tom Small wanted to know who was there with him. Mahler stammered, "Uh, well, this gets tricky. But I'm going to let you know. A gentleman I know just like—like with Conoscenti— can arrange it that there's company involved. I'm not going to call it 'prostitution.' I know, I know, you don't even care about that."

Bynum made it clear that they worked major crimes, not vice.

"Okay"—Mahler nodded—"it was a prostitute that I got through another gentleman who fancies himself a pimp. His name is Atticus King. He's a black guy, two hundred forty pounds, about five-eight. He's a taxi driver, uh, as a guise to transporting women."

"So, were you using cocaine at the hotel with King and the hooker he brought?"

"No."

"Were you high on cocaine at the Island Hotel in Newport Beach?"

Mahler confessed that he "partook a little bit." Small asked how much. "It was enough for me to enjoy myself and have champagne with strawberries." He claimed the client who met him there, and whose name he would never divulge, had given him the cocaine.

Small asked Mahler to reconstruct what happened in the few hours preceding his arrest. He replied that he had gone out with a few friends for Chinese food, returned home, got on the Internet, and made some cell phone calls. "And *bada-bing,* I started hearing banging on the front gate. And I'm thinking, someone's out there, and it's not Karl. I had just spoken to him. This leads me to a text message I had received, threatening me. It said, 'If you don't comply, you are the one going down. If you don't pay us . . .'"

Given the opportunity to explain, Mahler told a long story about someone who had borrowed $13,000 and hadn't paid it back. Kristin had mentioned knowing a person who could help collect it without going too far illegally. "The guy comes over. I give him a few bucks to do the job. The next thing you know, I'm [being] called every single freaking day for more money."

"What's the person's name who owes you the money?"

Mahler acted reluctant to reveal it, but he said, "Now you're getting into serious business because he's a [police] officer. I don't know how much you want to despair [*sic*] his department. You know what? I will give you the name, because I'm so mad that he hasn't paid me. It's Robert Jimenez. Do you know him? Well, there you have it."

The interviewers needed more details. Mahler said it was an extremely complicated matter and rambled on for several minutes. He said he had posted bail for Cheryl on a felony count. "I was on the hook for thirty thousand. Cheryl and I weren't even seeing one another anymore and it was too much money [to lose]. And she did wind up skipping bail. That's when I hired Jimenez for seven hundred dollars to bring her in. But he did a bad job. He failed to do anything right. But he comes over the next day, demanding money."

"When is all of this?"

"About a month ago. He started making threats, showing me a pistol." Jimenez, Mahler said, had coerced him into making a loan of $7,000. Kristin, Mahler purported, had then put him in contact with someone named Rick, who, for a fee, would persuade Jimenez to return the money. Rick had shown up at Cole Crest on Saturday night, just before Edmund made his appearance.

Mahler threw in another twist. He claimed that Kristi had called Rick to come and pick her up in Newport Beach and take her back to her home, but he had apparently let her down. "While they were in my house, they were bickering about it. I was in the middle of a dangerous mess. He started talking to me about wanting twenty-five thousand dollars. It was blackmail, extortion in my mind."

It became apparent to the detectives that Mahler's convoluted story of financial intrigue and threats was designed to throw them off the track and make them believe he feared for his life. Thus, when the officers showed up at Cole Crest the previous night, he had hidden in Jeremy Moudy's closet. How much of it was true, or what portions were fabricated, bore little relevance to the investigation of Karl Norvik's allegations that David Mahler had shot a woman named Kristin. Still, they dutifully took notes and kept open minds.

Mahler again mentioned that he had contacted Stacy and had asked her to come be with him. "We have plans to go out to breakfast together tomorrow morning." He expressed surprise that she hadn't arrived yet at the Hollywood Station.

CHAPTER 17
CLINGING TO PAST LOVE

The interview of David Mahler by Tom Small and Vicki Bynum had consumed nearly two hours, and it would last seven more. As it progressed, Stacy Tipton drove her red Jeep Cherokee from Visalia to Hollywood, about two hundred miles.

Mahler had reached her by cell phone after his arrest and asked her to come down. She had no idea what had happened to cause the police to pick him up, but she assumed it was either on a drug charge or related to some financial shenanigan. Or maybe he had slapped around one of his girlfriends. It probably had something to do with the blood found in his house. He had seemed nervous and edgy during her visit on Monday, less than a week ago. The idea of sleeping in a house with someone's blood on the carpet had freaked her out. So they had stayed at the Standard Hotel.

Driving alone gave Stacy the opportunity to mentally relive highlights and low points of their long relationship.

It had all started out so nicely. She loved the way he treated her in the early years, courteously opening doors, allowing her to enter a room in front of him, and ordering for her in restaurants. Even when they worked on business matters together in his apartment, they made it a team effort. She later described it. "He concentrated deeply and we kept conversation to a minimum. He spent a lot of time with intensive telephone conversations. But he would always break at twelve noon and we would have our little bagels with cream cheese and our fifteen minutes together in the kitchen. That's when we could talk. To me, that just showed how dedicated he was. Even though he was doing business at home, he would always dress professionally."

When Stacy met David's mother, it had been a thrill to hear her say that David had never talked to her about any woman in his life except Stacy.

The move West, though, had altered everything. Mahler's behavior had slipped downhill gradually. He became domineering and selfish. His desire for strippers, hookers, and porn actresses had hurt Stacy, but she didn't want to end the relationship. People feared him and he seemed to enjoy dominating them. Still, she clung to love ties.

The miles zoomed past Stacy as she drove south on I-99 and approached Bakersfield, where she and David had rendezvoused a couple of times. The corners of her mouth turned up in memory of the fun times, but other recollections pained her.

Stacy recently had found solace in her dogs. She had started raising pugs and would say, "They are the love of my life. I have owned three litters of the cute little pug puppies. They are my babies. Love me, love my dogs."

Once, a dog had been the start of an unhappy experience at Cole Crest. "I was outside, late at night, playing with my dog, and David was yelling at me about it, criticizing my doggy. I just walked away and went to a neighbor's house. It was cold and windy, and I had this light outfit on with my little dog in my arms—nowhere to go. Some guys had just moved into the house and were running some kind of computer operation. I used my cell to call a taxi and was waiting for it, but cabdrivers could never find their way up there. It was like hours. I wanted to get somewhere to get warm. Those guys invited me in and offered me a shot of tequila 'cause I was freezing and my nerves were shot. Finally the taxi showed up and took me and my pup down to a motel on Sunset Strip. Usually, I had very little money with me, but that time, fortunately, I had enough to take care of my expenses. The next day, I went down to Newport Beach, where I had friends. The point is, don't ever mess with my dogs."

Ascending a stretch called "the grapevine," over the Tejon Pass crest at 4,144 feet, and through the Tehachapi Mountains, along a stretch known for generations as the "Ridge Route," Stacy thought about the most recent argument with David. He had been furious because he expected her to be with him on that Sunday, May 27. But she had bought the new Jeep Cherokee and her father had insisted on some final mechanical adjustments, including assuring the door locks worked. She had tried to call David, but she hadn't made the connections. Then, on Monday, he had called to say he had been arrested. He was still angry at her for standing him up on the previous Sunday. But it had been so innocent. Perhaps, she wondered, if she had been there that weekend, she could have kept him out of the trouble he was in.

With about an hour more to drive, Stacy looked forward to seeing David and hoped things would turn out well for him.

CHAPTER 18

THEY WERE GOING TO LEAVE SOMEONE'S HEAD AT MY DOOR

Moving on after a short break, Tom Small asked if Edmund had been a drug supplier to David Mahler. He replied, "I'm not going to lie. Yes, I've gotten coke from him." He emphasized that it was for his personal use. "I have never sold any of it. I will admit that I once bought nine hundred dollars' worth of meth so Cheryl could have it at my house when she needed it. She had a real problem and that's partly why we broke up." He admitted that he had tried meth a few times for enhancement of sexual experiences.

Out of the blue, Mahler asked Small, "Are you married?"
"Yes."

"You seem like a genuine nice guy to me. You're the kind of guy that likes making love. You make love to your wife. You may have wild sex now and then to keep it passionate, right?"

The ploy of intimate personal ingratiation didn't fool Small. He answered, "Very interesting. Very astute."

"So you don't need a stimulant like meth for sex. But I'm in a different zone."

David Mahler had concluded that the police raid at Cole Crest must have been the result of an informant calling them. Dying to know who, and what the person might have said, he resorted to inserting inquiries into his answers in the hope that Tom Small or Vicki Bynum would reveal it. Speaking casually, Mahler said, "So I'm just thinking. We got Robert Jimenez probably calling you to give you information. Rick— now there's another guy I'm curious what he would do. And that guy Damien . . . You know who contacted you, and I don't. So I'm just trying to put the pieces together."

The bait didn't even tempt Small. He used the comment as a transition to his next question. "So what is Damien's play in this?"

"I told you. He's the guy who introduced me to Kristi. And he would call me every now and then and say, 'I got a girl here. You want to meet her?'"

To Small and Bynum, that description fit several people: Atticus King, Edmund, and now Damien. "How often do you get these girls?"

"Lately, not at all, because, remember, I've had girlfriends. I had my fiancée, Kitty, and Cheryl, and Stacy. So I haven't done it for a while." Mahler seemed to have forgotten speaking about having a prostitute at the Marriott Hotel with Atticus King.

Small brought up another subject. "We did a little check on you and we know you have guns in the house."

Mahler turned indignant. "You know I have guns? I do not have guns. If they checked my whole house today, you will see there are no guns there."

"No guns at all?"

"None at all. There was—at one point, there was a gun that Robert left there, but it was picked up."

"Other than that, have there ever been guns in your house?"

"Never." He guessed that Cheryl had told the police he had a gun, and then speculated it may have been reported by Karl Norvik. "Now, if that's coming from Karl, I'll be very honest with you. Karl sometimes gets a little riley when he gets drunk. I have a very real-looking water pistol. This drunken idiot sometimes—when he's drunk, I'll say, 'Get out of my room.' It's nothing but a water pistol."

At Small's request, Mahler described the toy in detail and said it could be found in a drawer under some black sweatpants.

"Okay, that's the only gun you have ever had?"

"That's it, in my whole life."

Veering away from that subject, the detectives spent some time hearing about Mahler's business and personal relationships with Sheldon Weinberg, and the links with Kitty, Cheryl, Kristi, and Michael Conoscenti who was also known as Damien.

Small's facial expression tensed. He asked, "Do you know where Kristi is?"

"No, other than the fact that I was told she was looking for drugs two days ago."

"Who told you that?"

"Rick."

To Small and Bynum, this made no sense at all. Rick, the guy who had been extorting money and threatening Mahler, was now feeding him information about Kristi searching for drugs?

"Where does she live?"

"She stays in Sheldon Weinberg's place, in Calabasas." Mahler gave them the address and phone number.

After a prolonged discussion about Mahler's cars, and his part ownership of a Mercedes and a home in Orange County, he admitted that they had been obtained from a relative of Karl Norvik through some financial arrangements.

"Where is Karl?" Small inquired.

"You know, it's funny you asked that, because it's freaking me out right now. I spoke to Karl [by phone] not thirty minutes before the officers arrived at my house and he told me he was in Orange County. But when the police came, I knocked on his bedroom door and someone said, 'Hold on.' I'm like, 'Karl, the police are here.'"

The detectives noted that David Mahler had given a protracted alibi of being frightened for his life, fearing that people who wanted to hurt him might have been outside. But now, he spoke of telling Karl the police were there. His inconsistencies weren't helping him.

Small said, "I'm going to ask you a question I'm really curious about. How did you wind up in Jeremy's closet?"

Perhaps realizing his mistake, Mahler tried to recover lost ground. "Scared shitless, okay? Here's why. I've had all these threats. After knocking on Karl's room, I hear someone screaming, 'Just a minute.' I know Karl is not there. I had just spoken to him in Orange County. My mind started saying, 'Is Robert up to something? Is Rick in there? Who is in Karl's room knowing the police are here and not answering the door?' I didn't even want to know. I went down to talk to Jeremy and I went in his closet. It's not like I was, you know—"

"Was Jeremy expecting you?"

"No."

"Did he and his girlfriend hide you in the closet?"

"No. I just wanted him to answer the gate and see what the police wanted. . . . I overreacted and got scared."

Small wouldn't let him off the hook. "Why didn't you go let them in? You are the main resident, and you knew it was the police. I'm just curious."

"I thought it was possibly someone setting me up. I had

received a text mail telling me that someone's head was going to be dropped off outside my door. I didn't know what to think, to be quite honest with you."

"Was there ever a head left at your house?"

"No."

"Were any kind of body parts deposited there?"

"Not yet. But that doesn't mean I'm not nervous about it. These guys are experts. I wouldn't put it past them to leave a head at my door."

A series of questions followed about Mahler's drug usage. He complained that he had already answered them several times. Small apologized. "Sometimes I forget what I have asked."

Mahler responded, "You don't have a short memory. You're smart. I'm a lawyer. I know the technique of repeating questions to see if the answers are consistent."

Vicki Bynum broke the growing tension with her musical laugh, saying, "That's better than admitting that we're really getting old and we don't remember."

Returning to the alleged incident of Edmund slapping Kristin in Mahler's presence, Small asked, "Did anybody else come to the room?"

"Donnie did. Remember, I mentioned that?"

"So Donnie saw Edmund and Krissy going into this little episode?"

"Yeah, and then he left right away. He was smart."

"Did you summon him up there, or did he just arrive on his own?"

Indignant again, Mahler snapped, "First of all, I've never summoned him up there. If I called him at all, it was in answer to him calling me first."

"Okay, how were you dressed when Donnie was there?"

Mahler wasn't certain. He said he could have been wearing shorts, his pants, or a bathrobe. Small wanted to know what kind of a bathrobe. Mahler said, "A white Marriott robe. I always take them from hotels. Sorry. Arrest me."

"At the time you had the robe on, were you wearing anything else?"

"I would imagine nothing. I'm not sure where this is going, but—"

Ignoring his concern, Small inquired why Mahler went to the Marriott that night. The reply came out sounding sarcastic. "Because that's where Atticus was. It's my favorite. You should try it. I had called Atticus and told him there was too much drama at my place, and he suggested we meet at the Marriott."

A harsh tone colored Small's next words. "So you go to the hotel, and right after that, Kristi turns up missing."

Mahler tensed. "Uh-huh, okay. Are you making an implication here?"

"I'm just trying to figure out where Kristi wound up."

"Okay. Well, that would be something that Edmund or one of her other friends would have to tell you."

"What do you think happened to her?"

"Well, I'm not so sure she is missing. I'm getting told from Rick just two days ago that she asked him for drugs. She and Rick are close enough that he wouldn't make up a story like that."

Small grew edgier. "We're trying to locate Kristi, and that's really what this is all about. And I think you can help us."

Mahler appeared to scramble. He suggested calling her cell phone and mentioned that she often stayed with a guy named Jeff. "Allegedly, he's the guy who picked her up from Newport Beach, so she says."

Small unloaded. "David, I think your story's full of shit!"

Mahler recoiled as if he had been shot. "Why?"

"Because Edmund wasn't in that room at the time you were prancing around in that bathrobe."

Quickly recovering his bravado, Mahler replied, "Why do you say that? I do it all the time."

"It comes from what people have been telling me. I think you are mistaken. Maybe you had a little too much vodka in you."

Sounding like his feelings had been hurt, Mahler whined, "But I'm not full of shit."

That's not what Small had said. He had told Mahler that his *story* was full of shit. But the detective didn't bother to respond and clarify the distinction. Instead, he said, "Maybe you're clouding things because something happened in that room you don't want to remember. Or maybe there was an accident. Something went on in there that left a lot of blood. And there's blood in other places in your house."

Still dancing around the main point, Mahler retorted, "I haven't had time to check the place out and look. I haven't even looked around. My concern was my bedroom."

Later discussing that segment of the interview, Tom Small said, "I lost my temper with him. I was fed up with his evasions and lies. He just wanted to hear himself keep talking. So I figured, why not push his buttons and see what happens?"

Turning to Vicki Bynum, Tom said, "You kinda kept the situation nice. I basically told him that everything he was saying was bullshit."

Laughing, Vicki complimented her partner. "It was an amazing game, mostly between Tom and Mahler. They were sparring with each other for hours."

Small explained, "Mahler didn't want to put it down. With him, everything is negotiable, so he started trying to set up some trading chips and negotiate his way out of being charged."

* * *

Keeping his focus on the main issue, Detective Small said to Mahler, "Until I lay eyes on Kristi, I have to consider her missing. No one knows where she is, but people did see you and Kristi together."

David Mahler muttered, "Who saw us together?"

"People we have talked to saw you and her in that room."

"She wasn't there that long."

"You were seen with her in that room—just you and her, with no Edmund." Small threw another boulder into Mahler's sinking boat. "You were seen waving that gun around, acting all crazy."

To this new and significant charge, Mahler could manage no more than "Uh-huh."

Unrelenting, the detective added, "You probably had a load on. You were upset. You were tired. You've had enough drama. Krissy's causing you grief. You want her out. You're pissed off about this Rick guy, right?"

Donning a cloak of calm, Mahler replied, "I'm listening to what you are saying."

Small queried, "Does it make sense to you? And then you summoned Donnie up there."

"Uh-huh. Donnie, yeah."

"Yeah," Small echoed. "He shows up, and you pretend like you're going to cap a round into him."

"Into him?" Mahler's question sounded as if he was incredulous that the round would be intended for Donnie rather than Kristi.

"It scared the crap out of him and he splits," said Small. "He closes the door and then hears the sound of a gunshot."

"Okay, if that's what you . . . if that's what you're—"

"That's what I got."

"You're telling me—"

"I'm telling you that another witness goes up and views her body in your room."

"With me there?" Mahler probably assumed Small meant Karl Norvik, but the detective's follow-up confused him.

"No. You weren't there. Can you explain all that?"

"In two ways. But first of all, there's—"

Small wanted no diversions. "How about the truthful way?"

At this point, Vicki Bynum stepped in to defuse the growing hostility with a little touch of "good cop" gentleness. She spoke sweetly to Mahler, hoping it might inspire him to reveal what he knew.

David Mahler remained on the defense. "I think you guys are insinuating that in some way I had something to do with her disappearance. I am stunned."

Suggesting that perhaps an unintentional accident had taken place, Small gave Mahler an opportunity to rationalize events. He rejected it. "If an accident happened, it wasn't at my hands."

Small felt fire in his belly again. "You were the only one there. And you are the only one with a gun in his hand."

"Donnie was there, first of all. I mean, I know Donnie was there, because he was in and out—like you say. Edmund was there too."

"So when the gun went off, were you shocked? Was it unexpected?"

"What makes you think—where is this coming from that the gun even went off?"

By this time, David Mahler certainly knew that Donnie Van Develde had provided the information leading to these accusations. "I don't know why he would say that. I have absolutely no clue other than the fact that we've had disagreements in regard to his paying the rent."

Small asked, "Did Kristi say something to you to get you going? She just wanted away from you."

"Kristi and I get along fine. Did Donnie say different?"

Using the present tense for Kristi made it sound as if Mahler thought she was still alive. And he seemed to have forgotten talking about the dispute that prompted him to abandon her in a hotel, and his description of ordering her to leave his house.

It hadn't left Small's mind, though. "Did she hold a grudge because you left her in Newport? Did she owe you some money too? Is she ripping you off?"

"No."

"Did she sic someone on you?"

Mahler asked if they could take a break. All three agreed, and Vicki Bynum left the room. Both men continued to chat, however. Mahler commented, "I'm a lawyer. When I go to court, I'm in control. I'm damn good at what I do. In this room, you're damn good at what you do. And you're good, because you knew exactly where you were headed."

"I'm just trying to find the truth," Small countered. "And I want to know where Kristi is."

Mahler gave the first hint of cooperating. "I know I can find that out."

They continued bantering in mutually complimentary terms. Mahler said, "I'm talking to you because I'm looking at you in the eyes and I'm saying, 'This man is good at what he does.' Maybe sometimes you've got to slide the truth, but [you are] always on the right side of the truth. And I'm telling you point-blank—what do you want or need from me so that I [can] sleep at home or in a hotel this evening and not in jail?"

To Detective Small, David Mahler had played his first bargaining chip. He had made clear his willingness to trade information in exchange for getting out of jail. Still, the detective needed crucial information. He met the offer with a curt reply.

"I'm not going to promise that you're going to sleep at home, and I'm not going to promise that you're going to sleep in a hotel. I can't make any promises, and you know that."

Disappointment clouded Mahler's face.

Offering a little leeway, Small said he thought the whole thing might have been an accident. "If that is so, you need to tell me about it. Otherwise, I'm left with what I've been told by other witnesses and by evidence we find."

Still probing for negotiation opportunities, Mahler asked if they had more than Donnie's version of what had happened. Small said that they did indeed have corroboration of Donnie's statements. "And I can tell you, we believe Donnie is telling the truth."

Vicki Bynum returned to the room. She again made an appeal to David Mahler, to think of himself and not waste his future by getting deeper and deeper into a hole.

He expressed his understanding of the situation and acknowledged that it would be stupid to force the detectives into writing a harsh report depicting him in negative terms. Mahler realized that he needed their presentation to the district attorney (DA) to be in as favorable terms as possible.

The trio batted the issues of "doing the right thing" versus "self-preservation" back and forth for the next hour.

For Mahler, the challenge seemed to be discovery of how much evidence and how many statements had been piled up against him, but the detectives let him keep wondering.

Regarding witnesses, Tom Small played another chip. "You called your best friend up and asked him to help you get rid of a body."

It sent Mahler into a dizzy spin. He replied, "I don't even have a best friend. Who are you talking about?" He puzzled over it and speculated, "The only person that could be is Damien. But I don't consider him as a friend. Have you looked into his history?"

Ignoring the comments, Detective Small reiterated, "Where are we going to find Kristi?"

Mahler deftly dodged it, pointing out that any kind of an answer, even if he had one, would incriminate him. After more jousting, he came up with an idea.

Mahler said, "Let's look at it hypothetically. Let's presume that I'm able to pinpoint her exact location. Let's further presume that once she's located, she won't be in good health." He wanted to know if providing "hearsay" information to help locate her would help him avoid being jailed.

A judge would have to make that decision, said Small. "I think it would carry some weight that you stepped up and did the right thing."

Vicki Bynum made a powerful appeal to Mahler's logic. "David, let's stop it now before it becomes an avalanche. Make it stop. . . . I know you are going to go the right way. I feel that about you. I think you are a decent guy, a smart guy, an accomplished person. But something has happened to you in the last six months. People I have spoken to say that something has changed in your demeanor, your behavior. I think that whatever's happened to you—whether it be drugs, financial, whatever—it has caused you to make this horrible mistake. You are not the kind of person to do something like that. But if you let it continue, it's not going to work in your benefit."

Tom Small returned to pragmatic basics. "I want to know three things. One, where she's at. Two, where the gun is. Three, who moved her? Was it you? Or did you have help?"

David Mahler snapped, "Those are three pretty serious, incriminating statements if I were to answer any of them, aren't they?"

Now Vicki Bynum grew impatient. "Look, we've been doing this job for a long time. And you know we're not bull-shitting you here, David. You know that."

Her language seemed to impress Mahler. "I wouldn't even be talking here if I thought you were. You don't think I'm disrespecting you, I hope."

Another half hour of gambits and verbal chess followed.

As the clock ticked close to noon, Mahler said, "I'm willing to meet you halfway. But you can't ask me to give you—

show you all my cards in hope that they're good enough. That's not fair."

Small put it in clearer terms. "What you're asking me is— 'Can we deal?'"

"Not necessarily 'deal,'" Mahler said, "but what can we do to minimize the charges?"

"I don't have anything to do with what a charge would be, other than present the facts as I obtain them."

"What charge would you recommend if everything got answered?"

After thinking it over for a moment, Small said, "If the evidence shows it was an accident, I would say it could be involuntary. It could very well be that. I don't know. Based on the totality of the circumstances as we know it right now, we are going to continue to investigate." He unequivocally stated, "I cannot play 'let's make a deal.'"

Mahler appeared to withdraw, so Small offered a tidbit of encouragement. "Look, if you are the kind of person who's going to stand up and tell us where we can find her, and you're going to help us complete this part of the investigation, the DA is going to know that you helped us."

Still dreading the thought of spending that Saturday night, Sunday, and Monday in jail, David Mahler asked if something could be done to request a judge to grant him freedom through bail or release on his own recognizance.

The subject of lunch came up at half past twelve. Mahler registered surprise. "I didn't know it was that late. Can we have a meeting with a judge in chambers before four o'clock?"

Bynum stepped out to arrange for food to be brought to the room for Mahler.

"Do you know where Kristi is?" Small repeated.

Mahler growled out, "At this point, it doesn't matter to me." Instantly realizing his strategic error, he tried to smooth it over. "I don't mean it like that. I can't even believe I said that. I take it back completely. Pretend I never said that. What

I mean is—this is my best bargaining chip, because her parents want her alive. Let me tell you this. The last time I saw her, she was alive."

Sensing an opening, Small bored in. "Where was she hit?"

For the first time, Mahler hinted that he knew Kristi had possibly suffered a life-threatening injury. "The last   you know, the last I saw her, there was movement and there was the attempt at speech. How long does that last? I'm no doctor."

With renewed energy, Small pushed even harder. "Where is she? If she's alive, we need to get medical attention to her."

Mahler, though, saw the slight admission as an opportunity to request an immediate hearing with a judge to seek release in exchange for information. He voiced the suggestion. Small remained tenacious. "So it's your belief we could probably find her?"

"With my assistance, I think it's possible. And I also think you can find the gun, and a lot of other things you don't even know about. . . . I want bail set so I can get out of here. And then you get what you want."

"You know I can't make any promises," Small reasserted. "Are you telling me that you are able to find a way to locate her?"

"I am able to find a way to find her, probably in one phone call, to tell the truth. What else do you want? You want the shells? Do you want the bullets? They're all in different places. But somebody—and I'm not saying who—knows where they all are. I know you don't want anyone else using that gun, do you? Now I'm not admitting anything here. And I'm not going to admit anything. I can help you, but it's not for free."

Putting on a facial expression of deep thought, Small said, "Let me make some phone calls."

An attendant showed up with a sandwich and soft drink for Mahler's lunch.

Accepting it, Mahler made a request of Small. Could he

also have his cell phone to call someone? He implied that it would be to the person who could supply information that the detectives wanted. In addition, he hoped to reach Stacy. "If you could work that out, that would be fabulous."

Small left Mahler alone in the room. But the suspect didn't realize that a video recorder, with a monitor in an adjacent room, kept running. It picked up Mahler's whispering, growling soliloquy of fury. "Asshole. I want to get the hell out. Goddamn it. Fucking Stacy. Why did I have to [do] the stupidest fucking thing I ever did? This is fucking ridiculous. (Inaudible) fucking, I want to leave. How the hell was I so stupid? I'm getting tired. That's why. I was just getting tired. I have one more thing to do, one fucking thing. Everything was fucking handled. (Inaudible) Sunday, Monday, Tuesday, Wednesday, every fucking night except Thursday."

It would be interpreted that he referred to being satisfied with Sunday, the day of the shooting, Monday and Tuesday at hotels, but furious at the events of Thursday. When the detectives replayed the recording, they realized he probably referred to the early-morning trip to the desert on that Thursday. Mahler's vulgar monologue continued. "I'm sick of this goddamn little room. It's not right. I'm fucking losing it. Waiting like an idiot in a closed room."

Vicki Bynum unlocked the door, swung it open, and found David Mahler lying on the floor near a tipped-over chair.

CHAPTER 19

REVEALING SECRETS

Detective Bynum gasped. "Are you okay?"

Mahler stirred. "I'm okay. I'm okay."

Realizing that the collapse was doubtlessly a ploy for sympathy, she again spoke in her usual sweet tones. "Oh, so you're just lying down?"

"I don't know. My head gets dizzy. It's my own fault. Don't worry about it."

Bynum asked, "So you are all right?"

He snarled, "I'm not all right, but let's—what the hell are we doing?"

Tom Small, who had seen the minidrama on the television monitor next door, rushed in and spoke, tongue firmly in check. "I heard this noise. I thought you were knocking. I thought, 'Dang, that sounds like someone knocking.'"

"Nah, I fell over. I'm okay, though."

Simultaneously both detectives asked, "Are you sure?"

"I'm cool. I'm cool."

Still disguising his contempt by being oversolicitous, Tom Small asked, "Was it the sandwich? Do you need some water?"

Mahler declined any more aid. Small announced some bad news. No judge would be available for an immediate hearing. Nor would they receive anyone in chambers under these circumstances. Instead, any judge would rely on information presented to the DA.

Obviously disappointed, David Mahler said, "I know you were trying to help out. Where do we go from here?"

"Well, that depends on you. Do you have anything further you'd like to tell us, because we have learned more? . . ."

"Why don't you just tell me what evidence you have? Because as far as I'm concerned, there is none."

Flexing his jaws, and giving Mahler a cold stare, Small said that he thought Mahler had probably been high on cocaine that Saturday night and Sunday morning. "The facts are that you shot and killed that girl in your bedroom. And you wanted to cover it up and maybe elicit some support from some of your friends. . . ."

"Oh, so you are saying that there were some phone calls recorded?"

The question gave Small and Bynum one more piece of the puzzle. His worry showed consciousness of guilt. Small kept talking. "If you want to put a better light on it and tell us everything you know, I will present that to the district attorney. Otherwise, I'm going to go with what I've got. And with what I've got, you are screwed." Mahler slumped and made innocuous quarreling noises. Small moved in. "No, no, no. Sit up to the table like a man. Let's go one-on-one. . . . I'm going to turn up the heat a little because I'm tired of goofing off with you."

Actually straightening his posture a little, Mahler uttered a soft "Okay."

"You know—this little charade about falling on the floor— I heard you kick the chair over. What is this, a game you are playing?"

"Why would I do that?"

"Because I think you've got a body hidden somewhere. You shot this poor girl."

With his eyes darting back and forth—worried—Mahler's retort made little sense. "Let's leave that out of it, 'cause that has nothing to do with it."

"No, we're not going to leave that out, because that's what it's all about."

"You think I'm—"

"At this point, I'm starting to think a whole lot different of you. I thought maybe you had some good in you. Look, I've given you lots of opportunities to help yourself and do the right thing. I'm not going to keep coming back with more."

Perhaps worried that he had blown a chance, Mahler played his next card. "So you are going to let her—no medical attention the rest of the weekend? You think she will last?"

Small barked out, "I think she's gone, and you know it."

"If you think that, why are you . . . ?"

"If you know where she is, you give it up right now."

Stiffening his spine, Mahler said, "Let's talk like gentlemen and try to get some results here."

Small shot back, "The results are you want a cakewalk out of here. Ain't happening, okay? You're here to stay."

Somehow interpreting the comment as a threat to raise the amount of bail, Mahler protested, "The bail should be two million. I've got it. Don't tell me I am staying. I ain't staying anywhere. I'll stay in town and I'll face the case."

The sparring continued for another twenty minutes with jibes, veiled insults, and no change in what each side hoped to accomplish. David Mahler's thrusts hoped to squeeze promises from the detective, and Tom Small adamantly stated he could make no promises. The exchange appeared to be stalemated several times, with both Mahler and Small ready to end it. But they continued.

Small asked, "Are we going to keep this adversarial, or [are] we going to talk turkey?"

Mahler snorted. "I'm trying to talk turkey. You raised the heat, thinking I'm going to back down like a punk, and I'm not." He accused Small of not being a gentleman.

Vicki Bynum interceded as a referee. "This is not getting us anywhere. Detective Small is always a gentleman. David, do you understand that what we think you are asking of us is something we cannot provide? Let's try to get this back to where we were before it got adversarial. Okay?"

As the tension lowered, Bynum spoke softly to Mahler, recognizing that he was probably confused, in denial, a little scared, and unsure just what to do. "I think you are acting as you would with someone you are representing in court."

"But you also think that I've done some things—more than I have really done."

In her usual, pleasant, melodic voice, Bynum said, "Well, I'll tell you what you've done. You've been on a drug binge. You've been partying. You've had problems with women. You've been kicked out of hotels. You've had fights at hotels. You've had fights with girls. You've had somebody let you down. You've been ticked off. All of this is coming around and spinning around. It's gotten out of control for you. That's what's happened."

Mahler nodded his agreement. "You're right on point on every one."

"And you were not acting maliciously or with the intent to hurt anyone when it happened. But it happened. And instead of just dealing with it, you spun out of control, maybe thought about flight. Maybe that's why you went to a hotel by the airport. You spent some time thinking about how to cover it up. And now, here you are, sitting here, and you've dug yourself into a hole a little bit. And we've been telling you for hours how all we really want to do is help you get out of this. But we're not going to do it much longer because we have a lot—"

Mahler corrected one point. "Not 'get out' of it, but diminish it."

"Okay. *Diminish it.* Thank you. And you're not going to get out of it—and we're trying to help you diminish it. But we're not going to sit here much longer because, personally, we're tired. We've got a lot to do. You can make our job a lot easier and we can present this in the best light possible. But we're just about done. You know we can't make any promises or represent the DA or speak for a judge. Okay? All we can do is complete our investigation and go from there. And, of course, we want to know where she is. By the way, I'm a mother and I have a daughter about the same age as this young woman, and I would be worried sick."

Bynum's intercession worked perfectly. Mahler said he would help them find Kristi if they would allow him five telephone calls. Bynum agreed on the condition he would first provide a list of names he planned to call. He listed Stacy, someone named Mark, who would know where "the piece" is, a bail bondsman, and Mahler's sister. He hadn't yet decided who the fifth person would be.

It seemed reasonable to Bynum. "For those phone calls, we'll be able to locate somebody who needs to be found. Is that what you are telling me?"

"That is correct. I'll put it on paper." However, Mahler added, he wanted it understood that he was making no admission of any crimes. "It will be information I have been provided from other sources, not personal knowledge." Bynum and Small concurred.

Apparently feeling generous, Mahler asked, "Do you know her last name yet? Does her family know yet?"

"We will be contacting them as soon as we have the

information we need," said Small. He wanted to know if the woman's name was really Kristi.

Mahler replied, "That's what her driver's license said."

Bynum asked, "Is she also known as Cheryl?"

Mahler's face turned pale. "No, no, no, no!" he shouted. "How is Cheryl involved in this?"

Startled, Bynum explained, "I was just asking."

"You're scaring me," Mahler bellowed. "Cheryl is not missing, is she? Cheryl, I do love. Is she okay?"

It settled him down when Bynum said she didn't even know Cheryl. Her name had been mentioned several times by Mahler, and the detective just wanted to avoid confusion in identities.

Eager to learn Kristi's last name, Small asked for it again and explained that if she had ever been arrested, he could perhaps find a photo of her "and see if this is the girl we're talking about."

With that kerfuffle settled, Mahler even offered to give the name and phone number of Kristin's "father." Evidently unaware that Peter Means was her stepfather, David said, "She talks more—she talked more about her father than she did her mother." It didn't escape the detectives' radar that he had changed his use of Kristin's name to the past tense, probably indicating knowledge that she was dead. Mahler drove home the point, again, that "there is no admission of guilt here. You've not heard me say anything about being guilty."

The deal, according to Mahler, would be for him to write down information the detectives wanted, and then fold the paper in half. They would wait until he made his allotted phone calls before reading it. He would trust them not to read it early, and they would have to trust him that the information would fit their needs. With the bargain sealed, he wrote and folded his document. He again barked out: "I just want to get my bail so I can get out of here. Then you get what you want."

The detectives escorted Mahler to a speaker-telephone, keyed in numbers he requested, and activated a machine to record them. He stated once more, "Remember, there is no admission of guilt here." First he spoke to Stacy Tipton on her cell phone. She said that she was en route, and very close to the Hollywood Station. Next he attempted to reach a business associate but got no answer. He was able to connect with a bail bondsman, who said he would be there right away. The fourth call went to his sister in another state, but she did not answer.

Following the phone calls, it turned out that Mahler had written on the folded paper the number of Sheldon Weinberg. He explained that Sheldon would have contact information for Kristin's family. Mistakenly, Mahler said the father lived in Hawaii. He had accurately noted Kristin's surname as Baldwin.

Small asked Mahler if he knew her age and full first name. Mahler said he didn't know, but added that he was going to provide information that would help with those details. "Just remember, I don't know who did it. Hypothetically, if I did, I wouldn't say. But her driver's license can be picked up—it was just put there recently—I didn't do it, but if I did, I deny it—it can be picked up along with her credit cards and other personal possessions at the intersection of Sunset Plaza and Sunset Boulevard. It's in one of the garbage cans outside of a restaurant. From what I understand, and the way it was relayed to me, the cans were almost empty when the stuff was dropped in there. So it should be relatively easy to find."

"Okay," said Small, "what about the other information I was asking for?"

Mahler vacillated, hinting that he had already met his part of the bargain and wanted some approbation for being so cooperative.

Ignoring the diversion, Small asked, "Is she going to need medical attention?"

"Do you want my honest opinion?"

"Of course, I do."

"I don't think—there's—I don't think she can be helped."

Vicki Bynum would later describe the comment as "real cold" and "evil."

The disclosure also bothered Tom Small, but it didn't surprise him. He still needed to know where she could be found. Mahler showed far more interest in his self-protection. "If I say more, it hurts my case. I know this will go to trial, and I'm hurting myself by telling you anything. How can I do this without self-incriminating? I think there is a way. I will sign a statement. I, David Mahler, via hearsay—underlined—have been hereby informed, not through personal knowledge, that Kristi Baldwin may or may not be, but—in all probability—is at the following location."

The offer stunned Tom Small. He asked, "How will that help you?"

"It's gonna help me more than just telling you."

"Okay. That's fine."

Vicki Bynum threw in her instant approval. "Let's go for it."

Mahler still wanted assurance they would portray him in the best possible light in reports to the DA. Small said, "The information will be passed along to those who need to know."

At three minutes past four o'clock, Mahler began printing on lined paper. He reminded both detectives that they must cosign the document. They agreed. As he printed the words, he read them aloud. He wrote:

6/1/07

I, David Mahler, accused suspect or party with alleged information, without admitting any guilt & denying __all__ guilt, through & by HEARSAY have reason to believe that Kristi Baldwin may be found at the following location.

Intersection of I-15 No. (above Barstow) and I-40 near hospital sign. This in no way shall be used to be incriminating Mr. Mahler as it's . . . voluntary and without coercion.

However, both Detective Small and Detective Bynum acknowledge their appreciation for this information.

Mahler signed his name in cursive letters nearly two inches high. Below that, Tom Small and Vicki Bynum entered their signatures.

While writing the portion about a hospital, Mahler said, "There is a hospital right there. That was purposely part of it. Okay? It was almost like dropping someone off at a hospital."

Small had doubts. "Okay, so she would have been noticed out in plain view and maybe treated by that hospital?"

Mahler agreed. "And possibly treated." He added that she had not, as far as he knew, been put in a place of concealment.

The reference to a hospital would turn out to be totally untrue. The site where Kristin Baldwin's body had been dumped was nowhere near a hospital. No hospital sign could be seen within a ten-mile radius.

Tom Small wanted more. "Any chance you would be able to include where someone might look for the gun?"

"What if I provide it to you? I'm going to be out of here in an hour. Can you stop that now?"

Small said, "I can't stop you. No. That's your right."

"Unless you charge me with something else, I guess."

"I have nothing else." He explained that he wanted to send someone out to pick up the weapon so it wouldn't fall into the wrong hands.

"Okay," said Mahler. "I'm even going to tell you where this gun came from. I'd love you to go talk to him, the son of a bitch. He's a cop. On the gun it says, 'Issued by the L.A. Police Department.' Son of a bitch shouldn't be giving out guns, should he? Sorry, I'm getting a little emotional about it. Jimenez, Robert Jimenez. You want his address? I'll give it to you."

"Is that where the gun is?"

"No, he doesn't have it now. He's the one who left it at my house—in my opinion, intentionally."

"Okay, then where is it?"

Once again, Mahler turned reluctant, complaining about possible self-incrimination, hesitating and asserting his innocence. Small asked if he wanted to write this information down too. Yes, Mahler said, but added, "I don't know if you're going to find it. That's gonna be tougher. You know, you guys talk to me for twenty hours, and all of a sudden I figure you are my friends. You're not my friends. You're here to get me."

"No," said Small. "We're here to find the facts and clear everything up."

Mahler proceeded to deliver another long-winded spiel of personal philosophy, but Small stopped him.

"Can we get to the gun, please?"

With an agreement by all three, Mahler put pen to paper again:

6/1/07 4:26 P.M.

I David Mahler hereby admit, swear & testify that one Robert Jimenez, purported officer at law and bail recovery agent, placed a gun/revolver into Mr. Mahler's home and did not remove it despite several requests to do so and as such the gun seemingly & apparently was the item involved with an incident re; Kristi.

No guilt to be presumed, assumed, or construed.

The gun was left intentionally by Robert Jimenez,

*labeled Prop of Police & claimed to be unregistered
& unlicensed.*

   *Mr. Mahler wishes contrition on having the gun in
the house & having handled the gun several times
before the alleged incident (i.e. 7 days prior) and
Detectives acknowledging this statement is given to
secure in the interests of public safety & not to
evidentiary incriminate or to further promote any
liability prior to 6/1/07 to David Mahler.*

   *It is hoped by Mr. Mahler that the State recognizes
his sympathy, remorse & cooperation.*

   *This gun is located, based on hearsay, at or about
1400-1600 Sunset Plaza Drive in a large green
Dumpster in a plastic bag.*

During the preparation of this second document, David
Mahler and Tom Small discussed each passage, while Vicki
Bynum took a restroom break. They decided the weapon was a
revolver, because it resembled a "cowboy gun." The subject of
liability for Jimenez came up. Mahler lamented that if the gun
hadn't been left in his house, the "incident" would never have
happened. He said, "I want this guy. As far as I'm concerned,
if not for ever knowing him, I wouldn't be in any trouble,
'cause I've never had a gun in my house." Mahler worried repeatedly about his culpability if investigators found the
weapon. He expressed the opinion, though, that he would never
be convicted of anything. "I haven't lost a case in eleven years."

He completed the writing soon after Bynum returned, and
all three of them signed it.

Bynum informed Mahler that she had learned, coming
back from the restroom, that his bail bond guy had arrived.
He perked up, believing he would be leaving within an hour.

He was wrong.

CHAPTER 20

LIES, LEGALITIES, AND LEGWORK

Locked in a jail cell, David Mahler fumed with outrage. Frustrated, disappointed, and boiling over with anger, he couldn't believe he had been outwitted. To him, the interrogators had cheated and used deceptive tricks. He had undergone the humiliating booking process under "probable cause" rules, in violation of *California Penal Code 187 (a), murder.* After being fingerprinted and photographed, Mahler found himself once more in a dreaded cell. He would have to remain behind bars at least until the district attorney filed charges on Monday morning. And if he faced first-degree murder, there could be no bail. From expectation of leaving the Hollywood Station on Saturday evening, Mahler knew he might be in jail for months while waiting for trial.

Stacy Tipton arrived just before the interview ended, and waited near the front desk. When she finally received permission to visit Mahler, Stacy worked hard to calm him down, but she had little success. Later speaking of it, she said, "I saw him in the Hollywood Station. He was still in his street clothes, a black jersey and dark slacks. I couldn't believe all of this had happened to him."

Directing his anger at Stacy, Mahler accused her of not being there for him in his hours of need. His slashing words seemed to blame her for failing to show up on Sunday, May 27, when the shooting had occurred in his bedroom. She stood her ground, and said, "David, I tried to call you and explain. My dad just wanted to make sure the locks and everything worked on my new car. You didn't answer your phone or call me back. You assumed I was standing you up. Instead of yelling at me for not being there, you should thank me for trying. I wanted to tell you to clean up your act and get rid of all this junk in your life. I was going to tell you if you did that, I wanted to marry you."

In recalling it, Stacy quoted David as saying, "Why didn't you tell me this before?"

Stacy would continue to visit him.

Dead tired after more than fourteen hours on the job, Vicki Bynum and Tom Small still had enough energy to feel a sense of triumph and attend to a few more details. They had laid out their game plan in advance, and played it perfectly. Less experienced detectives might have withered under the difficult challenge of interrogating a smug lawyer suspected of a homicide, or prying any useful information from him. And to elicit incriminating statements might have seemed impossible. Yet, Bynum and Small had turned Mahler's complacent arrogance into an advantage. So determined to wiggle his way out of a tight spot, and overconfident that he could outsmart a couple of cops, David Mahler had spilled more information than might be expected from uneducated street thugs. His glib effort to cast all of the information as "hearsay" turned out to be an inept failure. Bynum and Small's adherence to the rules of proper interview techniques, with no promises, had produced not only laudable results, but had been accomplished with the highest level of professionalism.

Tom Small would later say, "The thing about Mahler is, he thinks he can negotiate his way out of anything. He has a long pattern of doing that with everyone. It's what he can get out of it. He wants you to think he's got something on you so you owe him. That's the way he works. People around him know that and some of them have been sucked in by it before and don't want to owe him, so they stop having anything to do with him."

If there had been any doubt of Mahler's credibility, the interview had crushed it. He had been caught in at least a dozen misleading statements:

- Initially, Mahler said he hadn't seen Kristin from the time they met until a week or two ago.
- At first he insisted that he didn't know Kristin's last name, then later gave it.
- His tale of Edmund slapping Kristin was disputed by Donnie Van Develde's story.
- He said he registered at the Island Hotel in his own name.
- "I don't want drugs around me or in my house" was patently false.
- His denial of summoning Donnie to his room was belied by Van Develde.
- His assertions of calling Van Develde and Norvik for "advice" was untrue.
- Stacy lived in Visalia, not Bakersfield.
- More claims of not using drugs faded into admissions of frequent usage.
- He said he had not used any prostitutes lately, but actually had paid for one at the Marriott.
- "There have never been guns in my house" was a lie.
- He insisted he had last seen Kristin at 3:00 A.M. Sunday. Donnie said she was there at 6:00 A.M.

More probable lies became evident to Small and Bynum. Some of the deception lay in information that Mahler had provided by framing personal knowledge as "hearsay." Both detectives believed that he had shot Kristin to death and dumped her body somewhere. In addition, he had personally disposed of the gun in a trash bin at a construction site on Sunset Plaza Drive, probably when he drove from Cole Crest to the LAX Marriott on early Sunday morning, May 27. At the point where the street intersects with Sunset Boulevard, he doubtlessly had made a stop behind a Chinese restaurant and ditched Kristin's identification documents in a trash bin at one end of the parking lot.

Subsequent investigation of Mahler's statements would reveal even more duplicity. In a discussion about the interview, months later, the detectives explained how they could contain themselves during the arduous interview.

Small said, "I was acting the whole time, because I either wanted to strangle this guy, beat the hell out of him, or laugh."

Bynum confided, "It was a grueling nine hours. It was hard. A lot of people would have given up."

Small agreed. "They would have. But the whole thing was—the motivation for us was—did we have maybe a slim chance to find her alive? Do we have a chance? If there was any hope, and she was near a hospital sign, like he said, even though we doubted it, we had to take the chance. That's why we persisted. Otherwise, we would have booked his ass a lot sooner."

Before ending their long tours on that Saturday, Bynum and Small wanted to find a photo of Kristin Baldwin. They left messages with the California Department of Motor Vehicles and similar county departments in Hawaii, but none of these contacts would result in obtaining photos. Small tried one more source. Wondering if Kristin had ever been jailed, he accessed computer records and hit the jackpot. The DUI incident in Ventura County, a couple of years earlier, produced a mug shot, plus the recording of fingerprints, full name, and other information. Now the detectives had not only a photo, but they knew her name was Kristin Frances Means, aka Baldwin, with a birth date of May 6, 1969. So she had vanished from Mahler's Cole Crest house exactly three weeks after her thirty-eighth birthday.

Early Sunday morning, a team of searchers, including a helicopter, swept over the desert region near Barstow, concentrating on the intersection of I-15 with I-40. No hospital sign could be found anywhere in the vicinity. Nothing turned up to even hint that an injured or dead woman had been dropped off. A check with all the local medical centers was equally disappointing. Mahler's self-serving claims of Kristi being left near a hospital, where she could have possibly received treatment, proved completely false—more lies. They were probably efforts on his part to curry favor with the detectives by creating an image of his compassion. If so, he seriously misjudged Bynum and Small.

Other officers were deployed that day to drive the entire twisting three-mile labyrinth of Sunset Plaza Drive and hunt for the trash bin in which the gun had been discarded, according to Mahler's "hearsay." Hours of digging through all types of refuse produced nothing. They experienced the same results after rummaging through several trash barrels close to the Chinese restaurant. If Mahler had told the truth, either some "Dumpster diver" had beaten them to the weapon and the documents, or everything had been transported and buried at a disposal site. Neither the gun nor the identification papers would ever be found.

After a day of rest on Sunday, Tom Small, Vicki Bynum, and Wendi Berndt's homicide team resumed the investigation early on Monday morning, June 4.

Bynum arrived at the LAX Marriott by 6:00 A.M. and spoke to David Grant, director of loss prevention for the hotel, and security director Ken Van Meter. Both of them clearly remembered David Mahler's stay. At Bynam's request, they provided records of it. He had checked in at 6:57 A.M. on May 27, and left the next day at approximately 11.51 A.M., resulting in being required to pay for two nights. A total of $3,706.38 had been charged to Mahler's credit card. The room rate of $250 plus taxes per night accounted for a portion of it. Other assessments included two vehicles left in the valet's custody, room service charges of $415, a fee for smoking in a nonsmoking room, and several bottles of liquor. The cost had skyrocketed by an additional fee of $2,200 for the destruction of a wide-screen television set. Bynum marveled at Mahler's extravagance. She knew he had also paid $700 to a hooker, and probably paid Atticus King for his services. All of this took place after probably shooting a woman to death just a few hours earlier. The callous self-indulgence gnawed at the detective's stomach.

She also wondered if his choice of a hotel near Los Angeles International Airport signaled his thoughts of fleeing the country.

The hotel employee explained the procedure of allowing Mahler to check in under their "code blue" policy. "On occasion we have guests who want to remain anonymous for whatever reason, such as they don't want to receive incoming phone calls or if somebody were to call the hotel and ask for them by name. No one would know they were registered. And the reason we enter it as code blue is so the folks in security and other hotel personnel would be able to get in contact with the guest in case of emergency."

Security records indicated that Mahler's room had been visited several times by hotel officers, who requested that the occupants please reduce the noise level and stop disturbing other guests.

Bynum verified that the two vehicles handled by the valet parking service had been a 2007 dark blue Jaguar and a green-and-white van marked as a taxi. The license numbers matched information showing they were the ones driven by David Mahler and Atticus King.

While Vicki Bynum visited one hotel, Tom Small made a longer trip to another one. He drove to Newport Beach and arrived at the Island Hotel, just before seven o'clock that morning.

Small initially contacted desk manager Greg Squires and showed him the recent mug shot of Mahler taken at the Hollywood Station during the booking process. Squires's face lit up with recognition, not so much from Mahler's May visit to the hotel, but from last night's television news program that had covered the arrest. The desk manager escorted Small to an office, where the detective met security officer Jonathon Thompson, who described his duties as assisting guests with hospitality services, in addition to being responsible for safety and security of patrons, as well as staff. Both employees recalled that Mahler had arrived quite late on May 24 in a "blue expensive vehicle." He had been accompanied by a "thin, blond girl." They also had observed the couple teaming up with a husky, bald man, who arrived in a separate car.

Another matter had stuck in the officer's memory for a very sound reason. He said that Mahler and the girl with him had a "violent altercation" in their room. Security personnel had made several visits up there to quiet the situation, and Mahler had trashed the room. As a result, Mahler and his friend had been asked to leave the hotel.

Small asked to have a look at tapes made by hotel security cameras on or about May 24. The trio reviewed the videos and found a segment that Small had hoped for. Grainy color images showed David Mahler with a woman, presumably

Kristin, at the check-in desk. An inviting bowl of apples could be seen on the countertop. A burly, balding man wearing a Hawaiian shirt entered the scene. The trio appeared to have a conversation with the check-in clerk in the silent tape. Then, as they walked into the expansive lobby, Mahler put his left arm around the woman's shoulders in what appeared to be a show of affection. All three of them went to an elevator and entered it.

Hotel records showed that Mahler had checked in at twelve thirty, Thursday morning, but not under his own name. The room had been assigned to someone named George Goldberg (pseudonym), who had presented a gift certificate issued by a local automobile dealer. It covered the cost of the room for one night.

It didn't take Small long to find that Goldberg was a businessman who lived a short distance from the hotel. In a subsequent interview, Goldberg would acknowledge an arrangement to meet Mahler at the Newport Beach Marriott Hotel on the evening of Wednesday, May 23. Goldberg had arrived at about seven thirty to entertain another man, a client of Mahler's. Three hours later, at about ten thirty, Mahler showed up, accompanied by a woman he called Kristi.

Describing himself as Mahler's commodities broker, Goldberg estimated he and David had been linked in that business for about six months. They had conducted at least two or three transactions per week, by telephone, during that time.

According to Goldberg, after Mahler and the woman had made their appearance, all four of them sat around a table for about two hours. Mahler and the client immersed themselves in a business discussion, but Goldberg had paid little attention to what they were saying. Casually chatting with Kristi, he heard her say that she used to work at a couple of restaurants in Newport.

When the business discussion ended, the client left. Goldberg told Mahler he had reserved a room for him at the nearby

Island Hotel. He led the way in his car, while Mahler and Kristi followed in the Jaguar. When they arrived, he went to the check-in desk with them and produced a certificate for a free night. A local auto sales dealer had given it to Goldberg. To use it, Goldberg registered for the room in his name. Mahler, Goldberg said, had aggressively tried to convince the clerk to upgrade them to a suite, but he had failed. Goldberg had gone up the elevator with them, talked in the room for fifteen or twenty minutes, and then left to drive to his nearby home.

In regard to Kristi, Goldberg had the impression that Mahler "liked her a lot." But sometime Friday morning, Mahler had called him. "I remember that he was angered or upset. And he said, 'We got to get this bitch out of here. I hate her and I don't want to pay for a cab or a limo.'"

The turn of events had surprised Goldberg. Asked why, he said that Mahler had privately confided something in their conversation at the hotel. He had said that he loved her.

Additional footage from outdoor cameras showed Mahler's arrival in the blue Jaguar with Kristin. Later she could be seen alone in the lobby. Jonathon Thompson could recall that part of the sequence quite well, since he had been standing only a short distance away from Kristin. He told Small that she had appeared distraught. In his recollection, she met a male in the lobby and left with him in a taxi. He had formed the opinion that Mahler had left her stranded.

Upon returning to Hollywood from her trip to the LAX Marriott, Vicki Bynum joined Wendi Berndt to have a look at the Cole Crest house. While observing criminalists going methodically through the rooms, the two women decided to search for the single bullet that, in Donnie Van Develde's story, had killed Kristin Baldwin.

Thinking that it might have hit the fireplace, Bynum

The Mojave Desert near Dagget, California, where Allura McGehay avoided a deadly collision. Her near-miss led to an important discovery.
(Courtesy Los Angeles County Superior Court)

A reckless driver who didn't bother to stop forced McGehay's pickup truck to the sandy shoulder where her tires sank into the soft earth, leaving her stuck. *(Courtesy Los Angeles County Superior Court)*

Sheriff's deputy with Robert LaFond and Christopher DeWitt, who stopped to help the stranded woman. *(Courtesy Los Angeles County Superior Court)*

While they were searching for stones to put under the pickup's tires, sunlight glinting from a gold watch caught the attention of LaFond and DeWitt. *(Courtesy Los Angeles County Superior Court)*

Closer inspection by the Samaritans revealed an arm protruding from the shadows under this shallow bridge. The desiccated body had been there for over two weeks. *(Courtesy Los Angeles County Superior Court)*

Kristin Baldwin at age five holds her kitten. She and her family moved frequently from town to town on the East Coast. *(Courtesy Marie O. Dionne)*

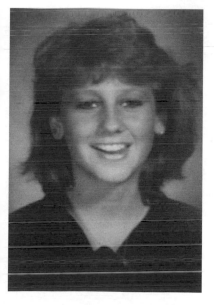

By the time Kristin reached age twelve, she attended school in California. Gregarious, athletic, willy and exuberant, she was voted Most Popular by her classmates. *(Courtesy Marie O. Dionne)*

Kristin's mother, Marie, gave birth to four children during two marriages: twins Robin and Rick, Kristin, and Stephanie. A third husband took the family to the West Coast. *(Driver's license photo courtesy Los Angeles County Superior Court)*

Peter Means gave Kristin and her siblings stability and a beautiful home in upscale Westlake Village. They regarded him as their true father.
(Author photo)

With her bubbly personality, Kristin loved to entertain kids. She thought about entering show business but never seriously pursued it. *(Courtesy Jennifer Gootsan)*

Jennifer Gootsan, Kristin's neighbor in Westlake Village, attended classes with Kristin from elementary school through high school. They remained lifelong friends. *(Author photo)*

A beautiful young woman after graduation, Kristin moved to Newport Beach and then later to Hawaii, where she lived for ten years. *(Courtesy Robin Henson)*

Kristin at a 1995 family reunion with her maternal grandmother, Frances O'Neill. *(Courtesy Robin Henson)*

The home on Cole Crest Drive in the Hollywood Hills where lawyer David Mahler settled after moving from New Jersey. He shared it with three male tenants plus a long line of women. *(Author photo)*

David Mahler and Stacy Tipton in Hawaii. His girlfriend for two decades, Stacy lived with Mahler in the East for two years and continued their fractious relationship after he moved to Hollywood and involved himself with a porn star and a stripper. *(Courtesy Stacy Tipton)*

In Hawaii, Mahler and Stacy argued. He abandoned her there, which was consistent with a long pattern of leaving her stranded and foreshadowing an event involving Kristin. *(Courtesy Stacy Tipton)*

Porn actor Michael Conoscenti, aka Damien Michaels, befriended Kristin and introduced her to David Mahler. *(Courtesy Los Angeles County Superior Court)*

Rock musician Donald Van Develde, aka Donnie Vie, witnessed Kristin crying and begging to go home as David Mahler furiously cursed and waved a gun in their faces. *(Courtesy Los Angeles County Superior Court)*

Detective Vicki Bynum worked numerous homicide cases in Hollywood. She and her partner investigated a strange call about an alleged shooting, even though no victim had been found. *(Author photo)*

Detective Tom Small, Bynum's partner on the Mahler case, atop the Hollywood station with the famous sign in the background. His powerful interview skills came into play with Mahler. *(Author photo)*

Vicki Bynum and Tom Small in the Homicide Bureau. During the filming of movies in this location, the detectives had met many stars, including Paul Newman and James Garner. *(Author photo)*

Vicki Bynum and her supervisor, Detective Wendi Berndt, stand near one of seven memorials for officers killed in the line of duty, including Detective Ian Campbell. Joseph Wambaugh's book *The Onion Field* told Campbell's story. *(Author photo)*

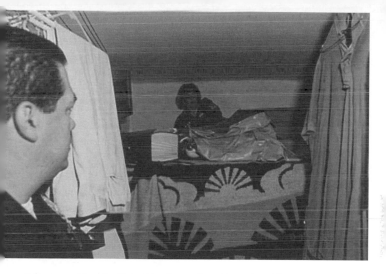

Police searching the Cole Crest house found David Mahler in a tenant's closet downstairs. Vicki Bynum demonstrates exactly where he attempted to hide. *(Courtesy Los Angeles County Superior Court)*

Officers transported Mahler to the Hollywood station for an interview. *(Courtesy Los Angeles County Superior Court)*

Tom Small and Vicki Bynum faced Mahler in a small room for nine hours. It turned into a game of wits between veteran detectives and a smug lawyer. *(Courtesy Los Angeles County Superior Court)*

Investigators search for evidence in front of the Cole Crest house. *(Courtesy Los Angeles County Superior Court)*

In Mahler's untidy bedroom, forensic technicians found blood stains. Donnie Van Develde had witnessed a frightening scenario play out in this same room. *(Courtesy Los Angeles County Superior Court)*

A forensic investigator checks blood spots on the back of Mahler's Jaguar, which indicated that Mahler had used it to transport a body.
(Courtesy Los Angeles County Superior Court)

Prosecutor Bobby Grace faced an uphill battle in the trial of David Mahler to prove murder rather than involuntary manslaughter. *(Author photo)*

A key piece of evidence came from a security camera next to Mahler's house, which showed his Jaguar leaving at times that linked him to killing Kristin and disposing of her body. *(Courtesy Los Angeles County Superior Court)*

During a break in the trial, Michael Conoscenti approached Bobby Grace's legal assistant, Armine Safarian, and invited her to be an actress in porn films. *(Author photo)*

Kristin Baldwin, making the "hang loose" sign popular in Hawaii, was remembered by her relatives at the sentencing hearing. Her remains were cremated. *(Courtesy Peter Means)*

Robin Means stepped up to the lectern, placed a wooden chest on it and said, "This is my sister." Tears could be seen on the faces of people in the courtroom. *(Author photo)*

The chest held the ashes of Kristin Baldwin. A portion of them were eventually taken to Hawaii and scattered in the sea she loved. *(Author photo)*

sifted through the ashes but couldn't locate it. She later said, "It appeared to me that he had burned some clothing in there, probably things that belonged to the victim. The cleaning materials certainly indicated that someone had tried to scrub away evidence at [the] crime scene. It sure wasn't because he was a neat person. This guy was a pig."

In the master bathroom, both women were struck by the picture of Al Pacino that Mahler had chosen to hang on a wall over the spa tub. Bynum later said, "Almost every thug, gangster, or doper fancies himself to be like Tony Montana, the role Pacino played in *Scarface*. Mahler is no exception. He runs around with the white robe open, with his little—his nonmanhood exposed, you know. There was some mention of him walking around naked all the time. He thinks he is Tony Montana, but he's not. And he lives in his fantasy drug-gangster world. What kind of a middle-aged person who has been to law school wants a picture of *Scarface* over their bathtub?"

Tom Small and Vicki Bynum teamed up again before noon on that Monday and paid a visit to the Clara Shortridge Foltz Criminal Justice Center, better known as the Criminal Courts Building, in downtown Los Angeles. In the district attorney's office on the seventeenth floor, they met with Deputy District Attorney (DDA) Cathryn Brougham in the Major Crimes Division. After reading their written report and discussing the Mahler case with them, Brougham filed one count of murder, a violation of *Penal Code Section 187 (a),* and one count of assault with a firearm, a violation of *P.C. Section 245 (a) (2)* against David A. Mahler. Another count would later be added: *P.C. Section 120022.53 (d), personal use of a firearm.* Now, with the charges made official, Mahler would be required to remain in jail until an arraignment.

Both detectives understood the difference between securing

charges against Mahler and providing enough evidence to convince a jury of his guilt. Information they had accumulated so far probably wouldn't even persuade jurors to agree on a verdict of involuntary manslaughter. The body hadn't been found, no murder weapon had been located, and blood evidence hadn't yet been matched to any victim. The statements of Karl Norvik and Donnie Van Develde might be eviscerated by a sharp defense attorney. Mahler could be portrayed in court as incapable of forming intent to kill, due to the influence of drugs and alcohol. His erratic behavior might be characterized as mental illness.

Still facing a mountain of obstacles and a staggering workload, Small and Bynum returned to the grind that same afternoon.

Tom Small, back at the Hollywood Station, prepared to interview Karl Norvik, who had agreed to drive in from Orange County.

Small hadn't expected search teams to find any trace of a victim in the desert near Barstow. Still, he felt a sense of disappointment. Maybe Mahler had lied about Kristin being taken to that remote area, but Small's intuition convinced him the tale held some elements of truth.

After filing a missing persons report on Kristin Baldwin, he teletyped a message and sent it statewide throughout California, Arizona, and Nevada. To be certain it reached the Barstow area, he sent it again to the Barstow Police Department (BPD), the San Bernardino County Sheriff's Department, and the California Highway Patrol (CHP).

MESSAGE FROM LAPD HOLLYWOOD
HOMICIDE—6-4-07

This agency is investigating a homicide of a Jane Doe whom it is believed died from a GSW. *(Author's note: gunshot wound)* The victim has not been found and was likely transported from the murder scene by the suspect(s). The investigation has revealed that the likely victim may be Kristin Baldwin, AKA Kristin Means. She is described to be a F/White, blonde hair, blue eyes, 5'5", 115 with a dob 05/06/69. The victim was wearing what was described to be white sheer pants with an unknown top. Baldwin is currently a missing person. Any information regarding this individual should be forwarded to the LAPD Hollywood Homicide Unit, Detectives Small or Bynum.

CHAPTER 21
A MATTER OF PERFECT TIMING

In the community of Simi Valley, beyond the northwestern border of Los Angeles County, Kristin's stepfather Peter Means received a call from Robin Henson, who sounded distraught. In recent days, they had exchanged text messages and telephone conversations asking each other if they had heard from Kristin. Robin now told Peter that she had been contacted by the Los Angeles Police Department about an investigation. A missing persons report had been filed, due to statements made by a tip they had received.

Another call came on Monday, June 4, this one was from Detective Wendi Berndt. She asked Means if he would be willing to answer a few questions.

Berndt and a lieutenant traveled more than twenty miles to Simi Valley and arrived after three o'clock that afternoon. Always a gracious host, Peter invited them into his immaculate, comfortable home. A remarkably unflappable, poised individual, Peter managed to hide his distress and fear of a worst-case scenario.

Answering their questions, he told them of Kristin's background, her ten years in Hawaii, and a few men she had dated. He clarified his role as her stepfather, and explained that they had an excellent relationship. Kristin, he said, had recently been living in a guest room at the home of a businessman who produced films. "The place was pretty dumpy, and she was trying to clean it up for him. He is elderly, spends a lot of time in bed, and has an adult son who also lives there. They needed some help. I think that he had been a porn producer."

Berndt wanted to know when Means had last heard from her. He told of receiving a message on his cell phone about ten days earlier, on Friday, May 25. She had said, "I'm at the Island Hotel in Newport Beach. Can you give me a call when you have time?" He had tried unsuccessfully to call her back.

"Were you normally in regular contact with her?"

"I usually heard from Kristin at least every couple of weeks. She almost never answered her cell phone. I'd call and leave a message, and she would get hold of me sooner or later. Probably like most young women, she would look at the name and say, 'Oh, it's just Dad. I'll get back to him when I can.'"

"Do you know if she was with anyone in Newport Beach?"

Peter did not. He had not yet heard the name David Mahler. And he had no idea how she had returned.

When bodies are found, police agencies often rely on dental records to identify the remains. Wendi Berndt tactfully asked Peter if he could provide dental records for Kristin, and he agreed to seek them out.

Before Berndt and the lieutenant left, Peter Means provided them with a photo of Kristin, much better than the mug shot they had been using. This one depicted her in Hawaii, making the well-known hand signal with thumb and little finger extended while all three other fingers fold like a fist. Its friendly meaning is "hang loose."

* * *

In Los Angeles, Detectives Vicki Bynum and Larry Cameron visited the LAPD Scientific Investigation Division to view footage recovered from the Cole Crest neighbor's outdoor security camera. What they saw quickened their pulses.

The tape, transferred to a compact disc, included dates and detailed timing of recorded events, down to the hour, minutes, and seconds.

The first clip showed Mahler's 2007 Jaguar backing out of the garage on Sunday morning, May 27, at 06:21:05. This corresponded perfectly with information that he had left Cole Crest that morning and driven to the LAX Marriott.

The next clip showed the Jaguar returning to the Cole Crest garage at 12:34 P.M., on Monday, May 28. This, too, fit the time frames of previous information. The next event caught the detectives' instant attention. Just six minutes after the 2007 Jaguar pulled into the garage, the black 1999 Jaguar could be seen backing out, turning around, and being backed into the garage. This would suggest that Mahler had gone inside and dragged the dead body from his bedroom into the garage. Dropping her near the side entry door, he had decided it would be easier to put her into the trunk by backing the vehicle into the garage.

A third clip showed the newer Jaguar pulling into the garage four days later, on Memorial Day, Thursday, May 31, at 1:54 A.M. Bynum knew David Mahler and Stacy Tipton had checked out of the Standard Hotel on the previous day, Wednesday, so the puzzle pieces seemed to fall into place. Apparently, the body had been lying in the house four full days.

Twenty-three minutes after the newer Jaguar arrived, the 1999 Jaguar pulled out in a forward direction at 2:17 A.M., and vanished into the darkness. It remained absent the rest of the night, and didn't return until seven fifteen in the morning. Four hours and fifty-eight minutes had elapsed. This time Mahler didn't back into the garage, but rather headed directly in.

To Bynum, the implications couldn't have been clearer. Mahler had taken a trip of nearly five hours and disposed of Kristin's body. If Mahler's statements of "hearsay" indicating she had been dropped off in the desert near Barstow were true, the timing would be just about perfect.

This information prompted the detectives to contact the provider of Mahler's cell phone service. Their records of calls made and received during those time frames might reveal exactly where he had driven. It is not common knowledge among the general public that locations from which calls are made can be traced later through documentation that identifies cell phone towers used to transmit the calls. Unfortunately for this investigation, the transmission records had been deleted.

A tiny tidbit of information remained, though. Mahler's cell phone had been used to call one of his friends at 1:19 A.M., about an hour before the 1999 Jaguar left. The same friend had been called again at 6:34 A.M., almost forty-five minutes before the car pulled back into the Cole Crest garage. No activity could be seen between those two calls. It suggested that he had perhaps driven a long distance, and contacted his friend en route back home.

Working long hours and feeling the pressure to locate Kristin Baldwin—whether deceased or still alive—the detectives needed some help. Vicki Bynum asked Officer Brett Goodkin and his partner, Officer Jerry Wert, to lend a hand in interviewing people involved in the case. The duo readily agreed.

Stripper Cheryl Lane, David Mahler's former girlfriend, was easy to locate. Bynum found her telephone number in Mahler's cellular directory. Goodkin gave her a call at three o'clock on that busy Monday. Cheryl said she would meet them the next day at a Starbucks on Sherman Way in Van Nuys. They set a time of 4:30 P.M.

Detective Tom Small sat in the Hollywood Station interview room with Karl Norvik at six o'clock, Monday evening. Nervous and perspiring, Norvik told Small about the living arrangements at Cole Crest for himself, David Mahler, Jeremy Moudy, and Donnie Van Develde. He had been there "for the better part of twelve years," but he now resided with a relative in Orange County. Mahler had been there about six years. "I used to handle the managerial duties, but David replaced me."

About the events of Saturday and Sunday, May 26 and 27, Karl said he was at the house when he saw Mahler and another man arrive at about seven o' clock, Saturday evening. The "client," according to Norvik, was a male Hispanic, fat, approximately five-eleven. He had seen the two men walk through the common area of the residence and down to either Mahler's bedroom or the office. The overweight man stayed only about forty-five minutes.

"Were you there by yourself?" Small asked.

"No. A friend of mine was with me until he left at seven thirty."

Karl had gone to his bedroom and retired between ten and eleven, he said. About four hours later, approximately three thirty on Sunday morning, he had been awakened by the sounds of loud shouting. He recognized Mahler's distinctive bellowing in argument with an unknown female voice. The prolonged disturbance had been so loud, Norvik had covered his head with a pillow to try to muffle it. He spoke of hearing a loud thud overhead, like something heavy falling to the floor. Also, he thought he heard a female voice scream momentarily, and then all was silent.

To Small's inquiry about hearing a possible gunshot, Norvik couldn't say he had.

At about six thirty, Norvik said, Mahler had banged on his bedroom door, yelling, "This is an emergency. I need to dispose of a dead body."

"I didn't believe him," Norvik told Small. "He seemed to be intoxicated. I opened my door and saw him standing there. He repeated his wild comments, and then led me upstairs."

In Small's written report of the interview, he entered, *Norvik observed a deceased female which he described as a "corpse," lying on her back, face up, palms up and arms angled out from her sides. The body was lying at the foot of Mahler's bed, about eight feet away from where Norvik stood to make his observations.*

His voice shaking with nerves, Norvik told Small that the woman was obviously dead, and it looked to him like she had been shot in the face from close range. He said he saw a large volume of blood on the victim's face and upper body.

Asked for a description of the woman, Karl stated that she was a white female, with bleached blond hair, wearing a halter top, and "sheer" white pants. The sight had been so emotionally disturbing that Norvik had to sit down on the exterior stair landing just outside of Mahler's bedroom.

Norvik recalled asking Mahler, "What did you do?"

Mahler, he said, replied, "I shot her over by the balcony. So you want no part of this?"

Norvik had replied instantly that he absolutely did not want any part of this and returned to his room.

Growing even more nervous, perhaps over the possibility that he might be charged with being an accomplice after the fact, Norvik told the detective that he waited about five or ten minutes, then went out on his balcony for a smoke and to contemplate what he should do. His downstairs neighbor, Donnie, also out on his balcony, called up in a loud whisper to Norvik to say that something bad had happened in Mahler's room. It involved "death and murder." Donnie, said Karl, used his hands to simulate the action of firing a handgun.

"I played dumb," Norvik confided to Small. He summoned Donnie up to his room to talk about it. "He gave me his story about seeing Mahler waving a gun around at the girl and at him." In Donnie's opinion, David was out of his mind on drugs. He had shot the girl right after Donnie stepped out of the room. Donnie left but came back a little later and saw her on the floor, covered by a bedspread, all but one of her hands. "We agreed not to call or tell anyone about it." Karl remained in his room for several hours, he said, and later heard what he thought was a vacuum cleaner being used in or near Mahler's bedroom.

Frightened that Mahler might come after him, Norvik said, he had left later that evening of May 27 and gone to Orange County. On June 1, he had called Donnie and told him he was about to notify the police.

In Norvik's view, Mahler was a "hot rocket" who used a lot of cocaine and methamphetamine in recent weeks.

Small asked, "Were you aware of any guns in Mahler's possession?"

Yes, said Norvik. Five or six weeks before the murder, Mahler had shown him a .38-caliber revolver, which he kept in a leather holster hidden in his closet. "I think it had either a four- or six-inch barrel." Uncertain of the weapon's color, Norvik guessed it was silver.

He stated that he thought he had seen a gunshot wound below the victim's left eye, but he couldn't be certain because her face was covered with blood.

As the interview ended, Karl Norvik quoted David Mahler warning him not to tell anyone about the events.

Working on Monday, June 4, Detective Lance Jurado, another member of the investigative team, located several links in the chain of Kristin Baldwin's life. Working from information Kristin had given at the time of the DUI arrest, Jurado went to an apartment on Woodman Avenue in Van Nuys, where Kristin had sometimes stayed. The manager recognized a photo as Kristin Baldwin and put Jurado in contact with a man who had been dating Kristin. The detective called and spoke to the former boyfriend. They had broken up two or three months ago. He remembered receiving a call from her sometime in May and that she appeared to be "troubled and distressed" because a guy named Damien had accused her of taking something of his.

So far, investigators had heard several references to a car that Kristin drove, but no records turned up to reveal any information about it. The former boyfriend told Jurado that she drove a blue or black Geo Storm hatchback. He also mentioned that Kristin had been friends with a woman named Kitty, who worked in the adult film industry. He gave the name and phone number of a producer who would know how to reach Kitty.

Jurado made a call and found that Kitty had recently been working for an adult-entertainment talent agency. He contacted the company and spoke to Kitty, who agreed to meet the detective at a nearby diner in twenty minutes.

At 6:20 P.M., she showed up with a male companion. Kitty easily identified the booking photo of Kristin. Regarding her own background, she said that when she came to Los Angeles from Florida, she had been introduced to Damien Michaels. He talked her into entering the porn film industry as a performer with him. Soon afterward, she moved into a house with Damien in Calabasas.

The relationship hadn't lasted long, said Kitty. She had broken up with him after a fight during which he bit her wrist. Damien then introduced her to his "personal attorney," a guy named David Mahler. Kitty and Mahler had started dating and were eventually engaged. However, they had a big argument when she found out that he was hot for Kristin, who had also moved into the Calabasas house.

"I confronted Kristi," Kitty told the detective. "She apologized, and we became good friends." Even though she and Mahler had split, they remained on friendly terms. A few days ago, said Kitty, a male pal had said he got a call from Kristin on Friday, May 25. She had been stranded by Mahler at a hotel in Newport Beach. Kitty had talked to Mahler since then by phone, and asked him how the trip to Newport with Kristi had turned out. He had acknowledged "some trouble," but refused to say any more about it.

Kitty gave Jurado a current address and phone number where Michael Conoscenti, known as Damien, now lived. She also revealed that Damien and Mahler were no longer friends, but maintained a business relationship.

Detective Jurado's interview with Kitty would be her final contact with investigators. Later speaking of her, Tom Small said, "I think Kitty was Mahler's one true love. She was a porn star, and that seemed to be right up his alley. She took off to Florida during the investigation, and we couldn't find her after that."

CHAPTER 22

STRIPPER'S STORY

Cheryl Lane showed up, as promised, on Tuesday, June 5, at a Starbucks in Van Nuys. Officer Brett Goodkin and his partner were waiting in the parking lot when she arrived by herself in a 1987 blue Chevrolet Camaro. They jotted down the license number.

After greetings, introductions, and orders of coffee, Cheryl sat at a table with the two officers. Both of them were surprised at her youth and diminutive stature. She produced a driver's license, which gave her birth date, and said she hadn't yet turned twenty-one. Only five-four, she weighed exactly one hundred pounds. With no hesitation, Cheryl told them she was currently employed as an "exotic dancer" at a gentlemen's nightclub. She performed as "Cherry."

Asked about her relationship with David Mahler, Cheryl said she had known him a little longer than one year. She had been introduced to him by Damien Michaels. None of the investigators had yet met Damien Michaels, so Goodkin asked Cheryl for a description of him. She said he was about five-eight, with brown eyes and brown hair, maybe touched up with dye, and wore a little goatee. She thought he was about fifty years old. It came as a bonus that she could also provide his current address on Gault Street, in Van Nuys, and his phone number.

Damien, Cheryl said, had once worked at the same night-club where she now performed. When she first met him, she told Goodkin, he had lived with a pornography producer in Calabasas. She thought they had also been business partners in the adult-film industry, but they had since terminated that arrangement. Cheryl didn't know Damien's real name was Michael Conoscenti.

Taking the officers through her extended affair with David Mahler, Cheryl told of his causing her to be fired from one club because of his belligerent, aggressive behavior there. She talked about their live-in relationship and their dispute over bail money he had provided when she was once arrested. "I paid him back," she said, "but he didn't think it was enough." On May 30, he had sent a guy named Rick to the club where she worked. Rick demanded that she cough up $7,000. She had contacted Mahler, who yelled at her and insisted that she pay the money to Rick. She didn't have it, and had been frightened ever since then.

"When was the last time you saw David Mahler?" Goodkin inquired.

She said it had been a little more than three weeks ago. He had sent her numerous e-mails and text messages threatening her, and even put scary notes on her social networking Web pages. Showing them a scar on her hand, Cheryl described the incident in which he had caused an injury by slamming a laptop computer closed, entrapping her hand.

Cheryl said she knew Kitty, the porn actress, and had seen "vicious physical fights" between her and Mahler. She had also met Stacy Tipton and said that Mahler had beaten her severely and been arrested for one such incident.

Goodkin asked Cheryl if she had ever seen Mahler take

drugs. She affirmed it, saying that drug usage was routine
with him, and he consumed large quantities of cocaine, meth,
and alcohol. Another habit of his bothered her even more.
Cheryl described David's regular need for prostitutes, who
were provided by a pimp named Atticus. She described him
as an overweight black man, who lived somewhere in the
South Bay region. She had never met Atticus, but she knew
the name from boasts made by Mahler.

"Have you ever seen a gun in his possession?" Goodkin
asked.

"Yes. About five months ago, he bought a handgun from
somebody. It was a small blue steel revolver with a short
barrel and brown wooden grips." She recalled that he stored
it in a nightstand next to his bed. Cheryl said she was terrified
at the prospect of David owning a gun, due to his violent and
unpredictable behavior. Out of fear of what he might do, she
had made a point of covertly unloading it whenever she was
in the house.

It had come as only a mild surprise when she heard that
Mahler had been arrested for murder. A bail bondsman she
knew had called her just a couple of days ago. He had expressed great relief when she answered; explaining that
when he heard Mahler was accused of killing a woman, he
had instantly thought it might be Cheryl.

Showing her a photo of the probable murder victim, Goodkin asked Cheryl if she recognized the woman. Yes, she said.
"It's Kristin. I saw her at David's, now and then, in the last
couple of months. One time I helped her fix her hair. We didn't
talk at great length, but she did tell me that she was struggling
with finances."

David had told Cheryl a strange tale of allowing Kristin to
live at a house he owned in Long Beach, but he had been
forced to evict her. Investigators would later believe that
Cheryl had mistaken Kristin for some other woman in David's

stable of hookers. Nothing about the fanciful allegations could be connected to Kristin.

Ready to conclude the interview, Goodkin's interest scale shot up again when Cheryl confided, "I'm not supposed to say anything about this, but you should talk to Damien." She said that after they both had learned of David Mahler's arrest, Damien had shared a secret with her. Mahler had said to him, "I need you to finish something that I started." Assuming that David had wanted his help in collecting a drug debt, Damien had replied, "Get the fuck out of here." But when he heard of the murder charge, he realized that Mahler had been asking for help in disposing of the victim's body.

To be certain that Cheryl hadn't played any part in the killing, Goodkin asked her to detail her activities on Saturday, May 26, through Sunday, May 27. She told of working at the club from ten o'clock, Saturday night, until about five, Sunday morning. But she couldn't recall if she went directly home or to the home of a male coworker. Her memory lapse stemmed from being "very drunk" and angry that she hadn't earned enough money in tips from stripping and doing private lap dances. Asked if she had any contact with David Mahler during that time frame, she responded, "I was so pissed off and drunk that I might have called his cell phone to yell at him or relieve my own rage." She had evidently not played any part in the tragedy in David's bedroom.

Mention had been made by other witnesses of a green-and-white van, operated by Atticus King, often parked all night outside the Cole Crest house. Goodkin asked Cheryl if she had ever seen a van there. She answered yes, but her recollection did not correlate with King's vehicle. Cheryl said she could think of only one person who drove a van: Edmund. She described him as a heavyset male Hispanic who had a small, dark goatee. Edmund, she said, drove a large blue van with a lot of dents and scratches. He often used it to deliver drugs to Mahler. The vehicle, she thought, had probably been damaged in relation to Edmund's day job as a construction worker.

Complaining about another matter involving Edmund, Cheryl said that she owned a 1991 red Toyota Celica and had frequently parked it near David's house. She had left it there for a period of time when she was unable to afford registration renewal. Spitting her words in fury, she said that David had given the car to Edmund in exchange for drugs, without her permission. About three weeks ago, she had been notified by the LASD that the vehicle had been impounded. Now it sat collecting dust at a sheriff's storage facility.

Another car had been the focus of a big dispute between David and Damien, said Cheryl. David had leased a BMW in his own name for Damien's use, on the agreement that he would pay the monthly fees. Even though Damien had been unable to keep up with the payments, he had refused to give the vehicle back to David. Cheryl blurted out another eyebrow raiser. "David was so enraged, he called Atticus, trying to find someone to kill Damien." Nothing came of it, though.

Instead, said Cheryl, David expressed his anger by ramming the gate at Damien's place with a car. Edmund had been sent out to repair it later.

Goodkin and Wert thanked Cheryl for her cooperation and returned to the Hollywood Station. Utilizing computer research, Goodkin found that Damien Michaels, adult-film actor, was actually Michael Lewis Conoscenti (date of birth, 01-23-53).

Following up on Cheryl's reference to the gentlemen's club where she worked, Goodkin contacted the establishment, spoke to a security guard, and learned that Michael Conoscenti, aka Damien Michaels, was no longer employed there.

A previous run-in with the law by Conoscenti showed up in computer records. He had been on parole at one time and currently was on probation for possession of methamphetamine. Goodkin called a detective in the West Valley Division who had made the arrest and learned that Conoscenti still lived at the Gault Street address in Van Nuys.

Cheryl had complained of her red Toyota Celica being taken and stored by the police. Goodkin made inquiries seeking verification of her story. The vehicle had indeed been impounded on May 19 for unpaid parking tickets, and remained in a storage yard.

At one o'clock that Tuesday afternoon, Vicki Bynum tried another number she had found in David Mahler's cell phone directory. The detective reached Tara Rush. Kristin's friend in Canoga Park had been one of the last people to see her alive. Tara said that she had met Kristin through a mutual friend about two years ago, and that Kristin had recently spent a few nights at her Canoga Park apartment. Recalling an alarming cell phone message from May 25, Tara reported that Kristin had called from Newport Beach. "She said some lawyer she was dating had abandoned her in Newport Beach. They had a fight and he left. It was scary, like she was screaming for her life." Tara thought that Kristin had taken a cab back to the San Fernando Valley.

Tara said she had seen Kristin on Saturday, May 26, at her apartment in Canoga Park. "She had taken a taxi there. She called the guy she went to Newport with and he came to pick her up." She met him in front of a liquor store.

Bynum asked what Kristin had been wearing at the time. Tara thought the apparel consisted of a tank top, plus a short white skirt.

As the investigation progressed, the Los Angeles County Sheriff's Department located Kristin Baldwin's car. They reported to Detective Tom Small the discovery of a blue 1993 Geo Storm. It had been parked for about ten days on Paul

Revere Road in Calabasas, not far from the home of Sheldon Weinberg. Sheriff's deputies impounded the dusty hatchback and towed it to a police storage yard in Hollywood.

Finding Kristin's old car offered important insight to Detectives Small and Bynum. It demonstrated another probable lie by David Mahler. He had denied picking up Kristin after her telephone call the day after she returned from Newport Beach. Tara Rush, with whom Bynum had spoken just a short time ago, had contradicted his story, stating that he had picked Kristin up in Canoga Park. The discovery of the victim's car in Calabasas seemed to lend credence to Tara's version of events in which Kristin had taken a taxi to Canoga Park, visited Tara, and then met Mahler at the liquor store.

On Wednesday morning, June 6, a tip came in of a possible body discovery in the hills around the Santa Clarita area, thirty miles northwest of Hollywood. For decades the remote peaks and valleys had tempted killers as a great place to dispose of their victims. Officer Jerry Wert climbed into an LAPD helicopter to help in an overhead search of the region. Nothing turned up.

Detectives Small and Bynum spent a good portion of that day speaking with an anonymous informant, but came away without any new or revealing evidence.

Wendi Berndt, working not just as a supervisor but also as a field investigator, found a listing on eBay offering a copy of the 1989 Westlake High School yearbook for sale. Kristin had graduated that year. Berndt arranged to acquire the book. While interesting to see photos of Kristin, and her selection as the most popular girl, it provided no forensic evidence. If the case ever came to trial, the information could be used to demonstrate to jurors that a decent person had been the victim of a killer.

* * *

The next day, Thursday, June 7, Officer Jerry Wert drove to Westlake Village for an interview with Robin Henson. She told him of her sister's background, the ten years Kristin had spent in Hawaii, a few difficulties she had experienced in recent months, and about the men Kristin had dated. Robin spoke of the close bonds linking the sisters and described her own tension brought about by the troubling absence of contact with her in the last couple of weeks. Robin had never met David Mahler, and Kristin hadn't said much about him. Robin did provide something that might turn out to be useful. She said that Kristin had a small tattoo of a blue dolphin on the left side of her abdomen.

In the early afternoon, the LAPD helicopter rose again to provide a visual check of the area around Cole Crest Drive for signs of a body or a recently dug burial site. It proved equally as futile as the earlier attempt in the desert.

On the morning of June 8, a tipster who had seen television news reports about the hunt for Kristin Baldwin called the Hollywood Station with a suggestion to search a wooded area near the intersection of Laurel Canyon Boulevard and Mulholland Drive. The aerial search team rose once more into the smoggy sky to zigzag back and forth over the Hollywood Hills in the helicopter. They found nothing. It turned out the information source had been a "psychic."

CHAPTER 23
OFF HIS ROCKER

Several attempts to meet with Michael Conoscenti, aka Damien Michaels, had turned into frustrating dead ends. Investigators had heard several accounts involving him, and they needed to hear *his* version of events.

The connection finally came about on Thursday, June 7, when Detective Lance Jurado reached the elusive porn actor by telephone at six o'clock in the evening.

Conoscenti said, "I've been waiting to hear from you guys."

"Why is that?" Jurado asked.

"I think you know. It is all about Dave." He agreed to meet Jurado and Jerry Wert on the corner of Sherman Way and Woodman Avenue, in Van Nuys.

Fifteen minutes later, the two investigators pulled into the parking lot of a chain restaurant. Waiting in his car, Conoscenti flagged them down. The ensuing conversation took place outside, in the lot.

Jurado wasted no time. "What did you mean when you said, 'it's all about Dave'?"

"Well, I was pretty certain you would eventually get

around to interrogating me, when I heard that Dave had been arrested for murdering a girl." Asked to tell about his association with David Mahler, Conoscenti said it started with his own arrest a couple of years ago for a narcotics violation. He had needed a lawyer, and his buddy Captain Bob had recommended Mahler. Over the next year, he had spoken numerous times to Mahler by phone, and finally met him face-to-face, all by coincidence, while visiting a neighbor on Cole Crest.

The detectives learned about Conoscenti's involvement in porn films and his business arrangements with Mahler, Sheldon Weinberg, and Kitty in Calabasas. They listened as he told of hooking Dave up with porn actress Kitty, stripper Cheryl, and finally with Kristin Baldwin. Anger creased Conoscenti's face as he described the falling-out with Mahler and the incident in which Mahler had damaged the gate at Conoscenti's most recent residence.

Getting to the crucial information, Michael said that two or three days before Dave had been arrested, something weird took place. "He came to my house, even though feelings had been pretty raw between us. He asked me, 'Do you know anybody who can do dirty work?' I said, 'What the hell are you talking about?' He wouldn't say exactly what he meant. Instead, he wanted to know if I knew anybody who could do a 'disposal' job."

"Did he explain what that was supposed to mean?"

"Not really. All he said was 'I got guys that already fucked it up.' He went on to say, 'They did half the job. And now they are after me.' I honestly had no idea what any of that crap meant, and asked him to explain. But he wouldn't do it. About that time, my roommate walked up, and Dave split. He took off. I still was in the dark about his whole pitch. But when he got arrested for murder, it started to make some sense."

"Did you talk to him again after that?"

"No. I called him the next day after he was at my place to ask him when he was going to have someone finish repairing my gate. He didn't answer, so I left him a message on his cell phone."

"Did he reply?"

"No. I guess he was pissed off at me. Sometimes, with Dave, you have to say things in the right way to make him happy. Then he might be a little more cooperative. So I left him another message saying, 'If you help me with my problem, maybe I can help you with yours.' But it didn't do any good."

"Do you know if he had any guns?"

Michael replied that about two months earlier Mahler had implied having possession of a gun. But it had been couched in code talk, which Dave liked to use. "He was all paranoid—like if someone was tapping his phone or listening from a van with sound equipment. I think he saw too many spy movies." Mahler had said something about buying a "G."

"I told him, I didn't know what he meant, so he finally came out and said he had bought a gun for self-protection."

"Was there any other source of trouble between you and Dave?"

"Yeah. I borrowed some money from him in the past to buy a car, but I couldn't make the payments and he took the car."

"Do you know anyone named Atticus?"

"I think you mean the pimp who supplied Dave with hookers and drugs." Michael described Atticus as a black male, overweight, about age thirty-five. "I met him about four times, always at Dave's house on Cole Crest Drive."

The detectives thanked Conoscenti and left the parking lot.

Michael Conoscenti, aka Damien Michaels, didn't know on that day in June that he was a doomed man.

With the investigation bogging down and producing no new leads or evidence, Vicki Bynum decided to drive two hundred miles north to Visalia and see what Stacy Tipton might be able to contribute. David Mahler had mentioned during his long interview that Stacy had gone to Cole Crest with him before they stayed at the Standard Hotel on Sunset Boulevard. Later discussing her, Tom Small said, "I think she knew enough about what happened to be scared. According to Mahler, she never went into the house because she was afraid. That's why they went to the Standard."

In Visalia, an agricultural city in the heart of the San Joaquin Valley, called home by more than 120,000 residents, Bynum and another detective visited Stacy. It produced only more disappointment.

Bynum later said, "We were let in and had to compete with about twenty puppies for attention. They were just old enough to be playful, and we were trying to interview her, with all these little guys peeing, pooping, and biting my feet. She appeared to be drinking something alcoholic and felt the effects. She did tell me she was afraid."

Stacy's fear, Bynum thought, accounted for her reluctance to say anything about David Mahler or what she had seen. Regarding attempts to clean up blood at Cole Crest, Bynum concluded, "I don't think she could have helped him."

David Mahler suffered another blow on Tuesday, June 12. He had been transferred to the Men's Central Jail (MCJ), known as the Twin Towers, the largest jail in the world. Near the historic Union Station rail center, it is only a few blocks from the downtown courts building, but still requires inmates to be transported back and forth by bus. On that Tuesday, officers took him to face a bail hearing. However, a judge rejected allowing him to be released. Sorely disappointed again, he returned to the Twin Towers to wait for a trial.

On that morning, as well, Detectives Wert and Goodkin paid a visit to Donnie Van Develde. They took with them a copy of Kristin Baldwin's booking photo. Without hesitation, he identified it as Kristi who had been in David Mahler's bedroom on May 27, crying and begging to leave.

As soon as they left Donnie, the detectives then drove to Calabasas to keep an appointment with Sheldon Weinberg.

Answering their questions, Weinberg identified a photo of Kristin Baldwin and stated that she had lived on his premises since about the first week of March. To help pay for it, she had assisted with some cleanup duties and some cooking. She had disappeared sometime during the Memorial Day weekend.

David Mahler, he said, had been a friend and business associate for about a year. He stated that before Memorial Day, he had given Mahler $15,000 in cash to deliver to a Newport Beach broker named George Goldberg to invest for Weinberg. With a note of worry straining his voice, Weinberg said he had never received a receipt from either Mahler or Goldberg. "I tried multiple times to reach David by telephone after the holiday weekend, but he didn't call back until a couple of days later. He apologized and said he had been very busy."

"When did you last see Mr. Mahler?"

"I saw him on Wednesday, May thirtieth, when he came over to fix my son's laptop computer. I had given him the money before that."

"Did he mention anything about Kristin Baldwin going with him to Newport Beach?"

"Yes. He said they were involved in some sort of a dispute at the hotel down there." Weinberg couldn't remember which day it had been, but he mentioned a phone call from her just before the holiday weekend. She said she needed money to pay for the hotel room. "I asked her why she was in Newport. She told me she had gone down there with David, but he abandoned her. And she was broke." Weinberg expressed surprise that Kristin had been with Mahler on the trip. "It was my understanding that he went there only to conduct some business on my behalf."

Weinberg's recollection of Kristin's reason for requesting money may have been faulty. Mahler had paid for the hotel room with the gift certificate provided by George Goldberg, and covered the remaining portion with a credit card. Kristin had probably asked for money or help with transportation back to Calabasas.

"Do you know if Mahler used drugs?"

"Oh, he was definitely a drug user, mostly coke and meth, I think."

Asked when he had last heard from Mahler, Weinberg said that David had made several collect calls on June 1 to say he had been arrested for murder.

Tom Small and Vicki Bynum filled in another blank spot on the canvas painted by David Mahler during his long interview. He had cursed and vilified a man named Robert Jimenez, identified him as a police officer, and named him as the person who had left the gun at Cole Crest. An officer brought Jimenez to the Hollywood Station that Tuesday morning.

Jimenez told the detectives that he worked as a bail recovery agent for a bail bonds agent in Torrance, twenty miles south of Hollywood, and had been so employed for ten years. Answering puzzling questions, he made it clear that he had never been a police officer for any agency in California, or in any other state. "I have the greatest respect for the profession," Jimenez said, and indicated he would like to pursue a career in law enforcement.

Providing requested information about David Mahler, Jimenez disclosed that he had met him a couple of years ago. Mahler had hired him as a bodyguard sometimes. On those occasions, Jimenez said, he was paid to meet Mahler at various strip clubs and accompany him inside. He wasn't quite certain why Mahler needed this service, but he had been well compensated for it, and didn't mind a job that allowed him to watch women strip.

He spoke of another service he had provided for Mahler. About eighteen months ago, he had been paid to pursue one of the lawyer's clients who had allegedly absconded from bail. Mahler had insisted that Jimenez arrest the girl, Cheryl Lane, who worked at a strip club in the San Fernando Valley.

"Did you have some monetary arrangements with him?"

Jimenez said he had experienced financial problems after a divorce and sought help from Mahler. David loaned him $6,500, accepting as collateral the pink slip for a motorcycle. Also, Mahler owed him $5,000 for bodyguard services. About three or four weeks ago, Mahler had given him a check for part of it. That was the last time he had seen David.

David, he said, could be obnoxious. Jimenez had often heard him making cell phone calls in which he always "seemed to be yelling at people. Sometimes he was really cuckoo."

Regarding possession of guns, Jimenez admitted that he had owned several firearms, but always wound up pawning them or selling them to friends. He adamantly denied any illegal transactions and emphatically denied ever giving, selling, or leaving any weapons with David Mahler.

"Mahler told us that you left a thirty-eight revolver with him."

Balling his fists in indignant outrage, Jimenez asserted, "I have never given him guns or sold him guns. This guy is off his rocker!"

Asked if he had ever met a woman named Kristin or Kristi, with or around Mahler, Jimenez said he had neither met her nor heard of her.

"Can you account for your whereabouts on May twenty-fifth through May twenty-seventh?"

"Sure," Jimenez replied confidently. "My girlfriend and I were staying at the Crowne Plaza in San Francisco. We were there over the full Memorial Day weekend, and didn't return until late Monday night."

Jimenez produced a hotel and rental car receipt to verify his statement.

The lie meter for David Mahler crept up a few more notches.

Another key player in the David Mahler drama had been elusive and difficult to round up. Officers had gone to the listed address for Atticus King in Hawthorne—a Los Angeles suburb in the South Bay region—several times but without any luck. At last, on the morning of Wednesday, June 13, Brett Goodkin and Jerry Wert found the rotund King at home. As soon as they introduced themselves and explained they were conducting an investigation, King said, "I know what you guys are here about, and I won't help you find that girl's body."

Goodkin shot back, "What girl's body?"

"Look," said King, "I know David Mahler, and I saw the news and stuff like that, but I don't know where that girl is."

With some friendly persuasion from two well-trained officers, King agreed to accompany them to the Hollywood Station for an interview with Vicki Bynum and Tom Small.

In the same tiny room where Mahler had sat and tried to make deals eleven days earlier, Atticus King told the detectives about being Mahler's friend for over five years. He admitted transporting prostitutes for Dave, but denied being a pimp. He was nothing more than a taxi driver. Yes, he said, David used a lot of drugs. Atticus spoke freely of events at the LAX Marriott Hotel, including the hooker, a violent altercation in which a television set was ruined, and the extravagant costs. It had been his idea, he said, to meet at the Marriott rather than the Beverly Wilshire, where Mahler wanted to go.

Soon after they entered the hotel room, King recalled, Mahler had started raving: "She tried to kill me! We were talking, having a good time, and then she freaked out. She pulled a gun on me!"

Small and Bynum both remembered that in Donnie Van Develde's account, Mahler had accused Kristi of pulling a knife on him.

Atticus said he had asked Dave, who was he talking about? Rolling his eyes and squinting as if in pain, Atticus admitted knowing that Dave was prone to exaggerations, so he thought the wild claim related to some dispute with a prostitute over money.

"Mahler just kept on a-hollerin'," King declared. "He tol' me, 'I took the gun away and killed her. Shot her!'" King said he hadn't believed Mahler. "I thought he was bluffin'."

Next, said King, Mahler had shut up long enough to order room service meals for both of them, along with a large bottle of Rémy Martin. "He left a tip of one hundred and fifty dollars."

Small asked if Mahler was on drugs. Yes, said King. "He was wiped out, going back and forth from the meth pipe to alcohol. Then he started yelling again. He said, 'The bitch tried to kill me! We were having a good time, having sex and getting high. She pulled the gun on me, and I wrestled it away from her and I shot her!'"

Snatching a multicolored baseball hat off his head to mop sweat from his wrinkled brow and from furrowed muscles on the back of his neck, Atticus spoke again, huffing as if he had just completed a one-hundred-meter dash. "I still didn't believe him. Then he passed out, or at least took a long nap. I stayed there to watch over him."

When Mahler woke up, according to King, he made a phone call to arrange for a prostitute to come to the hotel.

"All hell broke loose a few hours later," King complained. "When she said her price was two thousand dollars for the night, Dave flew off the handle. He refused to pay and started in to whop on her. Man, I never saw anything like it. He was crazy out of his head. It got so wild in there—he busted a nice TV set. I had to step in between them and get him settled down. And that girl, she ain't backin' down none."

A compromise had been reached, said King, in which he paid the hooker $700, with a promise to give her more on the next day. "Man," King huffed, "It's really hard to believe someone could commit murder and then turn around and party like Dave did. That sounds more like Ted Bundy. It's sociopathic."

Mahler's next request, in Atticus's recollection, had been out of bounds. Pronouncing the word "asked" as "axed," he said, "Dave asked me how much money it would take to get me to go to his house, clean it up, and move the dead girl out of there. I told him there ain't no amount of money would get me to do something like that."

"Are you telling us the truth?"

"I'm tellin' it straight. No way would I lie about this, even for David. I did not help him in any way to clean up or move the body. When I saw the news about this on TV, it cleared up my head about what happened, and made me think he actually did commit murder. I asked my wife what I ought to do, and she said to tell the truth. But I hoped to stay out of it and not get involved."

Small and Bynum arranged for Atticus King to be transported back to his home. Before he left, they advised him that if the case ever came to trial, he would probably be subpoenaed to testify in court. That prospect put a load of worry in his head and heart.

One other informant contacted the detectives, but the person's name would remain a secret. Wendi Berndt and her team used a code name for someone who supplied information but must remain anonymous. They referred to the individual as "Mrs. Beasley." In this case, Mrs. Beasley stated that David Mahler had made remarkable threats. He had said that if he could make bail, which he confidently expected to do, he needed to have a gun available to him. Mahler would use the weapon to eliminate a few crucial witnesses.

Donnie Van Develde and Karl Norvik had expressed fear of reprisals by David Mahler. Mrs. Beasley's information seemed to give credence to their fears.

CHAPTER 24

"IMAGINE STUFFING DOLLARS IN THAT G-STRING"

In a subsequent round-table discussion of the case, Vicki Bynum, Tom Small, and Wendi Berndt reflected on the incredible cast of characters populating the David Mahler case. Few movies have depicted such a colorful bunch.

Regarding Atticus King, each of the trio smiled. Asked what made King so likable and outstanding in their memories, Bynum said, "Because he was honest."

Small had reservations. "He's a pimp."

Her voice mirthful, Bynum replied, "But an honest one, so believable."

"Okay," Small agreed. "Atticus didn't want anything to do with this. He just wanted to play his role as a taxi driver who brings girls to Mahler. I don't think he really believed Mahler was capable of doing something like killing a woman. And so he was trying to be a good buddy. But when Mahler started talking about getting rid of a body, and when Atticus saw the news on TV, that's when he became a believer."

The interview of Robert Jimenez had revealed Mahler's odd need for a bodyguard when going to strip joints. Bynum had some ideas about that. "He was all about going to clubs, picking up some girl, and making them think he's someone he's not. He portrays himself like a bad version of Tony Montana. He paid Jimenez to walk in with him to those places, like a private bodyguard. Lots of muscle, you know. He's a big fake, and fraud. He could not impress a normal girl."

The reference to Tony Montana elicited more opinions from the detectives about Mahler's bathroom decoration: a poster of Al Pacino's character in the film *Scarface*. Asked if Mahler had placed it over his bathtub to impress women, Small chuckled. "Most of the women who came there were whores or strippers."

Of course, this characterization would not include Stacy Tipton, who had been in David Mahler's life for nearly two decades. Bynum also excluded Kristin. "I don't think she was like the strippers or hookers. Nobody ever said anything bad about her. She just got caught up in Mahler's trap." Small agreed.

Regarding the poster, Bynum said, "I think it's more than impressing women. I think it's how he fancies himself. I don't know any women who would be impressed by a picture of Tony Montana. It's like 'I'm a big bad dude,' the image of a gangster, a mover and a shaker in movie land. He thought he was the king of Hollywood Hills."

Berndt added, "It represented the evil side of Mahler."

Responding to a comment that the poster must have impressed Cheryl Lane, Bynum couldn't hide her negative impression. She and Brett Goodkin had paid a visit to Cheryl's apartment to ask a few more questions. They found it a disgusting mess. "She's on the bottom rung of those women who strip. Men who find her appealing would have to be really drunk, and it would have to be really dark. Imagine stuffing dollars in that G-string. Yuk! I guess Mahler thought he was running with the stars of adult entertainment. She would be like a cable version of porn."

Small observed, "She's a professional pole dancer, an acrobat out to make a buck."

Nodding her head in affirmation, Bynum commented, "That type of a woman, not to knock them, is just trying to make a living. To her, it was nothing but money. And that's what she saw in Mahler."

"He was just using her," said Small. "Cheryl was just somebody who owed him. It was a love-hate relationship—on again, off again. There was a point when he considered having her dusted off—killed. I think Kitty, the porn star, was his one true love."

"They're all tweakers." Bynum laughed. "Kitty, though, wouldn't bend to Mahler's tough-guy act. Larry Cameron and I went to her production company. It was a typical San Fernando Valley storefront, like in any strip mall, next door to a Subway store and a coffee shop. But inside was a porn business. You walk in the door and they are normal-looking people like us, sitting in offices. What struck me is right when you step inside, there are scales and a measuring tape. When the girls come in to get their assignments, you know, they get weighed and measured." Bynum paused a moment and said, "I'm sure they knew what we wanted and were not very friendly."

The subject of a blood trail at Cole Crest came up, and all three had individual opinions. "It was certainly a good educated guess that a body had been moved around and taken away," said Bynum. "One of the criminalists told us that a victim could not have lived with all this blood loss. I remember the blood smears going from the bedroom, the bathroom, around the corner, on the tile, through the carpet, and all the way out to the garage."

Small added, "The blood started on the bedroom level, but

as you go upstairs, you see blood transfers all up [and] down the steps."

Wendi Berndt speculated that David Mahler had dragged Kristin from the bedroom. "Then he took her up a short flight of stairs to the living room. To the left of that is a bathroom. Just in front of it is a blood smear on the tile."

Small said, "I think he rested the body there while he checked to see if anyone was outside, then opened the door and dragged her out to the garage."

Bynum had a slightly different view. "He left that body exactly where it had fallen. Covered her with the bedspread, tried to get people to help him, and then took off like a scared little boy to the Marriott. I don't think he moved the body at all, until he realized that none of his friends were going to help him." After a few more minutes of exchanged opinions, Bynum compromised. "It's possible that he moved her right then, though, and put her in the trunk of the Jaguar."

All three—Wendi Berndt, Vicki Bynum, and Tom Small— agreed that the next development in the case changed everything.

CHAPTER 25

THE HARDEST TASK OF ALL

The big break came on Saturday, June 16.

Sitting among a group of parents at his daughter's softball game, Tom Small heard his cell phone buzz at about ten o'clock in the morning. He flipped it open and listened to the voice of a female officer at the LAPD Command Post. She informed him that the San Bernardino County Sheriff's Department was working a crime scene near Barstow involving an unknown deceased female. She gave Small the telephone number of Detective Mike Gilliam.

Small immediately called. Later speaking of it, he said, "Gilliam advised that they were processing the scene of a body dump. The decedent appeared to be a female."

The Barstow Police Department, Gilliam told Small, had advised his unit that Hollywood Homicide was investigating the possible murder of a woman who might have been dumped in the Barstow area. They had seen the notification sent out by Detective Small. Gilliam couldn't be certain this was the one Hollywood sought. Three female bodies had turned up in the desert vicinity. He told Small these remains were in extremely poor condition, in a state of advanced decomposition, and somewhat mummified.

Small replied, "Well, maybe I can make it easy. What's she wearing?"

Gilliam said, "We can't really tell much about the top because it is so degraded. It looks multicolored. The pants are like very thin parachute material, almost transparent."

"It's gotta be mine," said Small. "That matches the description given to us of her clothing. It's probably going to be her, but we really won't know until we get her back here for an autopsy. Please do me a favor. Do a good crime scene on it and see if you can sift through some of the debris below her for a bullet."

The response from Gilliam sounded pessimistic. "There's really not much of anything here to help. But we will definitely sift the sand. We'll ask the coroner if they can lift some kind of a fingerprint." But, he said, the effects of wind and drifting sand would have long since eliminated footprints, tracks, and probably any other trace evidence.

"We believe our victim was shot in the face," Small said. "Can you see any sign of that?"

"We really can't tell. The coroner is here to take the remains away. Detective Chris Fisher is the lead on this case." Gilliam gave Fisher's phone number to Small.

Small learned of the body location on Nebo Street, north of I-40, close to old Route 66, and near Daggett. Other descriptive comments about the corpse convinced him that Kristin Baldwin's remains had been found. Closer examination of the clothing revealed a pink bra. A gold-colored wristwatch on the left wrist didn't help because Small hadn't heard of any specific jewelry worn by Kristin, but characterization of the long hair as dishwater blond seemed to fit. Those unusual, sheer white pants described by Donnie Van Develde and David Mahler sealed it for Small.

On Sunday morning, Small spoke to Wendi Berndt by

telephone, informed her of the news, and said he would follow up with Detective Fisher. That conversation took place later Sunday. Fisher gave Small a summary of how the body had been found when a pair of Good Samaritans had tried to aid Allura McGehay, whose pickup was stuck in the sand. Updating the crime scene investigation, Fisher said the area around the body had been "sifted and shoveled," but nothing turned up. They had collected some discarded plastic bottles and a few cigarette butts, but these didn't look very promising.

Later that same day, a call from the San Bernardino County Coroner's Department erased most of the remaining doubt about identification of the body. A specialist had utilized the Microsil process, squeezing gel compound from a tube directly onto the body's fingertips, allowing it to harden, and meticulously lifting it off. The procedure, requiring patient skill and extraordinary care, succeeded in obtaining partial fingerprints from the decomposed flesh. Because Kristin Baldwin had once been arrested on a DUI charge, her pitiful remains would now have a name.

Tom Small and Vicki Bynum received notification on Monday from Lieutenant Cheryl MacWillie, of the Los Angeles County Coroner's Department, that the body would be taken into custody from the San Bernardino County Coroner's Department. The remains would be transported that same day.

In the early afternoon, the two detectives arrived at the Los Angeles facility on North Mission Road just as the body was being checked in. Cheryl MacWillie allowed them a view before technicians began the process of preparation for an autopsy. Seeing the remains of murder victims had long since lost its shock value to Bynum and Small. However, they had been working so hard on this case for the last ten days, and had learned so much about Kristin Baldwin, this one impacted them a little differently. In most cases, they saw the bodies before learning anything about their backgrounds. Now it felt as if they had known Kristin for a long time.

Even though they had steeled themselves against the instinctive repulsion, this one still required strong constitutions. Small noted, "The body exhibited a large amount of insect activity and exuded a heavy putrid odor." The remaining skin appeared to be dehydrated and in a mummified condition. The cramped fetal position, with both legs pulled up tightly under the upper torso, led them to believe she had been manually forced into that position. Rigor mortis, which stiffens a dead body, begins about three to four hours after death. Approximately twenty-four hours later, depending on ambient conditions, it relaxes until completely limp. Kristin had probably been squeezed into this configuration perhaps two or three days after she died so she would fit into the trunk of a car.

Fluoroscope and X-rays of the corpse failed to reveal any bullets or fragments.

Making notes, Bynum and Small observed that the face was "skeletonized" with only a small amount of skin left clinging to the bone. The remaining long, wavy sandy brown or blond hair reached approximately to her shoulders. Bynum drew Small's attention to the perfect "French manicure" of the fingernails. Kristin still wore a bracelet, earrings, a ring, and a gold-colored watch that had glinted in the desert sunlight.

According to the official report, the shreds of discolored clothing, dirty and stained, consisted of:

1. A "Secret Pleasures," tanklike top shirt with pink flowers, short sleeve, size 3–5 with abundant decomposition fluid and beetles present. There is a single lower incisor tooth discovered in the clothing that is subsequently removed and placed in a stock jar.

2. A pink bra
3. A thong, small
4. Yellow and white pants, juniors, size 5.

All of the above clothing items, as described above show decomposition fluid that is dried with beetles present and dirt debris adherent.

Not long after the body had arrived, Dr. Louis Pena, deputy medical examiner (ME), conducted the official autopsy. Detectives Brett Goodkin and Jerry Wert joined Bynum and Small to witness the gruesome procedure.

Most autopsies of murder victims are performed on a complete human body. In this case, Dr. Pena had little to work with. In the routine preparation, he weighed the remains. Dehydrated and incomplete, the body tipped the scale at only thirty-one pounds. As he followed the normal progressive steps, the doctor spoke into a recorder, observing that none of the vital organs or soft tissue remained intact. "Portions of the trachea are present and are desiccated. The lungs are not identified. The esophagus, bowels, appendix, and pancreas are in advanced state of decomposition. A portion of the liver is present but extensively dehydrated. No assessment of the liver can be made. The gallbladder cannot be identified. The uterus, fallopian tubes, endometrium, cervix, and vagina cannot be assessed due to decomposition. The ovaries are not identified." The same observations applied to all of the abdominal cavity, heart, glands, the eyes, spinal cord, and brain tissue. "The breasts are difficult to examine due to the decomposed state of the body."

In his interview of Robin, Jerry Wert had learned that Kristin had a small tattoo of a blue dolphin on her lower abdomen. He and the other three detectives watched as Dr. Pena's examination revealed the dolphin on the leatherlike flesh.

All four detectives knew that witnesses Donnie Van Develde and Karl Norvik thought David Mahler had shot Kristin in the face. Hoping for some information related to gunshot injuries, they waited patiently, but even that turned out to be ambiguous.

Tom Small later said, "I observed the examination as the autopsy progressed. The body exhibited a circular hole or puncture on the upper right chest, near the neck. There was an unexplained hole inside the nasal cavity and another large hole at the base of the neck on the upper back. No apparent skull or facial fractures were noted. A tooth was recovered from the nasal cavity, and another tooth was recovered from the upper body clothing."

Dr. Pena found that "the upper right chest shows a round hole. . . . One cannot assess for soot or stippling." Also, "the posterior neck shows a large gaping hole, or defect four inches below the top of the head." In addition, he noted that radiology provided information of "metallic fragments present in the spinal column region and the rib, with acute fractures consistent with a gunshot injury." His eventual conclusion was that Kristin had died from a "gunshot wound of the torso."

Looking ahead to possible trial complications, the detectives hoped this finding would not undermine testimony from Van Develde and Norvik.

Before the day ended, Tom Small and Vicki Bynum performed perhaps the hardest job of all in a murder investigation. They contacted Robin Henson, Peter Means, and a few other family members of Kristin's to notify them that Kristin's remains had been found and positively identified.

Robin would later speak of a strange experience. "Not long after I learned that she was gone, I took my kids to school one day. When I came home, I could smell pancakes. My mind flashed back to those wonderful Sunday mornings when Kristin was staying with us and would make pancakes for our breakfast. The aroma would fill the rooms. No one had made them on that particular morning, and I had the strong sense that Kristin had been there. After that episode, I never felt her presence in my house again—like she had gone somewhere else. She had paid us a visit, said good-bye, and moved on. I hope her spirit went back to Maui and she is happy there."

Jennifer Gootsan had a similar experience. "Things had not been going well in my life and I was thinking about moving to Hawaii. I called a friend and said I was going to get Kristin and we are going to live over there. That night, when the call came with awful news, I was wearing a sweatshirt she had given me, with the name of Polli's restaurant on it." In telling this, Jennifer's voice broke and tears streamed down her cheeks.

CHAPTER 26

"HE WASN'T
HIDING IN GUATAMALA"

The Los Angeles County district attorney, ready to move ahead on the case against David Mahler, agreed with the superior court to set a preliminary hearing date of June 29.

Mahler needed to make a crucial decision.

With so much at stake, he would need the best defense attorney he could find. Would that be from a list of local top-notch defenders, or could he look closer to home—in a mirror?

In New York and New Jersey, he had successfully represented defendants charged with narcotics offenses and prostitution. However, he had never attempted to take on a murder case. Still, he held himself in high esteem for his courtroom tactics and skills in swaying a jury. So, should he risk it all by defending himself in court? Or should he take heed of an old axiom? "He who represents himself has a fool for a client" has convinced countless defendants to hire an attorney. Acting in pro per, the Latin term from *propria persona*—

meaning "for one's self"—may offer a few advantages but is loaded with dangerous traps. (In many states, the term "pro se" is used, instead.)

On the plus side is the opportunity to spend time in the jail law library, a welcome refuge from the noisy cell block. Other benefits include having a runner on the outside to bring documents and items supposedly for the preparation of the case. Pro per defendants often have use of computers for the preparation of their motions.

A defendant made world-famous by Joseph Wambaugh's book *The Onion Field* tried to use his pro per status to set up an escape attempt. Long before the advent of personal computers, Gregory Powell required the use of a typewriter. He persuaded a woman on the outside to buy one for him. It was delivered to the jail, but two small guns were found inside and the typewriter was confiscated.

During the trial, the prosecutor used the typewriter as a piece of evidence to convince jurors that Powell deserved the death penalty. One day, when the typewriter was placed on a counsel table, an attorney noticed a sprinkling of powder beneath it. He complained to the detective in the front row that they should have cleaned off the fingerprint powder. The indignant cop said they didn't dust the typewriter. Eventually it turned out the powder was cocaine placed in the roller by an outside accomplice for Powell's personal pleasure.

David Mahler had already experimented with defending himself in an earlier hearing. Unfamiliar with California law, he made motions without citing the correct code sections and seemed lost in regard to following proper procedures. A judge had recommended at one of the hearings that he needed an attorney. It probably rubbed his ego raw, but Mahler soon realized that even small errors in a murder trial could be disastrous. Without a doubt, the judge had been correct. A good

lawyer might be essential in guiding him through the most
important trial of his life.

One lawyer had already upset Mahler and been fired. He
had lost a hearing that might have allowed Mahler to be released on bail.

Considering the matter of new legal representation, he
weighed his options. Should he plead indigence and ask for a
public defender, or seek a private attorney?

Private criminal defense attorneys sometimes like to per-
petuate the myth that public defenders are only interested in
selling out their clients because they aren't highly motivated
by a large retainer. Public defenders, in reality, are trained and
have a great depth of experience, since they handle so many
more cases than the busiest of independent lawyers. Also, because of the high volume of cases, public defenders can be
more knowledgeable of the court system.

Fearful of being stuck with a young greenhorn, or perhaps
a veteran defender close to retirement age, Mahler decided
to seek hired help. Through his various contacts, he heard
about an aggressive criminal defense attorney named Andrew
Reed Flier.

The handsome, superbly dressed, and well-coiffed Flier
sported dark, wavy hair and handsomely chiseled features,
giving him a remarkable resemblance to the late John F. Kennedy Jr. Headquartered in Encino, another San Fernando
Valley community, Flier knew his way around the legal
system and demonstrated willingness to defend a broad spec-
trum of clientele, from celebrities to crime lords. He had recently completed a court case in which he represented Victor
Paleologus, who had murdered a young woman. His crime
bore eerie similarities to charges faced by David Mahler. Paleologus killed a young woman named Kristi Johnson.
Mahler had allegedly killed Kristin Baldwin, nicknamed
Kristi. The murder of Kristi Johnson took place in the Hollywood Hills, less than a mile from Mahler's residence, where

Kristin had apparently been shot. And Kristi's body, exactly like Kristin's remains, was missing more than two weeks before being accidentally discovered.

Paleologus had lured Kristi to the site by persuading her to "audition" for a role in a promotional film for an upcoming James Bond thriller. Flier neither won nor lost the courtroom battle because Paleologus decided, halfway through the proceedings, to change his plea. Fearing a possible death penalty, he negotiated a lesser sentence by pleading guilty to first-degree murder (see *Meet Me for Murder,* Pinnacle, 2008).

The financial agreement between Mahler and Flier was a private matter between the two of them, but it's a good bet that Mahler paid well for the lawyer's services. It has been suggested that it used up a significant portion of his wealth.

Preliminary hearings are held to determine if there is probable cause to bind an accused defendant over for trial. Unlike a full trial, there is no jury. The process requires the presentation of only enough testimony to convince a magistrate that sufficient evidence exists to proceed to the next step. The standard of proof is quite low, and hearsay evidence is allowable. Discovery rules—in which the prosecution must turn over to the defense, in advance, evidence they plan to present—do not apply. At the end of the hearing, the judge must decide if the defendant will be "held to answer." If so, he or she must next face an arraignment hearing and is subsequently tried by a jury.

The preliminary case of *The People* v. *David A. Mahler* came before Judge Daniel B. Feldstern on Friday, June 29, 2007, at 1:45 P.M. Prosecutor Cathryn Brougham would call only three witnesses: Donnie Van Develde, Karl Norvik, and Detective Larry Cameron. Detective Tom Small joined Brougham at the prosecution table.

Van Develde's nerves seemed tighter than banjo strings as he swore to tell the truth and took the witness stand. His eyes darted back and forth as if he expected to be attacked any minute. He identified the defendant as David Mahler, the person sitting at the end of the defense table and wearing a blue jail-issued jumpsuit. Machine-gunning his answers to Brougham, Donnie described the house on Cole Crest, the tenants' living arrangements, and his relationship with Mahler.

Brougham asked Van Develde to tell what happened in Mahler's bedroom early Sunday morning, May 27. He spoke of his wife being away on a trip, of his expecting to be paid by Mahler for some work, and being summoned up to David's room. There, he saw Kristi and recognized her from three or four previous meetings. Just as he had informed Tom Small and Vicki Bynum in the frenetic interview, Donnie delivered his story of David's displayed anger, being dismissed, and then summoned again, as well as David rambling around with an open robe, displaying his nudity. He told of David waving a gun, loading it with a single bullet, and clicking it in the faces of Kristi and himself. After exiting in panic, he had heard a single gunshot.

The testimony from Van Develde lasted nearly two hours, including cross-examination by Andrew Flier.

Detective Larry Cameron came next and recounted his experiences at Cole Crest on the first day of June. He described blotches on the master bedroom's carpet and a trail of spots leading to the garaged Jaguar. Criminalists, he said, had processed the suspicious stains and concluded they were human blood. Also, an assortment of cleaning materials and fluids indicated someone had tried to eradicate the stains. Cameron's turn lasted only twenty minutes.

* * *

Karl Norvik stepped up, obviously reluctant and nervous. He avoided eye contact with the defendant, David Mahler, while speaking of their relationship and his own shock at the events of that Sunday morning. Expressing himself in a vocabulary reflecting exceptional intelligence, Karl told of seeing Kristin's body, believing she had been shot in the face by Mahler, and refusing to comply with David's requests for help. He seemed apologetic that he had not called the police until several days later.

Norvik's testimony consumed the remainder of that Friday. Judge Feldstern ordered him to return on Monday morning.

It took another two hours on that day for Karl Norvik to answer questions from Cathryn Brougham and Andrew Flier.

With testimony concluded, the judge granted Andrew Flier's request to speak. The attorney stood and stated, "I have two issues. One is insufficiency of evidence, and the other is the bail status." Addressing the evidence first, he said, "They find a body (in the desert), but it is the defense position that there is no connection to that body and Mr. Mahler." Flier alluded to the circumstantial nature of the remains being identified as Kristin Baldwin. Partial fingerprints made from the Microsil process had been compared to her known prints, and that had shown strong similarities. A blue dolphin tattoo had also been noted. But none of this conclusively meant these remains were those of Kristin Baldwin, at least by legal standards, according to Flier.

Neither of the two witnesses who had lived in the residence, Flier asserted, offered any evidence that a murder had transpired. "Even if we accept that there was a dead body, there is no evidence about malice. There are no specific intent issues. And if you believe the first witness, Donnie, it is clear this happened over an argument or maybe even Russian roulette, which I think could mitigate this matter over to manslaughter. . . . There is no sufficient evidence to show that the body found is the same body that everyone is talking about . . . that it is the same person who presumably is on the [floor] in Mr. Mahler's bedroom."

Cathryn Brougham disagreed. First, no real doubt existed about the body identification. Second, "Donnie basically told us that the defendant had a gun, that he loaded that gun, and that the defendant was in a rage . . . toward the victim, Kristin Baldwin. Moments after he left the room, he heard the gun go off. And we have the fact that he received phone calls from the defendant in which he was basically admitting to the murder and saying that it was in self-defense." She also cited Karl Norvik's testimony. "The defendant comes to his room after [Norvik heard] loud thuds . . . and, in fact, asked him to dispose of a body." Norvik had actually seen the dead victim.

In addition, said Brougham, Detective Cameron had testified about bloodstains in the bedroom, the discovery of Mahler hiding in a closet . . . "And finally we have the identification of Kristin Baldwin's body. As the court may know, this was originally filed as a no-body case." She expressed relief that the body had been found prior to the preliminary hearing, and confidence that it added enough weight to the charges for the court to find against the defendant.

Andrew Flier briefly restated his opposition and then moved on to the issue of bail. In three previous hearings, Mahler's arguments to be released on bail had been unsuccessful. Judge Feldstern gave Cathryn Brougham the opportunity to speak first and explain why Mahler shouldn't be granted his request.

In the first hearing, Broughham said, the prosecution had faced the possibility of trying a no-body case, and the defendant had asserted in a police interview that he was the only one who knew where the body and the gun were located. If he had been released, he conceivably could have made certain the body could never be found. Then he had concealed the gun where it could never be found. "He also had told a third party that he wanted a gun to eliminate any witnesses in this case if he could get out on bail." The second and third hearings had relied on this same information to rule against allowing Mahler to go free.

"I know," said Brougham, "the defense is going to say that conditions have changed since we found the body, so the concern that there is going to be destruction of the evidence is gone. The people would respond to that by saying the gun is still outstanding, and we have concerns about the safety of witnesses. We also have concerns that the defendant will flee." She added that Mahler had bragged that he could easily post the amount of money required. "The defendant knows a lot about these witnesses, where they can be located, and they are very vulnerable to him." She requested that the order for no bail remain intact.

Flier stood and argued that the assertions by the prosecution were not entirely true. In the police interview, he said, "The awareness of where the body is, and the gun, is through hearsay. He never tells anyone that he killed anybody. It's in their own report—that his statements were all from hearsay." Furthermore, said Flier, this is not a capital case and there are no special circumstances so he is entitled to bail.

The possibility that his client, if freed, might have destroyed the body, said Flier, was preposterous. But even if it had been true, the issue had changed since discovery of the body. Therefore, the people's main argument no longer applied. In regard to the gun, he said, "I don't even understand that argument. [They] don't need the gun to prove a murder case. Only the body is needed. The gun issue is a red herring."

Flier also expressed doubts about the alleged threats to the lives of witnesses. Certainly, the lawyer said, his client could be monitored with a tracking device to prevent him from doing harm to anyone. "So we are doing everything to protect society and to protect his rights."

Judge Feldstern noted aloud that Karl Norvik had been asked if the defendant had ever directly threatened him. The answer had been "No, but . . ." This observation alarmed the prosecutor.

She replied, "Our concern is for public safety. We have a defendant who can easily flee—one who has resources to get whatever he wants done. And he has indicated that he would want to kill witnesses in this case. Mr. Van Develde and Mr. Norvik didn't come forward for five days because they were concerned for their safety. They believed he has the financial ability to harm them, either through someone else or doing it himself. To us, it is a major concern that the gun is still out there and accessible to the defendant."

Flier replied by pointing out that his client had not fled. "He went to hotels, but came back to his residence, where he was arrested—"

The judge interrupted. "He was hiding in a closet, covering himself up, secreting himself."

"He wasn't hiding in Guatemala," Flier riposted.

"Fair enough," said Feldstern, trying not to smile.

Forging ahead, Flier said, "My point is he was hiding in his own residence. He was concerned and didn't know who was trying to get into his home. You and I might not have hidden in a closet. The bottom line is he was there in his own home. I don't see flight risk." Flier again downplayed the alleged threats to witnesses. "The key issue is his right to bail, and that is all we are asking."

Both attorneys rested their cases.

Judge Daniel B. Feldstern spoke. "First of all, let me just comment on the issue of sufficiency of evidence. The court believes it is overwhelming. In my view, this defendant committed this murder and disposed of the body using his vehicle. There can't be anything clearer than that. He was in possession of a firearm. The body and the gun were [missing] at the time of his arrest."

Regarding the question of bail, the judge acknowledged that circumstances had been changed by discovery of a body. He also noted that bail is normally denied in cases of capital murder, but often allowed in lesser charges. "This is not a capital case. But there are exceptions where there is a substantial likelihood that defendant's release would result in great bodily harm to others. There is evidence here that he has demonstrated an intent and propensity to hide and destroy evidence exemplified by the movement of the body, to put it in some remote area. The gun has never been recovered. He has made statements about knowing the whereabouts. He is the only person to know about it."

After a brief pause, while referring to his notes, Feldstern continued. "He was found hiding in his house. There was some sort of detergent found near one of the bloodstains, which was about the size of a basketball. This tells me the defendant went back to the house for the purpose of trying to further destroy evidence in this case.

"Also, there have been some representations here about his desire to eliminate witnesses, should he be released on bail. And the fact that he was [near] LAX right after this event occurred is another demonstration possibly inferring that he had the intent to flee, even though he felt compelled, at some point, to hide the evidence further.

"So, in the totality of circumstances, it appears to me that the issue of public safety is valid."

With mention of erratic behavior, the use of a firearm, involvement of controlled substances, and the crime's seriousness, he said, "It is not unreasonable, under these circumstances, for the defendant to be held without bail. And that will be the court's order."

David Mahler grimaced and visibly slumped in his chair.

Judge Feldstern had not finished. "It appears to me from the evidence presented that the following offenses have been committed and there is sufficient cause to believe the defendant is guilty thereof." He cited them like a bell tolling doom: murder, felonious use of a firearm, and assault with a firearm.

Finally he set a date for the formal arraignment of July 16.

Certainly, none of this meant that Mahler was guilty of any charges. The preliminary hearing had only accomplished its purpose, to legally subject him to arraignment and a trial.

Reporters and lawyers, both defense and prosecution, almost unanimously agreed that a jury would have great difficulty finding him guilty of second-degree murder. The best that could be expected, considering his drug usage, volatile personality, and the circumstances of the shooting, would be a verdict of manslaughter—either voluntary or involuntary. If so, Mahler would probably serve a prison sentence amounting to no more than a slap on the wrist.

Chapter 27

A Look Behind the Scenes
By Ronald Bowers

I first came to grips with the David Mahler case a short time after the criminal complaints had been filed. Fellow prosecutor Cathryn Brougham stopped by my office on the seventeenth floor of the Criminal Courts Building and asked me if I had heard about the homicide in the Hollywood Hills. I thought, at first, she might be referring to Victor Paleologus, who had been tried for killing Kristi Johnson.

"No," my visitor said. "It's the one that took place above the Sunset Strip, and the police couldn't find the body." That rang a bell. I had recently heard a television reporter asking for the public's help in finding the body of a female murder victim, but I could summon up only a hazy recollection of the facts.

The Deputy DA tried to enlighten me. I listened intently as she spewed out a lot of names: Donnie, Karl, Jeremy, Atticus, Cheryl, Kitty, Stacy, Damien—all surrounding a lawyer, David Mahler. He had been arrested and charged with murdering Kristin Baldwin. To be honest, I struggled to keep the names straight. As Cathryn spoke, I pulled out a legal tablet and plunked it down on my desk. My ears perked up when she told me that Mahler was an East Coast lawyer who had been a criminal defense attorney. This could turn out to be intriguing.

For more years than I care to remember, I have been assisting prosecutors in the Los Angeles District Attorney's Office with visual aids to use in criminal trials. I believe our techniques for augmenting introduction of evidence has been one of the best in the nation. Our uses of Microsoft PowerPoint presentations have proven exceptionally helpful to prosecutors in aiding jurors to understand evidence and complex issues in a murder case. Colorful, well-designed images projected on a large screen replace the tedious drone of a speech and keep jurors' attention focused. Still referred to as "slides" from the old-fashioned 35-millimeter slide projectors, this modern technology allows text, graphics, movies, and gradual addition to the pictures arranged according to the user's wishes.

It has been my experience that careful organization of the facts and pictorial presentation of them is essential to success in any business, and particularly in this one. So, I penciled in the names of the characters as my colleague delivered information about them.

I never interrupt other attorneys when they describe their views of a case because I am particularly interested in how they tell the story. This is a precursor of how best to convey those same facts during the trial. I want to listen as though I were a juror to see if the message penetrates the target or if it misses the mark. After fifteen minutes of details flying at me, I agreed with Cathryn that she had a riveting case and said I would be glad to help structure the presentation. As she exited, I requested a copy of the police reports. They were delivered to me about an hour later by a law clerk.

After a meticulous review of the documents, I realized we had some serious obstacles to overcome in laying this out to a jury. It could be difficult to make a convincing argument that Mahler had murdered Kristin as opposed to overreacting to an argument. I anticipated that his defense would portray him as under the influence of drugs, drunk, and emotionally unstable at the time, making him incapable of forming the intent to kill. My experience had taught me that jurors' ultimate decisions in these types of cases often hinge on the shooter's state of mind when the trigger was pulled.

My first objective would be to help the jury keep the cast of characters straight. Experimenting with it, I created a visual chart, including photos displaying all of the parties present in the room at or near the time of the shooting. This included pictures of Mahler and Kristin, as well as Donnie and Karl, all superimposed over a photo of Mahler's master bedroom. To drive home the point, I inserted a graphic clip art of a revolver next to Mahler with an arrow extending from the gun barrel to Kristin's chest. Even though transcripts of interviews said that Donnie and Karl thought she had been shot in the face, I decided to go along with the coroner's report of possible bullet damage to the chest.

Next I needed a way to explain the configuration of David Mahler's house without baffling the jurors. Every time the investigators discussed the case with me, they would describe a labyrinth of rooms that defied comprehension. The structure stretched seven stories down a slope, and the upper stories were divided into split levels. Each descending level jutted out below the one above it. An interior staircase made it even more confusing. Anyone describing it would usually wind up by saying, "There is no way to explain the layout of rooms in there."

To clarify it in my own mind, I wrote:

Above garage—kitchen and dining room
Street level—garage and living room
Level 1—office (below living room)
Level 2—David's bedroom and master bath
Level 3—Moudy's studio apartment
Level 4—Norvik's studio apartment
Level 5—Van Develde's studio apartment

At last, using police photos, I diagrammed it and instead of referring to "floors" or "stories," they became "levels." To further clarify it, I attached photos of the rooms at each level.

Grappling with another problem, I tried to develop a time line of events. So many things happened between May 24, when Kristin went to Newport Beach with Mahler, and June 16, when her body was found. I couldn't keep it all sorted out. So how could I expect jurors to grasp it? I couldn't keep it straight as to when Mahler went to the Marriott or the Standard Hotel, let alone the comings and goings of his Jaguars. Even the date of the shooting kept slipping out of my mind. And how long was it before Karl called the police? Several attempts at making flow-charts failed before I found a solution.

A giant calendar page solved my problem. I combined May and June onto a single sheet, beginning with May 20 and ending with June 16, the day Kristin's body was discovered. In the block for each day, I entered the important events. So simple, yet effective. For example, jurors could easily see that five days elapsed between the time of the shooting and Karl's call to the police. They could also easily see Mahler's activities after he shot Kristin, until his arrest and the police interview. This would certainly reduce the amount of explanation by the prosecutor. (Note: It also provided an indispensable aid to Don Lasseter and Ron Bowers in writing this book.)

Perhaps this task might sound relatively simple, but it must be kept in mind that I was working on several other cases at the same time. The Phil Spector murder case gobbled up huge segments of my workdays and nights. In his two spectacular trials, covered by international news media, musical magnate Phil Spector had been accused of murdering Lana Clarkson in his mansion. It took awhile for me to connect the dots of similarity.

The parallels between Spector and Mahler were amazing. They both involved an arrogant, testosterone-driven—possibly drunk or drugged—male who snared a younger woman and steered her to his isolated house, where he could dominate her at his will.

When confronted with some resistance or rejection, both men automatically resorted to pointing a gun, allegedly without intent to shoot to force compliance with their wishes. Mahler told two tenants of the shooting and Spector blurted it out to a chauffeur.

I later learned of another link between the two cases. Karl Norvik, whose call to the police ultimately resulted in the Mahler mystery being solved, had been a good friend of Lana Clarkson! He had attended the funeral services after her death.

For months I had been working on ways to disprove Spector's defense that Lana had grabbed the pistol and stuck it in her mouth to commit suicide. I wondered if Mahler would try to craft such an absurd excuse. Or, as an experienced defense attorney, would he manufacture a more plausible story to explain the slaying?

While uncanny similarities were mirrored in these two cases, a major difference perplexed me. The news and entertainment media demonstrated an insatiable appetite for any tidbit of information related to Phil Spector. To me, he was an obscure, over-the-hill record producer. They virtually ignored the David Mahler case, despite one of the most colorful cast of characters I had ever encountered.

Whatever excuse Mahler would come up with, he would still need to reason away the trail of blood leading from his bedroom to the garage and into the trunk of his older Jaguar. A criminalist planned to testify that the pattern of droplets on the stairs indicated that the victim's body had been dragged by her feet, causing blood to spatter on the carpet and the stairs as her head bounced from step to step. Initially I thought I could use one diagram to illustrate this. But photos of the crime scene revealed the incredible length of the trail. I settled on using four photo boards with superimposed dotted lines to designate the long path of blood drops.

Jurors have inquiring minds, and I knew they would want some evidence to show whose blood made up the trail. Could Mahler have sustained an injury and bled as he walked from his bedroom to the garage? Or perhaps it had been left by one of the other residents, clients, or hookers who frequented Cole Crest. I needed a way to show the blood belonged to Kristin Baldwin. Usually, that is an easy task, since you need only to compare a DNA sample, from the victim or the suspect. When I asked the detectives for a comparison of Kristin's DNA sample, the case suddenly got complicated. They responded that no DNA sample had been taken from her dehydrated remains.

I never quite understood why. Yes, her flesh had turned almost to leather, but I had read of DNA samples being taken from King Tut's mummy. I don't know if a mistake in the coroner's procedures or the advanced decomposition had made it impossible. The pitiful remains had been cremated. But another option existed. A swab could be taken from the mouth of Kristin's mother for comparison. Since she lived in Vermont, it took some time to obtain and analyze. At last, upon completions of that task, we had proof that the blood in the house, by a high mathematical probability, had been left by Kristin. My challenge was to make it easy for jurors to interpret the numbers. I think my displays succeeded fairly well, even though the subject of DNA can be overwhelmingly complex for any jury.

One of the key pieces of evidence came from the security video camera of David Mahler's neighbor. We were able to capture images of Mahler's Jaguar backing into the garage late at night. It later left and was gone for nearly five hours. I saw the need for a visual display showing that Mahler had the opportunity to transport and dump Kristin's body in the desert near Daggett. By tracing the route on a map, from Cole Crest to the site where she was found, I saw it was 124 miles. An easy calculation proved that Mahler could have made the round-trip, even with the constraints of speed limits. He even would have a little time left over. To make it easy for jurors to visualize, I enlarged a map and inserted a photo of the Cole Crest house at the starting point and a picture of Kristin's body under the edge of a low bridge in the desert. I posted the mileage, the starting time of 2:17 A.M., and the return time of 7:15 A.M.

Later, just to hedge all bets, we asked DA investigator Ronald "Ron" Valdiva to drive the route and determine if it could be done within those time frames. He videotaped it and we planned for him to testify at the trial.

During all of this preparation, I had heard a lot about the house on Cole Crest Drive, the environment up there and the tortuous driving conditions in the neighborhood. A report from the detectives even noted that David Mahler's longtime girl-friend, Stacy Tipton, often traveled from Visalia to visit him but refused to drive up into the Hollywood Hills because it was too difficult. Mahler had to come down and meet her somewhere. I also knew of Mahler's alcohol and drug usage, and wondered how he could have negotiated the narrow, twisting roads while under the influence. I decided to see for myself what everyone was talking about.

After carefully planning my route, I left my office in down-town Los Angeles, behind the wheel of my aging SUV, and took the freeway to Hollywood. At the corner of Sunset Boulevard and Laurel Canyon Boulevard, I turned north and joined a line of BMWs and Mercedes-Benzes all going too fast. Within a few minutes, I came to the historic Canyon Country Store and swung left on Kirkwood Drive. Right away, I realized that neither maps nor written instructions, not even a sophisticated GPS system, reveal the true story.

At first, Kirkwood Drive gives the impression of a rustic, pleasant mountain road. Petite wood-frame houses, with mini-mal front yards, are crammed into the hillside, with tall trees providing a sun-blocking canopy. The "pleasant" part vanishes as the lane constricts and begins twisting and turning like a roller coaster. As I climbed higher, I could see rows of houses on the right side jutting out over a bottomless ravine. Some structures rest on stilts, and others are secured to a few feet of bedrock and cantilever out over nothing but air. All the homes cling to the street, tied to it by concrete driveways.

What becomes immediately apparent to any visitor is the

harsh parking environment. As Kirkwood narrows, parking is legally permissible on only one side of the street. This makes the passage of two vehicles in opposite directions next to impossible. Large vehicles left along the curb bring two-way traffic to a halt and precipitate the negotiating game to see who will be the first to pull into someone's driveway so the other can pass. Nonaggressive types could never survive the drive up the hill, since staring down the other driver for passage is a survival skill. I had the feeling that daily users of the street must be type A personalities and don't want to back down for anyone. David Mahler would fit in quite well.

I spotted a few trash barrels, and tried to imagine the horrors of collection days, with two large recycle bins for each household blocking the shoulders on both sides, narrowing the artery like plaque clogging the passage of blood supply. I realized that Mahler would have had infinite opportunities to drop the gun, wrapped in a plastic bag, into any number of trash bins.

The supreme hindrance for the first-time visitor is trying to locate the names of the streets. While moving up Kirkwood, I passed unidentified streets, alleys, and private driveways, desperately looking for a Grand View Drive sign. But street markers seemed deviously hidden, perhaps by reclusive residents who don't want outsiders to venture into their private world. Forks in the road create moments of indecision whether to turn or proceed straight ahead. While I hesitated for an instant, some jerk from behind in a flashy sports car laid on his horn, announcing his impatience for my indecision. Making the wrong turn can be costly in more ways than one. The problem is that such an error may cause you to meander for miles, on narrow roads, eventually terminating in a dead end, with no place to turn around.

Kirkwood finally ended, and decision time arrived. Road forks are bewildering. I twisted my neck about 220 degrees and miraculously spotted a small sign whispering: GRAND VIEW DRIVE. Eureka! That is the next street to turn on, but this was much easier said than done. It required an abrupt left turn to proceed up an incline that demanded every bit of power my SUV could muster. The road snaked up the hill as though it was carved into the side of the cliff, leaving nothing on the other side. No guardrail protects the motorist from careening down into the bottomless canyon below.

First-timers are paralyzed with fear as they inch their way upward, come to rest at a blind corner, and pray that no one is coming down. As I climbed, I could make out another road to the right angling skyward. Finally I saw a sign announcing: COLE CREST DRIVE. However, I could see no way a car could steer such an abrupt turn to the right leading up a precipitous incline on a single-lane road. Surely, I thought, the city street sign was wrong. No city planner would allow such a dangerous intersection. Cole Crest Drive looked more like a private driveway. I had to pull up, back down, restraighten the car, then ease forward while tugging the steering wheel to the far right. At this point, any normal person would ask for heavenly help to prevent a car from coming down the steep hill and force him or her off the slender edge.

As I rounded the sharp corner, I was treated to a breathtaking, panoramic view of the entire Los Angeles Basin and the city skyline, making me feel as if I were on top of the world. No other city—not New York, Chicago, London, or Paris—can provide such a magnificent view from a hilltop. Now I could begin to understand why residents of the Hollywood Hills were addicted to living up on the Heights.

Around another short turn, Cole Crest gave me more views over the canyons below. I could see the iconic HOLLYWOOD on a distant ridge. Just ahead, about the length of a football field, the little street came to a dead end. Mahler's domicile was on the right, a few yards from the terminal point. It gave me an odd feeling to know of the deadly life-and-death drama that had played out inside the rather ordinary-looking house.

Across the narrow street from Mahler's two-car garage door, a ten-foot concrete wall stood against the upper slope. A towering row of eucalyptus trees reached skyward atop the hill. I could see on the ridge's crest a recently built lavish mansion, and to the right of it, three or four expensive homes.

It still puzzled me how Mahler could have frequently driven the dangerous route I had just completed, especially when he was feeling the effects of drink or drugs. I also recalled some mention of him traveling down to Sunset Boulevard via Sunset Plaza Drive. Neither my map, nor my visual inspection, revealed any possible way to do this.

Exploring the terrain on foot, I discovered an amazing secret. What appeared to be a private driveway to the palatial homes above actually passed through those properties and offered access to Blue Heights Drive, which curves downhill to Sunset Plaza Drive. Either by permission of the homeowners, or per-haps by a city negotiated right-of-way, the few people who lived along the north side of Cole Crest Drive could use this drive-way as a shortcut. This revelation changed my entire perspective of Mahler's comings and goings. It also cleared up my under-standing of his interview statements in which he said the gun might be found in a large container somewhere along Sunset Plaza Drive.

Using the newly discovered route, I retraced Mahler's prob-able drive down to Sunset Boulevard. Rubbish receptacles along the way could very well have been where he had tossed the gun. When I reached the Sunset Strip intersection, I could see the Chinese restaurant parking area where Mahler had said Kristin's driver's license and other documents could be found in a Dump-ster, which never panned out.

Back in my office that afternoon, I resumed preparation of the visuals, incorporating dozens of photos and creating charts for the upcoming murder trial. My experience in negotiating the treacherous roads to the top of the Hollywood Hills certainly enhanced my understanding of the entire scenario and gave me insights for helping the jury to comprehend what were sure to be some complex issues.

Reflecting on the incredible panorama from Cole Crest, I could only describe it as a killer view.

CHAPTER 28

"THE ELEPHANT ATE MY JACKET"

It came as a pleasant surprise for Ronald Bowers, often known as Ron, to learn that his colleague Bobby Grace had been chosen as a last-minute replacement to prosecute the Mahler case. They had collaborated previously, and Bowers enjoyed working with the intelligent deputy.

Grace had earned his place as one of the most highly respected members in the district attorney's office, having worked more than fifty murder trials. His performance in several high-profile cases had won admiration from not only his bosses, but from his colleagues as well.

In a trial that had ended just a couple of weeks before Kristin Baldwin was shot to death, Grace had handled the court case of Chester Dewayne Turner, termed one of L.A.'s most prolific serial killers. The jury had delivered eleven guilty verdicts.

Another triumph by Grace had riveted the nation in April 2008. Two elderly women, seventy-seven-year-old Helen Golay and seventy-five-year-old Olga Rutterschmidt, were accused of murdering a pair of homeless men and collecting $2.8 million dollars in life insurance policies. The scheming septuagenarians had provided living quarters and food for the victims over a period of two years, while paying the expensive insurance premiums.

As the prosecutor, Bobby Grace worked to overcome a possible backlash of sympathy by jurors due to the women's age. The defendants gave the appearance of innocent grandmothers who were just trying to help out the less fortunate. Using a PowerPoint slide show, Grace demonstrated their devious planning, which demonstrated extreme premeditation and deliberation. These women, he said, had meticulously spent two years planning to kill the victims. Gradually the jury began to understand that selfish avarice was not limited to youthful killers. They found both defendants guilty of first-degree murder. Handing down sentences of life in prison for each of them, Judge David S. Wesley commented, "These unfortunate men were sacrificed on your altars of greed."

As firm believers in the use of audio-visuals, Ron Bowers, Bobby Grace, and Grace's assistant, Lea Malit-Crisostomo, teamed up to prepare PowerPoint shows. They had developed the process so perfectly, it operated like a well-oiled machine. Grace could hand Malit-Crisostomo a basic outline of what he wished to accomplish, and Lea would soon deliver a draft for his opening statement, as well as the argument. Malit-Crisostomo, who had formerly worked for Ron Bowers as a paralegal, called him to help supplement and improve the presentation of the Mahler case that Ron had previously prepared for Cathryn Brougham. Their smoothly honed teamwork from past cases helped immensely in the hurry-up preparation for the pending Mahler trial.

* * *

Robert "Bobby" Grace credited his family and their lineage for much of his success. "My great-grandparents were slaves. My grandparents were sharecroppers, harvesting cotton in Texas. My father was a career military man who fought in World War Two as an infantry soldier in General Patton's Army. Later, in Korea and Vietnam, serving as an officer in the air force, he was the director of MASH units. He was not a doctor but an administrator. Back in the States, he was the director of a hospital at March AFB, in Riverside County, and at Norton AFB, near San Bernardino. My mother was a housewife. They are both deceased."

Born in San Bernardino, California, Bobby started kindergarten in that town and stayed all the way through high-school graduation. He will never forget an incident that happened to him in the fourth grade. Only Grace can tell the story properly:

"I was a pretty good kid, and my mother was strictly a no-nonsense person. People who grew up in Southern California know that in the late winter or early spring it gets cold in the mornings, but will warm up in afternoons. So you have to start the day with a jacket of some kind, but eventually take it off when it gets warmer. In the fourth grade, I would go out in the play yard, and wind up losing my jacket, leaving it somewhere on the grounds, never to be seen again. So my mom would get a little crazy buying me three or four jackets every school year. Finally she went to Neiman-Marcus in L.A. and bought me this really nice jacket with a fleece-lined hood. She said, 'Bobby, if you lose this jacket, there will *not* be any discussion. I am just going to immediately beat your behind.'

"I was sufficiently afraid of that, and really tried to keep a lookout for my new jacket. I was attending a Catholic school, and we went on our annual field trip to the San Diego Zoo. We are all running around, so I come up with the ingenious plan to tie the jacket sleeves around my neck so I couldn't mislay it or lose it.

"We lined up for a class picture, next to the elephant enclosure, with our backs to the fence. The photographer is getting ready to take the picture, about to say, 'One, two, three . . . cheese.' All of a sudden, I feel myself being lifted up into the air. Everybody is looking, like 'Why is Bobby rising up in the air?' It turns out the elephant thought the fake fleece lining in my hood was hay, and was trying to eat it. I'm pretty much suspended in midair and, luckily, he finally freed the jacket arms from around my neck and I fell to the ground. So the elephant had my jacket for lunch.

"I'm in a panic during the bus ride all the way back to San Bernardino because I know there is no way my mother is going to believe what happened. One of the nuns said, 'Don't worry about it, Bobby, we are going to call your mom. Don't worry.'

"A friend's mother arrived to take us home, and she kept asking, 'What's wrong with Bobby?' Her son said, 'Aw, his mom is going to beat his butt 'cause the elephant ate his jacket.'

"'Oh, don't worry, Bobby, she will believe you.'

"So I get home, and I'm hoping and praying the nun has called ahead so I don't have to explain. I go in, and soon as I hit the door, Mom asks, 'Bobby, where is your jacket?'

"So I told the truth. 'The elephant ate my jacket.' Of course, she didn't believe me. She got my dad's belt and I got a really big whippin'. I'm in my room afterward, silently crying to myself. The phone rings and my mother answers. It's the nun. 'Oh, I forgot to call, but I just wanted to let you know that an elephant ate Bobby's jacket. We're going to pay for it. So you can believe he is telling the truth.'

"So my mom calls me out and said, 'The nun called and told me what happened.' I'm standing there waiting for an apology.

"'I told you the elephant ate it.'

"My mom said, 'Shut up. That was for all the other jackets you lost.'"

Following graduation from San Bernardino High School, Bobby attended the University of California, Los Angeles (UCLA), from 1979 through 1984. He served as student body president in his senior year. Bobby's parents wanted him to be a doctor, and he took medical courses at first. "I went to a math class, Math 31B, and couldn't understand any part of it, so I switched to political sciences. Pretty much all of my friends were involved in student politics and went on to law school. That sort of drew me a road map. . . . It seemed like the thing to do."

After UCLA, he entered Loyola Law School, earned his Juris Doctor, and passed the state bar exam on his first try.

Looking back in time, Grace recalled, "At UCLA, I had a friend-tutor-counselor for incoming freshmen named John Caldwell, one of the most brilliant individuals I've ever met. He's a lawyer now. In addition to being very smart, he had a certain charisma as well. On the other hand, he could be a little grating at times. He came to my group of incoming freshmen and said, 'Look, I'm the smartest guy around here, but I'm not popular. You guys want to be popular, but if you will follow me, you can help me spread my gospel.' We wondered if he was crazy. He was overweight, but had been a basketball player at Fairfax High School. He asked, 'What would you guys like to do?' We thought we could trick him into playing basketball, to show him up a little. 'Okay,' he said, 'let's go play basketball.' We played one-on-one, and without any trouble, he beat four of us in a row. Believe me, he got our respect and attention right then. Then he started talking about some things we thought were important, which at that time was trying to get the UC system to divest some of its investments in South Africa. He explained the only way we could influence that change was to take control of student government. We had doubts. How could we change the system that had prevailed forever, with a BMOC from an influential fraternity always being the student body president? He said if we used the right strategy, we could do it. He was right. We created a coalition of groups—black students, Asian students, Latino students, and Jewish students, pretty much everybody who thought they were locked out of student government. We were the first ones to coalesce. We realized the only way to gain any power was to create a body of activists out of nothing. That was John's genius, pulling together what was thought to be disparate groups, to become a majority. My involvement in that process led to becoming the SB president. And we finally did get the student union at UCLA to divest itself from South Africa. The UC Regents followed up by changing their financial portfolio too."

Athletically inclined since childhood, Bobby Grace was active in high-school football and basketball. He was chosen the most valuable player (MVP) on the football team where he played tailback and defensive linebacker. After college he decided to take up skiing. "That's a big hobby of mine, skiing and running, and the Lakers. I've skied nearly every major area in North America. My favorite is Whistler (site of the 2010 Winter Olympics), outside of Vancouver."

From the first grade until his sophomore year in high school, Bobby attended Catholic schools. "I finally got a reprieve from my parents, allowing me to go to public school. The nuns are pretty much as they are portrayed in the mass media. They have their rulers, and they will whack your hand if you do something wrong. At that time, the parochial schools were pretty much no-nonsense. You are here to be educated, and everyone is on a college prep track. I got along pretty well as the reader at mass and as an altar boy. I wasn't out for athletics until [the] last two years of high school. I played Pop Warner football and YMCA basketball. So school was entirely academics."

The David Mahler case first came to Bobby Grace's attention through television news reports. "It caught my interest due to the fact he was an attorney in New York and New Jersey accused of killing a young woman, whose body was found in the desert." Grace's assignment to prosecute the case came at the last minute, due to shifting workloads in the DA's office.

Speaking of the obstacles he faced, Grace said, "There were a number of issues I wasn't aware of until I got into it. I was surprised that no DNA connections had been made, so we arranged to get that taken care of. I was also concerned at the absence of any direct evidence connecting Mahler to the victim's death. The other thing is, Mahler never actually confessed to killing her. Circumstantial evidence led to him as a suspect. But when we looked at the witnesses we had to rely on, in terms of what he did or in terms of causing her death, they were not the best people to rely on. From a character standpoint, these could be the worst witnesses you could ever get. We had an alcoholic, a drug addict, and a porn star."

To get a feel for how Donnie Van Develde would conduct himself on the witness stand, Grace arranged for him to come downtown for an interview. "Donnie was probably one of the most interesting witnesses I have ever encountered. I came from a gang prosecution background, so you expect to cope with witnesses who don't want to be there and don't want to testify. And for the most part, they have legitimate reasons for this reluctance. Loyalty to a gang or outright fear of gang retaliation can be terribly intimidating. So when we get what we call 'civilian witnesses,' we hope they will be cooperative and remember things—generally, go the way you would like them to go."

Bobby Grace could only hope that Donnie Van Develde would testify in a coherent manner. The entire lineup of witnesses worried the prosecutor. Would a jury accept any of them as credible? If not, the case was going to be the first major loss in Grace's career.

Chapter 29

Laboring at Law

David Mahler once again mulled over the possibility of defending himself in the upcoming murder trial. The bottom-line results of Andrew Reed Flier's defense efforts in the preliminary hearing had left Mahler infuriated. Not long afterward, he and the attorney separated company.

Still believing he could probably handle it in pro per, Mahler wrestled with the obvious risks. He hated being locked up and set his goals high: to be exonerated and released back to full freedom. Mahler understood that the main impediments would be testimony from Donnie Van Develde and Karl Norvik. Convinced that his skills at cross-examination would easily make them out to be liars, Mahler thought long and hard about tactical problems. He wanted to take the gamble; but at the end of the day, he went shopping again. Hoping for an expert defender at a moderate price, he screened a long list of candidates for replacement. At last, Mahler settled on a middle-aged defense attorney headquartered in Downey, ten miles southeast of downtown Los Angeles.

Lawrence "Larry" Young had earned his law degree at the

University of Southern California (USC), which was also the alma mater of Ron Bowers. As the head of his private law firm, Young took on a large variety of cases, from capital murder to domestic violence.

Affable, courteous, and obviously intelligent, Young avoided the garish image of some defense attorneys who dress in expensive, tailored, monogrammed shirts, Italian silk ties, off-the-rack Bottega Veneta suits, and Manolo Blahnik shoes. Many of them pull their long hair into ponytails. Young preferred the comfortable look of slacks, a blazer, and sometimes a pair of brown boots. He kept his thinning, sandy hair closely trimmed.

Young had achieved numerous successes in court. In 2003, he had won a verdict of not guilty for a young man accused of second-degree murder and vehicular manslaughter in a street-racing incident. Young said, "I was pleased at the jury's decision because the Norwalk courthouse has a national reputation for having some of the toughest prosecutors and the toughest juries."

Other victories included:

- Exoneration of a Long Beach defendant accused of kidnapping and forcible rape. He broke down in tears when the jury found him not guilty.
- A verdict of not guilty for a man charged with the attempted killing of two LAPD officers
- After two trials with hung juries in a capital punishment case, convincing a prosecutor to accept a manslaughter plea
- A verdict of not guilty for an ex-felon accused of attempted murder

Journalist Jeanne Gallagher wrote an article praising Young for *representing one of America's Ten Most Wanted, numerous shooting and murder cases, and a controversial patricide case.*

"Sometimes it is easy for the general public to wonder how defense attorneys can fight for someone accused of a savage crime. The majority of accused killers are found guilty. So, are these defense attorneys heartless professionals interested only in the money?

A notable public defender once explained it. She said, "We truly believe that everyone accused of a crime is innocent, unless proven guilty by the evidence. And some of them truly are innocent. We can't make that distinction in advance. One of the cornerstones of our democracy is the assumption of innocence and the right to a trial by jury. If attorneys failed to step forward and defend people accused of crimes, there would be nothing but kangaroo courts in our nation. If you were facing a trial for something you did not do, despite public opinion and some faulty evidence, wouldn't you want a good defense attorney?"

While Larry Young felt justly proud of his accomplishments in the courtroom, he took much greater delight in speaking about his personal efforts in aiding homeless and hungry people. He was instrumental in founding an organization called the Adams Harbor Food Kitchen for the purpose of feeding and clothing needy, disenfranchised street wanderers. Young's generosity, along with a band of other Good Samaritans, set up a kitchen and dining room at St. John's Episcopal Cathedral in Los Angeles.

Young reportedly kept the kitchen alive, even when funding diminished, by providing nearly 90 percent of the costs over a period of fifteen years. Young proudly said, "This has been the most enriching and one of the major challenging experiences in my life. . . . It is my fervent wish that it continues to receive the support it so desperately needs."

As a person deeply concerned about social problems, Young actively worked to end gang warfare. He spoke about the death of a young man who had been killed near the Adams food bank and pantry. "I have heard it all. . . . I have seen it all . . . more bodies in the last five years than in my entire lifetime. What has happened to our young people causing them to run in packs like wolves and cowardly kill from a speeding car, justifying the act with inane reasons? They rationalize, 'He was in our territory. He disrespected us. He belonged to a rival gang.' The urban violence hit close to home when Miguel was cut down. Another young life lost to senseless violence. . . ."

Compassionate and driven by a deep morality, Larry Young accepted the challenge of defending David Mahler. From what he could see by the evidence available, it certainly appeared that Mahler had been influenced by drugs, alcohol, and a severe mental disorder.

Working feverishly as the trial approached, on schedule for August 2009, Larry Young began the process of building a powerful strategy.

One option would be to let David Mahler tell the jury that a man named Edmund had been roughing up the victim and Donnie Mahler had left the premises. But the jury might give more weight to the eyewitness statements from Donnie Van Develde and Karl Norvik. And most defense attorneys are absolutely against letting their clients take the witness stand, since it opens a volatile Pandora's box of problems in cross-examination.

Another possibility could center on Mahler's original assertions that Kristin Baldwin had attacked him with a knife; thus he had acted in self-defense. However, her diminutive stature and the absence of any history of violence on her part could sink this defense right into a vortex of quicksand.

The issue of Mahler's hinting, in the long interview with detectives, that he might know where the body had been dumped created more problems. The "hearsay" protection he had tried to create would probably be no stronger than wet newspaper.

Even though Mahler would doubtlessly resist a defense of admitting the shooting, and rationalizing that it happened while he was under the influence of drugs and liquor—this looked like the most feasible strategy. Young could even bring in a psychiatrist to testify that Mahler suffered bipolar disorder and could not control his angry impulses. This could eradicate the element of malice, which is required for a murder conviction. The act of playing Russian roulette with no real intent to kill might very well convince a jury to deliver a verdict of involuntary manslaughter, which would allow Mahler to serve a relatively short prison sentence. Young knew that his client passionately wanted immediate release and freedom, so it might be a hard sell to obtain his agreement to this plan.

Larry Young met frequently with Mahler to work out a mutually agreeable solution.

David Mahler's trial would be held on the ninth floor of the Clara Shortridge Foltz Criminal Justice Center in downtown Los Angeles. On that same floor, a long list of notorious defendants had faced judges and juries. This included Phil Spector, O.J. Simpson, "Nightstalker" Richard Ramirez, the slayers of Dr. Haing Ngor, in the infamous *Killing Fields* case, and many others.

Department 102, at one end of the ninth-floor hall, was the domain of Superior Court Judge David S. Wesley. Highly respected as one of the most energetic, hardworking people ever to wear the black robes, Wesley had presided over Bobby Grace's prosecution of the elderly Golay and Rutterschmidt, plus several other trials.

Expressing his esteem for the judge, Grace said, "He's

very collegial with the attorneys who come in the courtroom. He often shares stories of when he was in practice, and can be very funny. But when he's in trial, he's all business and very much in charge."

In contrast with the severe facial countenance worn by some judges, Wesley's expression appeared relaxed. Even during stressful moments in a trial, he could break into a grin. With light brown hair parted neatly on the left and angling down over the right side of his forehead, and blue eyes highlighting an unlined face, he looked much younger than his sixty-one years. His six-foot stature gave the appearance of an athlete who regularly worked out.

A Los Angeles native, Wesley labored as a youngster at his father's butcher shop in the western side of the city on Fairfax Avenue. Asked about the salary, Wesley smiled and replied, "I was working for my dad. I didn't expect to be paid." Graduation from Alexander Hamilton High School in 1964 put him on an alumni list with other legal eagles, including Robert Shapiro, one of O.J. Simpson's defenders in the notorious murder trial, and William Ginsburg, who represented Monica Lewinsky during the investigation of her relationship with President Bill Clinton. Sportscaster Al Michaels took his diploma there in 1961.

Wesley attended California State University, Northridge (CSUN), for one year and decided to join the U.S Marine Corps Reserve with a few of his childhood pals. Following that stint, he worked for a while in the finance industry before returning to CSUN to earn a degree in political science. His Juris Doctor came in 1972 from Southwestern Law School, about three miles west of his future office in the downtown courthouse.

After easily passing the bar exam, Wesley interviewed with the district attorney's office and with the public defender. Greater freedom in decision making, he explained, guided his choice to do defense work. After nine years of representing

accused killers—many of them in death penalty cases—
Wesley and three buddies formed their own private law firm.
With higher income, he treated himself to a brand-new 1982
Porsche 928, and he still owns it today.

In addition to courtroom defense work, Wesley volunteered with the Los Angeles County Superior Court as a
juvenile referee. In this role, he counseled young people in
trouble. "I loved it," said Wesley. He wanted to steer youthful
offenders in the right direction "before they got entrenched
in crime."

Following several more years of defense work with his firm,
and a period of time as an independent lawyer, he changed directions in 1993 and became a state bar court hearing judge. In
1995, the superior court made an offer he couldn't refuse, to
become a court commissioner. Two years later, Governor Pete
Wilson appointed him as a full-fledged judge.

It didn't take long for Wesley's colleagues to perceive his
amazing skills. In addition to a reputation for an encyclopedic
understanding of the law, Wesley earned praise as an effective
manager. Litigators in his court understood the necessity of
avoiding unnecessary delays. One defense attorney said, "He
puts in enormous hours. And when you go into his court, be
prepared, because I guarantee he is."

Bobby Grace agreed. "You want to be on top of your game
when you are in front of him."

Fairness became a major hallmark in Judge Wesley's style.
Another colleague complimented him for his consideration
of not only lawyers, but defendants as well. "He treats everyone with dignity."

Apparently blessed with infinite energy, Wesley also
could find time for another important activity. At least twice
each month, he showed up at Dorsey High School in West
L.A. to preside over a teen court program. Instead of being
turned over to the juvenile justice system, students charged
with minor offenses face a jury of their peers after school.

Wesley's remarkable guidance caused the program to expand to nineteen schools.

Judge David Wesley, prosecutor Bobby Grace, defense attorney Larry Young, and dozens of staff supporters worked long hours in preparation for a trial scheduled to begin in the last week of August 2009. It promised to be a colorful drama, with an amazing cast—and no predictable outcome.

CHAPTER 30

"WE GOT TO GET THIS BITCH OUT OF HERE"

The opening act in a trial is selection of the jury. Each side, the prosecution and the defense, forms certain goals about what types of people they would ideally like to retain. By questioning (voir dire) each candidate, from a pool (the venire) often exceeding a hundred mostly unhappy people, the attorneys and oftentimes the judge gradually whittle the crowd down. Each side is allotted a certain number of peremptory challenges in which no explanation is necessary for excusing the individual. Other candidates are eliminated through "for cause" reasons.

In a death penalty case, the voir dire is far more complex in order to unveil biases or religious and moral viewpoints held by the candidates. In the case of *The People* v. *David Mahler,* this did not apply since the DA had chosen not to seek capital punishment.

It can be a long, tedious, boring process, but sometimes

quite entertaining to hear the various excuses people come up with, trying to get out of serving.

On the morning of Wednesday, August 26, 2009, the final day of jury selection for the Mahler case, the pool had grown dangerously small, threatening the possibility of Judge Wesley ordering another herd to be brought up from the crowded jury assembly point on the fifth floor. Defendant Mahler, wearing a light tan suit, white shirt with no tie, white socks, and jail-issued slippers, watched with acute interest at the selection of people who would hold his future in their hands.

One woman being questioned said, "I can't judge anyone due to my Catholic religion." Wesley responded by pointing out that the Catholic religion does not preclude jury service. Still, he allowed her to be excused. Another woman told of someone firing a gun at her and how it had made her permanently terrified of firearms. A venireman could be seen playing with a handheld computer game during the voir dire. When his turn came, he announced that he might not follow the law, which the judge would explain, and added, "I think the defense attorney seems shady from the objections he has been making."

Larry Young, justifiably distressed, asked for specifics, but the candidate could not name any. Observers concluded the man just wanted out of there.

Young's questioning had certainly been fair and reasonable, while also giving hints of the strategy he planned to employ. Many of his queries centered on understanding and experience with bipolar disorder.

Among the crowded gallery, seated on thin blue pads that did nothing to make three rows of hard-back benches any more comfortable, Jennifer Gootsan observed in fascination. Her friend Robin Henson waited out in the hall with other scheduled witnesses. At one point, David Mahler, seated at the defense table, turned around and appeared to glare at her, even though the two had never met.

* * *

Finally, at 2:20 P.M., seven men and five women, along with three alternate jurors, were sworn in. Only three candidates remained in the selection pool.

Judge Wesley turned to the prosecution table and asked, "Mr. Grace, are you ready with your opening statements?"

"I am, Your Honor," Bobby Grace replied. Impeccably dressed in a navy blue suit with a red patterned tie, he rose and approached an invisible mark on the floor about one yard from the jury box. He had long ago learned not to invade the so-called comfort zone of those twelve people. Studies have shown that jurors dislike attorneys standing too close to them, especially during delivery of passionate argument. Grace also avoided using the lectern as a protective shield, preferring to give the listeners an impression of openness with nothing to hide. Instead, he moved adroitly around, often with at least one hand in his pocket, sometimes both. Using no notes, but referring periodically to PowerPoint images on a large screen across the room, Grace spoke in a soft voice, sometimes inaudible to the gallery's back row. Jurors, though, had no trouble hearing him.

During the next half hour, he outlined what he expected the evidence to show. He spoke of the events in David Mahler's bedroom in the early-morning hours of Sunday, May 27, 2007. Witnesses, Bobby said, would testify about Mahler's behavior, his loading a single bullet into a revolver, aiming it at the heads of Kristin Baldwin and Donnie Van Develde, and finally pulling the trigger and ending Kristin's life. The defendant, Grace said, had been interviewed by detectives, who would testify about his statements.

Vickie Bynum sat at the prosecution table, as she would for the entire trial. She wore a white blouse with blue pinstripes covered by a rust-colored suede jacket and black pants. Few observers could guess that this lovely woman, with her collar-length blond hair, glasses, and a pleasant, sweet look on her face, was a veteran homicide detective.

Mahler seemed transfixed on the screen images, which included several photos of Kristin, some as a child, the Cole Crest house, his Jaguars, and a mug shot of himself. With glasses shoved up to rest on his forehead, he glowered and kept a fist lodged against his mouth.

Jurors and several people in the gallery gasped when horrific photos of Kristin's body, lying under the edge of a bridge in the desert, appeared on the big screen. Jennifer put her hands to her face and lowered her head, trembling and trying not to cry aloud.

At four ten in the afternoon, Grace concluded his gripping presentation and sat down.

Larry Young stated he would reserve opening statements until ready to present the defense's case.

Judge Wesley nodded, and gave Bobby Grace the signal to call his first witness.

Robin Henson walked into the room. She wore a long-sleeved white blouse, with large hoop earrings showing under her shoulder-length, left-parted dark hair. To Bobby Grace's questions, she told the jury of her sister's blue dolphin tattoo, gold watch, ear piercings, and an anklet. Several of these items appeared on the screen, informing jurors that they had been found on the body. Robin, obviously struggling to hold back the tears while dabbing at her eyes with a tissue, identified the watch found on Kristin's wrist. Everyone in the room had seen the contrast of glinting gold against the dark leathery arm that protruded from under the desert bridge.

As Robin stepped down from the stand after only five minutes, Jennifer rose from the gallery bench and joined her to leave the courtroom. Mahler twisted around in his chair to watch them walk out together.

Witness number two, Monique Wood, an assistant officer manager from the Island Hotel in Newport Beach, answered Grace's questions and verified documents showing Mahler's stay there, with a female guest, on May 24, 2007, under the name "Goldberg." He had checked in at 12:30 A.M. and had checked out twenty-four hours later. The witness's testimony lasted only sixteen minutes.

A long day in court came to a close, and Judge Wesley instructed everyone to return the following morning.

Jonathon Thompson, security officer for the same hotel, seated his substantial frame in the witness chair at nine forty, Thursday morning. Holding his mouth in a tight grimace as if unhappy to be testifying, Thompson said that he had provided a compact disc of security camera images to detectives. Bobby Grace had the CD projected for jurors to see. Even though a bit grainy, the sequence depicted Mahler and Kristin at the check-in counter, along with a heavyset, balding man wearing a Hawaiian aloha shirt. No sound accompanied the action.

Grace asked, "Is the woman that appears in the right part of the screen known to you?" Thompson said yes, that it was Monique Wood, the previous witness. This established that Wood had, indeed, seen Mahler and Kristin checking in.

"On that date," Grace inquired, "did you have contact with the other woman depicted on the video footage?" He referred to Kristin.

Thompson said he had seen her in the lobby at around eleven thirty that night. "When I first saw her, she was charging her cell phone. Her luggage was outside in our valet parking area. I would say around twelve thirty in the morning she left in a taxicab."

Defender Larry Young had no cross-examination questions for any of the first three witnesses.

* * *

George Goldberg came next on the stand, wearing a gray T-shirt and black short pants. He didn't appear very thrilled with being subpoenaed.

Bobby Grace opened with, "Mr. Goldberg, do you know the defendant in this case, Mr. David Mahler?"

"Yes." He pointed toward the defense table and said, "He's at the end of the bench right there in a tan suit, with glasses above his eyebrows."

Projecting a photo on the screen of Mahler and Kristin checking in at the Island Hotel, with Goldberg standing next to them, Grace asked the witness if he recognized it. He replied, "It is David and a girl—Kristi, I think her name was." He spoke of having talked to Mahler frequently by phone, including a conversation prior to the hotel meeting. They had met at another hotel in Newport a few hours before driving over to the Island Hotel. The entire session had been to discuss a business investment. "I was his broker. He opened a trading account with me. He also did some, you know—wrote some legal work for me."

"When you got to the Island Hotel with them, was it your plan to stay there overnight?"

"No. I live there locally in town. I had a certificate for a free night that I told David I would give to him. I checked in under my name, but he used the room."

"Approximately how long did you remain at the hotel with David Mahler and Kristi?"

"I would say maybe a half hour. Checked in, went up to the room and then sat and talked for fifteen or twenty minutes. Then I left." Goldberg said he had not consumed any alcohol, nor had he seen David or Kristi drink any.

Grace wanted to know if Mahler had been temperamental, aggressive, or belligerent. Goldberg replied, "He wasn't argumentative. He tried to get an upgrade on the room, you know, nothing unusual—like anyone else might have asked for. He was just trying to get the clerk to give him a better room, but he kept on going, going, going. I don't think he was argumentative or contentious, as you say, but you know, he was working her pretty hard to get an upgraded room."

"Did you have any contact with Mahler after you left there?"

"He called me—I think two or three times the next day, which was not unusual for him to do, because he was checking the market and business things."

"At some point in time, did you have a conversation with him over the phone about Kristi?"

"Yeah, he said he liked her a lot." Pushing the point, Grace wanted to know about any additional comments from Mahler about the victim. Hesitating as if reluctant to say anything negative about his friend and business colleague, Goldberg muttered, "He asked me if I knew anybody who could give her a ride back to Calabasas. I told him I would find out and call him back."

Urged to elaborate, Goldberg said, "He wanted to not . . . She wanted—I guess, to go home. And he didn't want to pay for a limo or . . . it was too expensive. I'm not sure. But he asked me if I, you know, if I knew anybody who could give her a ride."

Grace glanced through a thick police report, which had been prepared after detectives interviewed Goldberg. With the judge's permission, he handed a few selected pages to the witness and asked him to read to himself. When Goldberg looked up, Grace asked, "Now, did that refresh your memory about what David Mahler said to you on that second phone conversation?"

"Yes."

"What do you now remember him saying about Kristi?"

Still exhibiting reluctance, Goldberg fidgeted and replied, "Well, I remember he was a little angered or upset that she wanted to go home and . . . you know, he wanted her to leave. Do you want me to state exactly what he said?"

"Yes, I need you to say it exactly."

"He may have said that, you know, he wanted to get the bitch out of there. He says, 'We got to get this bitch out of here. I don't want to pay for a cab or a limo. . . .'"

"Did you have any more contact with the defendant concerning business after that day?"

Goldberg mentioned a vague recollection of Mahler inviting him to go for dinner, but couldn't say exactly when that call took place.

For the first time, Larry Young rose to conduct cross-examination. His initial questions focused on the business relationship between George Goldberg and David Mahler, perhaps to establish an image in the jurors' minds of his client's serious professionalism, as opposed to a temperamental scoundrel who would abandon a trusting woman in a hotel.

Moving on to Kristin, Young asked Goldberg's impression of her. The witness said, "Well, I had . . . She was fun, you know. She was bubbly and, you know, we talked, had good conversation, and joked. She had lived in Orange County and had worked there a little bit as a waitress. She was entertaining."

"When you saw them together, then, initially they seemed to be getting along really fine? Is that right?"

"Absolutely."

"Did he ever tell you that he loved her?"

"Yes."

"And then later on, did he tell you that he hated her?"

"Yeah."

"So this is flip-flop, flip-flop, flip-flop?"

"Yes."

Observers could see the first seeds being planted by Young

portraying Mahler as suffering from bipolar disorder. "By the way, did you know whether or not he used drugs?"

"Yes, I think he liked cocaine."

The word "think" brought Bobby Grace to his feet. "Your Honor, I'm going to object unless the witness has personal knowledge."

Judge Wesley sustained it.

Young rebounded. "How would you have personal knowledge as to whether or not he did illegal drugs?"

Goldberg admitted, "I was with him one night. . . . He had gotten . . . I believe he did some cocaine in front of me. You know, it looked like cocaine."

The ambiguity gave Grace another wedge. "I'm going to object again, unless the witness has some special knowledge." Wesley overruled him this time.

Young wanted jurors to have no doubt. "When you say he did some cocaine, in what manner was it taken?"

"Snorted through the nose."

"And he did that in front of you?"

"Yes."

"In your relationship with him, did the fact that at one point he's telling you that he loves the girl, and then hours later he's saying he hates her—did that seem unusual in regard to his usual behavior?"

Goldberg gave a rambling reply, perhaps still unsure if his words could hurt or help his friend. He tacked on, "It seemed to me, they had gotten in some kind of an argument to switch emotions like that."

Young asked, "It did seem rather odd, didn't it?"

"Yes"

On redirect examination, Bobby Grace wanted to know when the cocaine-using incident had happened. George Goldberg replied that it had been approximately a month or six weeks before the hotel incident.

Grace inquired, "Did you continue to do business with the defendant after you saw him snorting cocaine?" The question contained several implications that made Goldberg appear to squirm, but he replied in the affirmative. The prosecutor wanted to know if the drugs seemed to have any effect on Mahler's business efficacy.

"Nothing changed," said the witness. "It didn't seem like anything was different to me."

When both attorneys indicated they were through with the witness, Judge Wesley thanked him and said he was excused. George Goldberg asked, "Can I go home now?"

Suppressing a smile, Wesley said, "Yes, you can."

Bobby Grace and Larry Young had both scored a few points. The defender managed to introduce erratic behavior by his client; while the prosecutor had shown that David Mahler knew what he was doing, even under the influence of drugs.

CHAPTER 31

ROCK STAR IN COURT

Cory Keitz, a former male friend of Kristin and porn star Kitty, settled into the witness chair at ten fifteen in the morning. Bobby Grace asked him about a phone call in the early hours of May 25, 2007, the time when Kristin had been stranded in Newport Beach. Keitz recalled the frantic contact from Kristin and said that he had planned to drive down there from the San Fernando Valley. However, she had called back a short time later to say she had made other arrangements.

Grace asked, "Did you ever see Kristin Baldwin alive again after that?"

Keitz gave a simple one-word answer: "No."

The defense had no questions, and Keitz left after spending less than two minutes as a witness.

Cory Keitz was followed immediately by Jeremy Moudy, one of the Cole Crest tenants. Wearing a horizontal-striped T-shirt and sporting a short, dark beard with mustache, Moudy had no trouble recognizing or identifying the defendant. Asked how long he had lived in the residence, he replied that he had rented a room there for about two years.

Moudy named the people who called Cole Crest home. "Well, there was David, myself, Karl, and either a couple or a gentleman for sure that lived . . . I guess it was in the bottom apartment. I'm not a hundred percent sure about him." Moudy had seen the man, but he couldn't recall his name. He spent several minutes answering Bobby Grace's questions about the layout of the home, allowing jurors to get a better grasp. To help them, Grace's assistant operated the Power-Point show Ron Bowers had developed to provide photos and a diagram of the structure. The witness also described the two Jaguars that David Mahler parked in the garage. One of the cars would become a crucial piece of evidence for the prosecution.

"To your knowledge, what was the defendant's occupation?"

"He was an attorney. And I heard him discussing trading stocks. I think he worked out of the office near his bedroom. I would see him on the computer and assumed he was trading stocks."

Zeroing in on the time frame shortly after the shooting, Grace asked, "Were you at home on June 1, 2007?"

"Yeah, I was, if you are referring to the early morning that the police came to the residence. My girlfriend and I had gone to bed and were awoken early in the morning."

"Okay," Grace replied. "Were you at home on Sunday, May twenty-seventh?"

Moudy explained that he had gone to Bakersfield that weekend. "I didn't come back home until Sunday late afternoon or early evening." Explaining being awakened so early, on Friday, June the first, Moudy said, "I heard somebody at my door, which connects to an interior staircase. I had been asleep and I think it was somewhere between midnight and two o'clock in the morning. I went to the door, opened it, and found David standing there. He said something about the police being at the residence."

"Did he say the police were trying to get in or that he wanted to get out?"

"I think both. There was a short conversation and basically I think he was trying to get into my room so he could exit through that side door. And he was just saying the police were there. At the same time this was going on, I could hear through the intercom system. I could hear the doorbell going off, over and over again."

"Okay, what's the next thing that happened after this short conversation with the defendant?"

"He wanted to get in. And I told him he couldn't. My girlfriend was sleeping. And I don't remember exactly what happened, but I closed the door behind him. And I was heading upstairs to see what was going on or who was at the door, or let the police in. I thought David followed me and went into his own bedroom. And I went all the way upstairs to the front door."

"And was it, in fact, the police?"

"Yes, and I let them come in. They immediately had me sit down on the couch in the living room. I assumed they were searching the house. After a while, they brought David up the interior stairs to the living room."

Grace asked, "When you got home from your trip to Bakersfield, did you notice anything unusual inside the house?"

"I don't know exactly when I noticed it—but at some point in time, I saw what appeared to be red stains in the living room. And then later I found some more—a droplet or another red stain in the garage, close to the washing machine."

"Did your girlfriend live there with you?"

"No, but she was there with me sometimes."

* * *

On his cross-examination, Larry Young wanted to know if Jeremy Moudy had a "close relationship" with David Mahler. No, the witness said, he could not classify it as a close relationship. "In your contacts with him, were there times when he seemed to have a . . . what you might call a volatile temperament?"

Moudy thought about it for a moment, and said, "There were times I would hear him yelling. Yes. I don't know I'd classify it as 'volatile.' But there have been times that I have heard him yelling either in his office or arguing with someone over the phone."

The answer seemed to please Young and he turned the witness back over to Bobby Grace.

The prosecutor said, "You stated that you would not classify his temperament as volatile. Did he appear to be a guy that was angry all the time?"

"I would not say 'all the time.'"

"Did he seem unusually forceful?"

"I would say he could be very persuasive."

"Did he get upset with you or any other tenants about late rent payments or that kind of thing?"

"With me, he was always—I was late a couple of times. He was always willing to work with me. He never really got upset at me, that I recall."

Bobby Grace sat down, and Larry Young immediately leaped up. "Did you hesitate a little on that question about him being angry all the time? Were there times when you saw him in an angry state?"

Moudy repeated his assertion of hearing Mahler sounding upset during telephone conversations.

Young asked, "Have you ever seen him drunk?"

"I saw him drink wine a few times and assumed he was intoxicated. When I would be going to my room through the stairwell, and his door was open, he would sometimes have a bottle open on the nightstand next to his bed."

"The times you saw him screaming, did you have any idea of what the context of that situation was?"

"Sometimes he was trading stocks—and, I guess, they weren't going very well—so he would, you know, be yelling because I guess he was losing money. And there were a couple of times we had conversations about 'Oh, I lost X amount of dollars,' or something like that. And other times I would hear him yelling or arguing with someone in a different level in the house."

Young, perhaps a little disappointed, had no more questions. Grace agreed the witness could step down.

At 11:35 A.M., jurors and observers watched with interest as Donnie Van Develde entered the courtroom. In Bobby Grace's opening statements, he had given hints that Donnie would be a key witness.

Wearing faded jeans and a dark T-shirt, Van Develde appeared nervous and edgy from the outset. His unkempt dark blond hair reached just below his shoulders, with hanging tendrils that looked unwashed. Two rings on the fingers of his right hand and three on the left provided eye-catching decoration. Both arms bore garish tattoos. Quite slim, he bounded into the room like a sailor walking the deck on a stormy sea.

In the witness chair, Donnie never seemed to make contact with the seat. He glanced everywhere—except at David Mahler, who stared at him with laserlike malevolence.

Bobby Grace opened by asking Donnie about his profession. In a loud, clear voice, he said, "I am a rock music star." He certainly looked the part. Explaining his background, Donnie spoke of having some good years and some bad ones. Recently, though, he had reestablished his band and claimed to have a new recording contract and numerous play dates.

It apparently aggravated the witness's frayed nerves when Grace asked if he knew David Mahler. Yes, he said, and commented that he and his wife had lived in the same house as the defendant. It unnerved him even more when Grace asked Van Develde if he could see Mahler in the room. Forcing his eyes to meet Mahler's, Van Develde made the requested identification.

Quickly breaking the visual contact, Donnie answered the prosecutor's questions in rapid-fire words, with incomplete sentences and overlapping subject matter. Judge Wesley interrupted several times to caution the witness. "Please listen carefully to each question and do your best to answer it without extra commentary." Donnie nodded his head in agreement, and then continued to give replies that overflowed with too much information.

Describing the residence on Cole Crest, Van Develde informed the jury that he had lived in the bottom apartment, down the hill, accessible primarily by an exterior fifty-four-step stairway. All of the apartments, he said, were connected by an interior stairwell, too, but the one into his unit had been blocked off.

"What was your relationship with Mahler?"

"Well, we had a landlord-and-tenant relationship, and also in the last few months before all of this happened, we had sort of established somewhat of a friendship."

"And when he wanted to speak to you, how would he contact you?"

"By telephone—either he would call me if he wanted me to come up with something, or I would just come up the stairs and ring the front doorbell and he would buzz me in. I didn't have a key to the front gate." Donnie described Mahler's two Jaguars and the garage interior, where they were usually parked.

* * *

After a ninety-minute lunch break, Donnie Van Develde resumed his testimony in the afternoon, at one forty-five, with the gallery nearly full of expectant observers.

Bringing the witness's attention to May 27, 2007, Bobby Grace said, "Okay, now I want to ask you some questions about what happened at that time. Do you remember going up to the defendant's bedroom?"

"Yes."

"Tell us about that. Why did you go up there?"

"I had been waiting for him to come home before—my wife went out on vacation . . . went back to her hometown, like a few days. So I worked out an arrangement with David to do a few little repairs around the house to make a few extra bucks, and I was waiting for him to give me a couple of hundred dollars he agreed to pay me. And I guess he went somewhere for a few days, or whatever. And I was waiting for him to come back and give me the money. He came home, and I think he called me about five thirty in the morning. So I went upstairs to get my money."

"What happened when you got up there?"

"Somebody hit the buzzer to open the gate and let me in. I go to this bedroom, but he wasn't there."

"Who was there?"

"The girl named Kristi was in there all alone, sitting in a chair."

"Had you ever met her prior to that date?"

"Yes, three or four times."

"Did the defendant come into that room?"

"After Kristi and I had a brief conversation, he came in. He was really very angry about something and asked me if I would go back down to my apartment for a while, because he had something to talk about with her."

Bobby Grace leaned over the prosecutor's table, checking some notes before proceeding. He wanted to be certain not to omit anything essential. Donnie's stories, as told during the interview with Detectives Bynum and Small, and in the preliminary hearing, seemed to vary somewhat. Grace needed to elicit from him the clearest possible narrative about crucial events leading up to the shooting of Kristin Baldwin. He asked, "Did the defendant tell you what he was angry about?"

Still agitated and constantly shifting his weight in the chair, Van Develde replied, "I didn't really . . . couldn't make out too much of the conversation. I just know he was very upset, and something had happened, and I guess that upset him and he wanted to—needed to—discuss it with her."

"How was he dressed at the time?"

"He was wearing regular street clothes." Donnie told of leaving the room, descending to his apartment, and waiting for maybe fifteen or twenty minutes. "He called me again and said he was through talking to her and for me to come back up there."

Van Develde said that he ascended the lengthy exterior stairs, and was buzzed in.

"When you arrived, what was David wearing?"

"He had a white bathrobe on. It wasn't tied or anything, and was open, and he didn't have anything else on."

"Where was Kristi at that point?"

"She was sitting on the floor, Indian style, right in front of the fireplace." Asked what she was doing, Donnie said, "She was going through her bags and looked like she was crying."

"Can you tell us about the defendant's behavior?"

"He was walking around, with his bathrobe open, talking a bunch of gibberish and ranting nonsense. It seemed like he was out of his mind. . . ."

Defender Larry Young could be seen rapidly entering notes on lined yellow paper.

". . . He was like hot and cold. One minute he was joking

and being friendly, and then in another minute, he was upset and it just . . . it was very weird."

Bobby Grace asked if Donnie had noticed Mahler drinking. The witness turned vague about this, said he wasn't certain, but David might have been consuming some wine.

"You said he was ranting. Could you be more specific about what he said?"

"I couldn't tell what he was really angry about. I don't think . . . It seemed to me that he didn't know what he was angry about. He would just get fired up, and then chill out, and then get hot again."

"Did you see a gun?"

Speaking even more rapidly, Van Develde told of seeing Mahler disappear into a closet and return with a revolver in his hand. The witness said he had seen it a couple of weeks earlier when Mahler had shown it to him.

Asked what happened next, Donnie said Mahler had pointed it at Kristi and pulled the trigger. It clicked, and Mahler did it again.

Now perspiring and twisting with even more animation, Donnie told of being rattled by Mahler's display of the handgun and pointing it at Kristi's face. "One time he kind of ran up at her and, as I said, he was like—like hot and cold. He was going at her and yelling at her, and then backing off and laying down on the bed. And then going back, and when he had the gun, one time he ran toward her and, like, almost up to her."

Mahler, he said, somehow came up with a single bullet, loaded it into the cylinder, and pulled the trigger again. "I didn't actually see him go to any specific place to get the bullet. Just one minute, there was no bullet, and the next minute, he had one."

"Then what happened?"

"He was arguing a bunch of gibberish again, running hot and cold. He would argue with her, and then he set the gun down on the bed. That's when I went to pick it up, because I wanted to see if I could throw it or hide it or something like that. And he grabbed my hand and stopped me from getting it. He picked it up again and was just holding it." Donnie waved his hand around in circles and thrust it forward, as if demonstrating Mahler's threatening gestures with the weapon.

Grace said, "You are making motions. For the record, is that how he was waving the gun around?"

"Yes, and he was talking, like spurting out comments and more—more of whatever he was upset about toward Kristi and things about life in general or whatever. I couldn't tell you exactly."

In his previous reports to the police, and at the preliminary hearing, Donnie Van Develde had said that Mahler also pointed the loaded weapon at him and clicked it. But to several questions from Bobby Grace about that, Donnie's memory failed him.

To be certain the jury knew of the previous version, Grace asked Van Develde if he remembered testifying at the preliminary hearing that Mahler had pointed the gun at his face. Donnie said he might have misunderstood the question at the prelim. Trying once more, the prosecutor asked, "Did he click it at you?"

Donnie couldn't recall. However, the nervous witness did add a new element. "He seemed to settle down and chill out for a while."

"What made you think he was chilled out?"

"He made some comment, something to the effect of some sort of sexual thing that he was . . . he had in mind."

"For Kristi?" Yes. "Do you remember what the comment was?"

Donnie, seemingly embarrassed, muttered, "Something to the effect of a threesome."

"What did you do?"

"I said no. No, thank you. I am a married man and I wasn't interested in that." Afterward, said Donnie, he decided to leave. "I had enough of the whole situation."

"Were you scared?"

"No, not really. I had just had enough."

"And what happened when you left?"

"As I went to shut the door, I heard the gun shoot. I heard the bang of a gun firing."

Jurors and spectators alike sat frozen in their chairs or on the bench, gripped by the dramatic climax, as if they had all heard the deadly explosion. No movie plot could equal the impact of this real-life pivotal moment.

"What did you do?"

"I kept going and went to my apartment."

Another memory issue came up when Grace asked Van Develde, "Do you remember telling detectives that Mahler said to you, 'I am so pissed off I could kill someone'?"

Hesitating and glancing around with apparent fear, the witness replied that Mahler may have said something to that effect, but he couldn't be positive.

According to Donnie, he had left the bedroom after hearing what sounded like a gunshot, returned to his room, and tried to think of what he should do next. Mahler, he said, tried to call him five or six times, but Donnie refused to answer. "I didn't feel like dealing with it anymore." Eventually, though, he changed his mind and accepted the call. Mahler had started talking about Kristi coming at him with a knife, so he had been forced to protect himself. Also, Mahler said he had left the house and was with a buddy who would help him.

Grace attacked the theory of self-defense by asking Donnie if he had seen any sign of a knife in the room, or in the possession of Kristin. He answered in the negative.

Through more interrogation, Donnie told of going back upstairs about forty-five minutes later. Mahler was nowhere to be seen. By climbing through a garage window, he gained entry and also noticed that one of the Jaguars was missing. Donnie went to the master bedroom door, looked inside, and saw a bedspread on the floor with Kristin's hand, palm up, extending from underneath. Only then did he believe that Mahler had actually shot her. "Then I hightailed it out of there and went downstairs to my apartment and started kind of freaking out a bit."

With an admission of not calling the police, Van Develde explained, "Partly because he was my friend, and because I would be afraid, you know, of him doing something. If he shot her, he might shoot me or my wife."

On his cross-examination, Larry Young worked to place the emphasis on David Mahler's angry, erratic, illogical behavior. In several forms of the question, he asked what David was like that morning. Donnie Van Develde provided exactly the answer the defender sought. "He was out of his mind."

Through his questions, Young stressed the "hot and cold" conduct Donnie had repeatedly mentioned. Observers understood the direct implications of bipolar disorder. Young also inquired about Mahler's drug and alcohol usage, as witnessed by Van Develde.

During a whispered sidebar conference between the judge and the lawyers, Donnie could be seen risking a glance at the defendant. The two men locked eyes for a few moments, and it seemed to generate a charge of electricity in the room.

The cross-examination by Young, brief redirect questions from Bobby, and a final recross by Young consumed the remainder of the day. Young said he still needed to ask the witness a few more questions. Donnie Van Develde slumped when ordered by the judge to make himself available for more testimony on the next day.

Judge Wesley advised jurors not to discuss the case with anyone and to avoid television or newspaper accounts of the trial, ordered them to return at nine the next morning, and bid them a good evening.

Later discussing the trial testimony of witness Donnie Van Develde, Bobby Grace expressed disappointment, especially with the alleged loss of memory about David Mahler pointing the gun at him. Grace recalled, "Probably about ten or fifteen percent of what he said on the stand was usable. On any given day, Donnie would tell you a different version of how this all happened, and, more critically, he would change his story about what happened when Mahler produced that gun—when he first showed it, when he put the bullet in and pointed it at both Donnie and the victim. I think we got enough out of him that the jury understood. For example, only one shot. Also, it made sense to me, in one of Donnie's versions, that the reason he left the bedroom was because Mahler had at least once pointed the gun toward him."

CHAPTER 32

"IN THIS INDUSTRY, NOTHING IS SURPRISING"

Friday dawned with a thick haze of smoke hovering over the entire Los Angeles Basin. The largest fire in the county's history had been started, probably by an arsonist, two days earlier in foothills above the La Cañada Flintridge community, about ten miles north of the courthouse. Voracious flames rapidly climbed into mountains of the Angeles National Forest and grew into a major conflagration. It would destroy more than two hundred homes, blacken over 250 square miles, and kill two firefighters. Countless wild animals lost their lives. A metal forest of television towers atop Mt. Wilson would also be in serious danger. Fire departments from dozens of cities would take six weeks to completely extinguish the blaze, at a cost to taxpayers approaching $100 million.

Jurors, lawyers, and court watchers filing into the courthouse buzzed endlessly about the dangers and the tragic losses. Flames and smoke could be seen from vantage points on the ninth floor.

Prospective witnesses who seated themselves on benches outside the entry to Judge Wesley's courtroom included Donnie Van Develde and Karl Norvik. Because witnesses who had traveled a long distance took priority, neither of the two men would be called on this day. They would be required to show up again on the following Tuesday, since no session was scheduled for Monday.

The judge seated himself shortly after nine o'clock, scanned the jury box to make certain all were present, and, without wasting a moment, told Bobby Grace to call his next witness. The prosecutor summoned Marie Means Dionne, Kristin's mother. A picture of her on the large screen appeared for a few minutes before being replaced by a smiling photo of her daughter. In Marie's mind, Kristin might have been wishing her a happy birthday, which would come on Saturday.

Marie's experience as a witness lasted only three minutes. Grace first asked her to identify the projected photo of Kristin, and then confirmed that a sample swab had been taken from Marie's mouth for DNA analysis. It had been used to establish a link between the victim and bloodstains found inside the Cole Crest house.

Larry Young wisely and compassionately chose not to cross-examine.

Detective Christopher Fisher, from the San Bernardino County Sheriff's Office, came next. A stoutly built man, with dark hair trimmed into a flat top and downward-sloping shoulders of an athlete, Fisher spoke in a deep, slightly hoarse voice.

With a photo displayed on the screen of the desert site where Kristin's body had been discovered, the detective, now a sergeant, told of responding to the scene on June 16, 2007. Pointing to projected maps and photos, he verified the setting. Upon arrival at the crime scene, Fisher said, he saw the pickup truck stuck in sand, but he didn't meet the owner or the two men who had tried to help her. Bobby Grace asked, "From the street level, was it possible to see the body . . . below the bridge?"

"No. You actually had to walk to the edge of the dirt shoulder and look down into the wash area to see the body."

Signaling the PowerPoint operator to change the projected photo, Grace waited until a ghastly picture of Kristin's remains appeared in full color for everyone in the room to see. In the gallery, Robin Henson clasped her hands over her face and bowed, looking toward her knees. Her body shook with sobs.

The prosecutor said, "Showing you what has been marked as People's [Exhibit] sixty-one, Sergeant, does it show a closer view of the victim's body?" Fisher said it did. He briefly described the search for evidence.

In cross-examination Larry Young referred to an aerial photo of the scene. Judge Wesley offered him the use of his laser pointer to make it easier for everyone to understand. Young accepted it. He asked the witness if it would be possible for someone to drive a vehicle in the wash where the remains lay. Sergeant Fisher said it would probably require a four-wheel drive to do so. "Even then, I think it would be very difficult."

Pointing out that the body appeared to be partially under the bridge, Young asked if the detective had any theories about how it got there. Christopher Fisher replied, "My two theories would be that somebody stood at the edge of the roadway and dropped the body straight down. Or someone took the body down to that area."

"Assuming that someone may have taken the body down, did you take any soil samples from around the body? Not where the decomposition is, but the rock and gravel and the type of dirt it is? And did you take any samples of the plant material from around there?"

"We took none of those things."

"Well, shouldn't that have been done in case someone had, in fact, taken that body down there and inadvertently on their shoes or their pants or their clothing picked up some particles of that dirt or some of that plant material?"

Fisher replied in a dry, matter-of-fact tone, "It was my decision. We did not take any soil samples or vegetation samples."

To casual observers, it might appear that Young had revealed an oversight. But most investigators would realize that traces of desert sand on a suspect's shoes or clothing would prove nothing, other than perhaps the individual had been somewhere in the Mojave Desert at some vague time.

Bobby Grace rose to ask questions regarding the point, but he changed his mind. Judge Wesley excused Sergeant Fisher.

The next witness, Minh Tran, walked into the courtroom with the grace and appearance of a fashion model. The black suit she wore minimized her female charms, and no one would have guessed that she had worked for San Bernardino County as a criminalist. Now with the FBI, Tran spoke of the desert heat on June 16 where the body was found. She had spent hours looking for evidence at the crime scene, all unsuccessful.

A nice-looking young man named Rick Stadd replaced her on the stand. He wore a dark suit and styled his hair in a somewhat spiked, modern fashion. A DNA specialist, Stadd worked for a Dallas, Texas, firm. The swabs from the mouth of Kristin's mother and samples of bloodstains from Cole Crest had been submitted to him for analysis.

While Stadd answered questions from Bobby Grace, the big screen showed charts Ron Bowers had prepared. Jurors could see, against a dark blue background, the left column containing photos of the Jaguar trunk, plus five sites inside the Cole Crest house where samples of bloodstains had been

lifted. Below that, on the seventh line, a photo of David
Mahler appeared, and on the bottom were pictures of Kristin
and her mother. Ten columns depicted the various numerical
categories of DNA makeup. Chart number one indicated
strong similarity between the mouth swabs from Marie
Dionne and blood found at Cole Crest. Chart two showed that
all of the bloodstains in the house had come from the same
person, and that they were not from the defendant. A high
mathematical probability indicated that Kristin Baldwin's
blood had stained the carpet, floor, stairs, and the Jaguar.

Larry Young's cross-examination underlined the absence
of positive proof that the blood could not have been left by
anyone else.

During Stadd's testimony, David Mahler had appeared
highly animated in his whispered conversations with Young.
He did not look happy.

When the judge called for a fifteen-minute break, a journalist approaching the men's restroom door overheard Karl
Norvik talking to Donnie Van Develde. Karl, apparently
under considerable stress and perspiring heavily, growled,
"Some choice! Go to prison as an accessory to murder or turn
state's evidence." He laughed raucously and then entered the
restroom, where he spent several minutes at a washbasin
brushing his teeth.

More DNA testimony followed. Faces in the gallery reflected
boredom, confusion, or total incomprehension. Jurors, who at
first seemed to be taking copious notes, soon stopped writing
and watched the screen. Without the graphics, understanding
of the information might have been virtually impossible.

The witness stepped down a few minutes before noon.
Judge Wesley, who had other necessary commitments for
the remainder of the day, excused the jury until Tuesday
morning.

* * *

The fires still raged up in the San Gabriel Mountains on that Tuesday, September 1, 2009. To make matters worse, the late-summer temperatures topped 100 degrees. The courtroom, though, had been air-conditioned to a chilly 70 degrees.

David Mahler was led in by a bailiff, who removed his handcuffs and watched him sit down. An observer noted that Mahler wore the same clothing day after day. His closely trimmed, thinning hair seemed darker than usual, almost a shiny black. Could he have hair dye available in a jail cell? In a whispered conversation, it was speculated that maybe he used black shoe polish.

The gallery gossipers also took notice of the prosecution's table versus the defense attorney's space. Bobby Grace, neatly dressed in a dark pinstripe suit with a red tie, kept his binders and notebooks in meticulous order. In contrast, Larry Young, wearing a gray suit coat with black trousers and a blue shirt, with a multicolored tie, seemed to have trouble with tabletop organization. His notebooks, yellow legal pads, and a variety of assorted paper were scattered across the surface.

To Donnie Van Develde's relief, he finally heard the call to resume his testimony. Larry Young's cross-examination over the next hour concentrated mostly on Donnie's allegation of David Mahler pointing the gun at Kristin Baldwin. He appeared to suggest, through his questions, that his client had been attempting only to scare the woman, and had no intent of harming her.

During one animated sequence, Young charged across the space from his table, moving in the direction of the witness stand, with his hand formed into the image of a pistol. He asked if that's how Mahler had done it, or if it was less aggressive in nature. During most of the session, a picture of

Kristin frowning remained on the screen. Jurors could be seen frequently glancing at it.

At 10:15 A.M., Donnie finally breathed a huge sigh of relief when Judge Wesley said, "You are excused."

In the hallway, a journalist asked Donnie if his real name could be used in a story about the case. He appeared to think about it and replied, "Sure, use my real name. I need the publicity for my music." With that, he hurried toward the elevators.

Karl Norvik would still be required to come back and wait for his turn to testify.

After the break, the next four witnesses completed their testimony in less than an hour.

Anna Marie Nack, with the San Bernardino County Coroner's Department, described how she used the Microsil process to lift prints from Kristin Baldwin's dehydrated fingers. Nack even showed the jury two tubes, resembling over-the-counter ointment containers, which contained the pastelike compound used.

The Cole Crest neighbor whose security video camera captured Mahler's comings and goings late at night, and the long absence during the early morning of May 31, spoke for five minutes. Observers agreed he certainly looked the part of a Hollywood Hills resident, perhaps in his forties, with black hair in a buzz cut, a two-day growth of beard, faded blue jeans, and a long-sleeved black jersey featuring gothic white markings. He said he had installed the cameras about four years before the incident and confirmed giving the contents to LAPD officers.

At Bobby Grace's request, David Grant, director of loss prevention for the LAX Marriott Hotel, examined what he called a guest folio. "It's like a record of guests who stay at the hotel." The folder's contents contained documents related to David Mahler's brief stay there on May 28.

Opening it, Grace asked, "Does it indicate approximately how much money was spent over the time period he was there?"

"Yes, it does. If you look toward the bottom of that form, that's the total amount charged to this customer's credit card."

Grace spoke the question slowly. "Is $3,706.38 correct?"

A gasp could be heard from a spectator, and jurors' eyes seemed to bulge.

Using another PowerPoint slide so everyone could see the amazing bill, Grace asked if the bulk of the charge related to a damaged television set.

Nodding his assent, the witness said, "That's correct, sir."

The remainder of the bill came under scrutiny, showing the room rate at $250, the cost of liquor, and the charges for room service. An additional fee had been tacked on for someone using cigarettes in a nonsmoking room. Grant also explained Mahler's request to be anonymous under the hotel's code blue policy.

Larry Young leaped on the astronomical charges, eager to show it as a demonstration of his client's extreme behavior, typical of bipolar disorder. "What was going on in that room that would have four hundred fourteen dollars of room service in one day and two thousand two hundred dollars' damage? This was not a rock star band in there, was it?"

"Not as far as I know, sir."

"Did you get any reports of someone not in control in that room?"

"No, sir."

"Do you have any knowledge of David Mahler, whether he asks to be anonymous all the time when he goes to hotels?"

"I don't know, sir. I have no knowledge of that."

"Could you tell what he did to that television set?"

"No, sir."

"You don't know if he kicked it, threw a bottle at it, or picked it up and threw it out the window?"

"He could not have thrown it out the window. Our windows are sealed, sir." Even with this explanation, Young had succeeded in implanting an image in the minds of jurors of irrational, violent behavior—a person out of control due to drugs, booze, or a mental disorder.

Young risked putting it into words. "Wouldn't you agree, looking at the entire bill, for one person, that it indicates someone out of control?"

"I wouldn't say 'out of control,' sir."

The answer appeared to catch Young by surprise. He responded, "Well, if you're in control, you're not going to do twenty-two hundred dollars' worth of damage and drink four hundred dollars' worth of alcohol, are you?"

The witness calmly explained that such charges can add up very easily, and the damage to the television set could have been accidental.

Young retorted, "I'm just saying it's rather surprising, isn't it?"

With a wry look on his face, Grant said, "To me, sir, being in this industry, nothing is surprising." The calm, collected witness stepped down at 10:37 A.M.

Then a retired detective from Vermont, Jody Small, no relation to Tom Small, spent five minutes on the stand telling how he had used swabs to collect a DNA sample from Marie Dionne, Kristin's mother, and forwarding them to a DNA lab for analysis.

Insiders familiar with the case had been hoping to hear from Detective Vicki Bynum. She took the oath at 11:05 A.M.

But her testimony would disappoint her observers; she was on the stand for only six minutes.

After identifying David Mahler, Bynum told of the protracted interview she and Tom Small conducted on June 1, 2007. Afterward, she had taken a buccal oral swab sample from the suspect.

Bobby Grace asked, "Can you explain to us exactly what you did?"

Bynum, in the melodious voice her friends had come to know very well, said, "It's very similar to the way Detective Jody Small described—using some swabs that are provided to us through LAPD's supply unit. They are sterilized, basically cotton-tipped swabs, each one with about a five-inch wooden handle. I've been trained to wear gloves when doing this process. So I put on the gloves, brought two swabs that are sealed, removed the paper wrapper, took the swabs out of the plastic containers, and asked Mr. Mahler to open his mouth, which he did. I rubbed one along the left inside of his cheek, and then rubbed the other on the right inside of his cheek. After that, the swabs were placed into a locked, secured evidence area, where they are air-dried. They were later booked by one of my coworkers."

Larry Young approached and asked where the process had taken place. Vicki Bynum said it had been in the Hollywood Station room where they had interviewed him.

"Did he appear to know what you were doing?"

"Yes." She said he had cooperated.

Detective Bynum, having completed the final duty in her twenty-six-month dedication to the David Mahler case, stepped down at 11:11 A.M. She would continue to attend and sit at or near the prosecution table.

* * *

One of the desert Good Samaritans, Robert LaFond, took her place in the witness chair. Perhaps thirty years old, less than six feet tall, with a shaved head, goatee, and mustache, he wore a plaid short-sleeved shirt and jeans.

A photo of LaFond at the desert site where Kristin Baldwin's body had been found appeared on the big screen. Bobby Grace asked, "Is that you?" La Fond said it was.

Answering a series of questions accompanied by color photos on the screen, he took the jury through his and another helper's efforts to assist a woman whose pickup truck had been stuck on the road shoulder. "It was hot that day, so I just pulled over and asked if she needed help." He described his search for rocks or sticks to place under her tires, descending down a slight slope to the wash, and spotting something that immediately caught his attention. "I saw a hand with jewelry or watch, and that kind of gave me an odd feeling. So I glanced over again and saw maybe blondish or brownish hair. And then I ran back and told the other gentleman."

A gruesome picture of Kristin's body appeared on the screen. Sitting in the gallery, Marie Dionne lowered her head and wept silently. Several jurors noticed.

"Were you able to see that from where you were originally on the overpass?"

"No, sir, I wasn't."

Larry Young asked the same question he had put to Detective Christopher Fisher. "Could you drive a vehicle down to that spot?"

"No, sir."

"How did you get down there?"

"I walked. The road has kind of a bend, and they were parked near the curve. It's sandy desert, and if you park on the side of the road, it's really soft. So I walked through the desert, about twenty yards, and that's how I found the body."

"Did it appear that any car had stopped in that—that dirt next to the road?"

"No, only where that lady ran off the road and got stuck. I didn't see no other tracks."

La Fond concluded his testimony at 11:20 A.M.

CHAPTER 33

"AND WHO ORDERED THE PROSTITUTE?"

Judge David Wesley did not allow time to be wasted. Instead of closing down for lunch at 11:25 A.M., he told Bobby Grace to call his next witness.

Karl Norvik had been waiting in the wings since the trial's beginning. The long period of suspense had frayed his nerves even more. Wearing black slacks and a black T-shirt, Norvik raised his visibly trembling hand to be sworn in. He immediately asked for some water and took a long drink.

Having told his story repeatedly, first at an interview with Vicki Bynum and Tom Small, at another interview with Bobby Grace, and at the preliminary hearing, Norvik dreaded going through it all yet again.

Perhaps the most difficult part came early when the prosecutor asked Norvik to look over at David Mahler to identify the man who had asked for help in getting rid of a body. The witness said, "He is the person sitting at the defense table, wearing a tan suit and pin-striped white shirt."

Spectators and jurors took notice of Norvik's ability to speak in crisp, articulate terms using a high-level vocabulary and sounding as if he had probably earned advanced college degrees.

Grace asked, "How long have you known the defendant?"

"Approximately twelve and one-half years," Norvik replied.

"How long had you been living at the house on Cole Crest Drive?"

Norvik instantly realized the error in his previous answer. "About twelve and a half years. Allow me to correct my testimony. I have known Mr. Mahler for six and a half of those years during which I lived in that house." He named the other residents and explained the layout of the house, calling the kitchen, office, and living room "common areas," which he and Mahler shared.

"Did the other tenants have access to the common areas?"

"Not without invitation."

"On May 27, 2007, would you characterize your relationship with the defendant as a friend?"

"Yes, I would say we were very good friends."

Asked to tell, in his own words, the events that weekend, Karl said, "I had been in Orange County working on a project in my profession. I came up for a dear friend's baby shower in Bel Air. Another gentleman was there with whom I am affiliated. He and I went to Cole Crest at approximately eight thirty that evening. We were together in the living room, working on a couple of computers over some business matters. I would say within thirty or forty minutes of our conference, Mr. Mahler entered with a Latino or Hispanic gentleman. They went down to his room, I would imagine, because the living room is just one floor above Mr. Mahler's room."

"Do you remember telling the detectives about that?"

"I am trying to recall. Please understand that this is so

traumatic and shocking, it's difficult to recall in precise detail." He spoke of being distracted by the business discussion, so the entrance of Mahler and another person wouldn't have made much of an impression.

"Did you see a woman there at any time?"

Norvik said he had not. Allowed to proceed with his story, Norvik told of his guest departing, of his going to bed at about 11:30 P.M., and being awakened early Sunday morning by loud "vitriolic" noises from the upper floor. Most of it sounded like Mahler screaming profanities, but he also heard a shrieking woman's voice.

The conflict upstairs hadn't surprised him because it had happened previously when women stayed overnight. His attempts to fall asleep again were interrupted by distinctive thumping noises, like something falling to the floor and being subsequently dragged. To demonstrate the sound of dragging, Norvik used a trick he had learned as a sound technician. He rubbed his arm against the microphone in front of him. He said that after a period of quiet, an alarming loud "insistent" banging on his door at 6:25 A.M. had caused him to jump out of his bed. He dressed quickly, opened the door, and saw Mahler standing there.

"What did he say?"

"He looked panicky and shouted, 'I have a major emergency! I need to dispose of a dead body.'"

"What was he wearing?"

"He was fully dressed in a dark suit." Karl added that Mahler appeared intoxicated. "His voice was slurring and he seemed unsteady on his feet."

At Mahler's request, said Norvik, he had followed the defendant upstairs. Just outside of Mahler's bedroom door, the defendant had stated, "I shot her near the balcony."

Judge Wesley's call for a lunch break reminded observers

of cliffhanger television shows in which the viewer can't wait for the next episode.

At one forty-five in the afternoon, the drama resumed, not only in Karl Norvik's story but in the courtroom as well. As Norvik began speaking, David Mahler glared daggers at him and muttered something in an unintelligible growl. A bailiff instantly appeared behind him and escorted Mahler through a side door. A few minutes later, they returned with Mahler's wrists in handcuffs behind him. He would remain shackled throughout the remainder of Norvik's time on the stand.

Picking up where he had left off, Karl wiped perspiration from his forehead and continued his narrative. After David opened the door, Karl said, he could see a woman's body lying on the floor near the bed, with what appeared to be a bullet hole in the left side of her face. He had been stunned by the bloody vision.

Bobby Grace asked the witness, "Did the defendant say anything at that time?"

"Yes, he blurted out, 'So, are you going to help me?'"

"And how did you respond to that?"

"I unequivocally told him that I would not help him. I went back downstairs to my room, and just before I entered, he yelled, 'Well, don't tell anyone.' When I got inside, I rushed into my bathroom and threw up, more than once."

"Can you describe the person you saw lying on his bed-room floor?"

"She had bleached blond hair, Caucasian, not very tall. She wore what looked like a gold halter top and white pants."

"Do you remember telling a detective the pants were 'sheer'?" Norvik said he had probably used that terminology.

"Did you see any movement at all, any signs of life?"

"No—no signs of breathing, and it looked to me to be very much in a dead state."

"When the defendant told you he had shot her, did he say anything about it being in self-defense'?"

"No."

"Did he ever tell you she had a knife?"

"No."

Asked about having any knowledge of Mahler possessing a gun, Norvik said, "A few weeks before that awful night, I was in one of the common rooms and he told me, 'I have a surprise.' He went to his office, one floor above, and brought back a silver revolver. I would say the barrel was about four to six inches. He took it out of a leather holster, the kind you would put under a jacket. He said, 'Be careful, it's loaded.' I asked him what kind of a gun it was, and he said it was a thirty-eight. From having watched cop shows, I thought it was what is commonly called a Saturday-night special. He indicated to me that it was, quote, 'clean,' meaning unregistered and with no serial numbers."

Directing the witness's attention back to his room after seeing the body, Grace asked what took place. Norvik described his sickened feelings and confusion. A little later, he said, he had a balcony-to-balcony conversation with Donnie Van Develde, in which he "played dumb," pretending that he hadn't yet learned of the shooting upstairs. They discussed the event further when Donnie came upstairs to Karl's room, and agreed to keep their mouths shut. Both men kept mum until Karl decided, on the last day of May, that he had to call the police.

Explaining why he had not called sooner, Norvik admitted abject fear of Mahler. "Here's a person who is showing me a dead body, asking me to dispose of it and be an accessory to murder. I had knowledge of his unregistered weapon. I had seen a big bullet hole in the victim's face. A lot of thoughts went through my mind. This man was a powerful, wealthy attorney with a lot of contacts. It seemed to me I was in a dangerous, untenable position."

* * *

Bobby Grace turned the witness over to Larry Young an hour later. The defender asked questions designed to reveal more about his client's drug usage, drinking habits, and volatile, inconsistent behavior. Karl Norvik's concentrated stare into Young's face, showing his determination to respond forcefully, reflected his indignant feelings about David Mahler.

After a relatively short cross-examination, Karl Norvik glowed with relief when the judge said, "You are excused." He wasted no time in making an exit.

Judge Wesley turned to David Mahler and explained the need for handcuffs during Karl's testimony. "You were obviously getting very upset at the witness." This type of behavior could not be allowed, nor could any potential threat to the person testifying. Mahler apologized and said he would not repeat the conduct.

At 2:45 P.M., everyone in the room turned to watch a true heavyweight make his appearance. Atticus King lumbered through the doorway like a professional wrestler making a grand entrance into an arena. Dressed in a glowing white jumpsuit with a blue Los Angeles Dodgers baseball cap atop his shaved head, King seemed to be moving in the beam of a spotlight. He had what film buffs refer to as "screen presence."

Huffing for breath, he took the oath and laboriously climbed into the witness chair.

From the outset, it became obvious that King did not want to testify against his buddy. His monosyllabic answers came with painful reluctance.

Bobby Grace asked, "Mr. King, directing your attention to the month of May 2007, did you know the defendant in this case, David Mahler?"

In a nearly inaudible grunt, King said, "Yes."

"Do you see that person in the courtroom today?"

"Yes."

"Can you please point him out?"

Atticus waved a chubby finger in David Mahler's direction.

"Where is he sitting at the table?"

"Third."

"At the end of the table?"

"Yes."

"Thank you," Grace said with exaggerated gratitude. "And how long had you known the defendant, David Mahler, prior to the date of May twenty-seventh of the year 2007?"

King generously extended his answer to four words. "At least six years."

Covering a budding smile, Grace asked, "Sometime during the early-morning hours of May twenty-seventh, did you get a phone call from the defendant, David Mahler?"

"Yes."

Even Judge Wesley appeared to be trying not to laugh.

Grace turned toward the big screen. "Directing your attention to the exhibit that appears up there, are you familiar with the LAX Marriott?"

"Yes."

"Did you suggest that you and the defendant meet at the LAX Marriott sometime on the morning of May 27, 2007?"

"Did I?" King nodded his head.

"Is that a yes?"

"Yes."

"And did you, in fact, drive to the LAX Marriott?"

"Yes."

Observers couldn't help but contrast King's single-word answers to the loquaciousness of the previous witness, Karl Norvik.

"When you got to the LAX Marriott, was the witness already there?"

"Yes."

Aficionados of prosecutorial techniques began to see exactly what Grace was doing. He certainly had realized King's unwillingness to say anything potentially harmful to Mahler. So Bobby Grace had designed his questions to allow only "yes" or "no" answers, avoiding a confrontational appearance.

"Are you familiar with the defendant's vehicles?"

"Yes, I am."

"What vehicle did the defendant drive, if you know, to the LAX Marriott?"

"Blue Jag convertible." King concurred that he had seen it in the valet lot upon arrival. Perhaps he realized he couldn't win this little battle, and decided to open up slightly.

Grace inquired, "Approximately what time did you arrive at the hotel?"

"It was after six in the morning. Between six and seven."

Several more "Yes" answers verified that King knew Mahler had checked in, and that the two of them went up to his room. The first "No" response came when Grace asked if the witness had been in the room during Mahler's entire stay. King didn't explain, but according to previous interviews, he had left at one point to bring a prostitute up there.

The next question from Grace elicited a veritable verbal essay from King. "Did the defendant tell you anything about having shot a woman?"

"It wasn't like he shot her, you know, like just shooting somebody. He said that they had been partying and having a good time, if I'm not mistaken, all weekend, and she just flipped out. A gun came into play. I think she pulled the gun and he wrestled with her, and it went off."

Grace sounded dubious. "He told you that *she* pulled a gun on him?"

"Yeah, he didn't say he pulled no gun on her. He said that—that it just went off, you know, him trying to get the gun away from her to—I would assume—stop her from shooting him."

"And he told you the gun went off?"

"Yep."

In the gallery, observers had split opinions about Atticus King's integrity. Some believed his honest answers simply reflected what David Mahler had told him. Others thought he wanted to protect Mahler, even if it required lying.

"At some point, did he ask you if you could help him dispose of her body?"

King's darting eyes and flexing jaw suggested a struggle on how to answer this one. He replied, "Well, when he said that, I was like, 'Man, you're not going to kill nobody or let nobody get killed.'"

Grace would not accept the ambiguity. "I understand that, but let me stop you. My question was—at some point in time, did he ask you if you could help him dispose of the dead woman's body?"

Partially caving in, but hedging about a faulty memory, Atticus King said, "I think so. But I really don't remember that very well, because I didn't believe him."

"Did he ask you how much you would charge him to go clean up his residence?"

"No, I don't remember him asking me no price, because I felt there wouldn't be no price. I didn't believe him no way, so—"

"Did you tell the defendant that you would not help him get rid of the body?"

"I didn't have to tell him that. It wouldn't happen, because I didn't believe him. It's kind of vague, but, you know, the way I remember it . . . I'm looking at him and I'm trying to see if he's serious. And when I look back, you know, I know it had to be an accident, so it was like, hey, you know, he didn't ask me to get rid of no—no body."

Calm and collected, Grace asked, "He did not ask you that?"

Atticus backed off slightly. "He may have. I don't know what he said, but I just . . . I can't remember all of what was said. I remember when he told me they was wrestling and—and then a gun went off."

Acknowledging a recollection of being interviewed by a detective, King said he remembered Vicki Bynum, but he couldn't recall the specific questions.

Grace inquired, "Did the detective ask you about a conversation you had with defendant Mahler on the morning of May 27, 2007?"

"I know she did. She had to, but I just can't remember."

Grace countered, "How many interviews did you have at the Hollywood police station?"

"One."

"Okay, and how many times have you ever been interviewed about a murder?"

"Well, you came and interviewed me. That's two." Suppressed chuckles could be heard in the gallery. Perhaps enjoying his own performance, Atticus added, "And then they came once, so that's three times."

"Have you ever been interviewed before about a murder?"

"In my life?"

"Yes."

"Oh, probably when I was younger."

Grace's aplomb remained, but he knew he had taken a wrong turn with this gambit. "Okay. I'm talking about the very first interview you had with anybody about this. Was it with the police at the Hollywood Station?"

"Yes."

"Mr. King, do you recall being asked by Detective Small and Detective Bynum specifically about whether or not defendant Mahler asked you to help him in any way dispose of a dead body?"

"No."

Grace brought out a police report of the interview and asked Atticus King to read a portion of it to himself. It contained a passage in which Atticus King had said, *"Dave asked*

*me how much money it would take to get me to go to his
house, clean it up, and move the dead girl out of there. I told
him there ain't no amount of money would get me to do something like that."*

When the witness finished silently reading the report,
Grace asked if that had helped refresh his memory.

King replied, "I don't remember it but if—if the detective . . . if it came to her notes, I must have said it, but I don't
remember. I don't think she'd lie on me."

Now Vicki Bynum could be seen covering her mouth
while her eyes twinkled with humor.

"Well, Mr. King," said Grace, maintaining his polite demeanor, "in fact, you do kind of remember, don't you? Because the police were investigating you to see whether or not
you may have had something to do with the removal of the
body. Is that right?"

King looked heavenward, as if praying for a little help. He
replied, "Yes, but let me back up a little bit. When I say, I
don't remember . . . She was pretty cool. I mean, she's a detective, but she was pretty cool. I remember when [David]
said . . . I don't remember him saying get with it, you know,
go up to his house, clean it up or nothing. He was so upset because he knew . . . I mean, he was panicking. It was an accident. He didn't know what to do. . . ."

"Let me stop you, Mr. King, because that's not respon-
sive to my question. I'll ask it again. Do you remember this
interview in which the police were asking you if you were
involved with getting rid of that dead body?"

"Right."

"And were you pretty concerned about the fact that the
police might have suspected that you had something to do
with it?"

"At first, you know, I mean . . . yeah, I mean, somebody
accuse you of getting rid of a body—"

Grace interrupted again. "Okay, so you were very clear

when the police were interviewing you, that they were asking you questions about the dead woman's body and where that body could be found?"

"I remember they were asking me. That's right."

"Okay, so I'm going to ask you again. Did Detective Small ask you specifically what did [Mahler] offer you in regard to that, cleaning up or getting rid of the body?"

"See, what did he offer me? He didn't offer me anything. I just can't remember him offering me nothing to go up there and clean nothing up. I mean, I can't remember."

Bobby Grace's frustration finally leaked through. "You can't remember, or you don't want to remember?"

Larry Young objected to it as argumentative, and Judge Wesley agreed. He also decided that everyone needed a short break. With the jurors out of the room, Wesley's face broke into a broad smile and he commented, "I can't help but like Mr. King."

With the break over, Bobby Grace tenaciously resumed trying for an answer to the same question, but Atticus King continued his rambling evasions for another ten minutes. The prosecutor at last resorted to reading aloud questions Detective Small had asked, with King's answers, and asking him if he recalled these conversations. This allowed the jury to hear that King had indeed been asked by Mahler to help get rid of the body and clean up the house.

Winding down, Grace asked, "You consider yourself to be friends with the defendant. Is that right?"

"Yes."

"And you really don't want to be here testifying. Is that right?"

"I was subpoenaed."

"You came, but you didn't want to be here. Is that right?"

"No, sir." The response probably meant that Atticus King

did not want to be there—but, literally, it meant that Grace's suggestion was not right.

Shaking his head in disbelief, Bobby Grace turned the witness over to the defense.

Larry Young took the reins and asked how long King had known David Mahler. Eight or nine years, the witness said.

"Do you pick up girls and deliver them for him sometimes?"

"If he ask me to go pick them up."

"Do you pick up drugs and deliver them to him?"

"No."

Producing the Marriott Hotel bill, Young asked a couple of questions about the room service charges and heard vague replies equal to what Grace had suffered. Turning to the tab of over $400, he asked if it was mostly liquor.

"Not really," King replied. "He was a big tipper. He told the guy if you bring the food up in fifteen minutes, I'll give you a hundred-dollar tip."

Young uttered, "Wow!"

Atticus King warmed to the subject. "And if you bring my booze up here . . . and the guy was running like a rabbit in a race. Shoot. The guy was getting the money. It wasn't no meal, 'cause steak and eggs and Rémy Martin don't cost no four hundred bucks." The witness displayed remarkable recall of these details, considering that he couldn't remember being asked to get rid of a murdered body.

Returning to the ongoing theme of Mahler's inconsistent behavior, Young asked, "How did he appear emotionwise and sobrietywise when you were there at the LAX Marriott, when you saw him?"

"He was tired. He was just tired, but he was cool."

This is not what the defender wanted to hear.

"Was he doing drugs?"

King said, "We were drinking."

"Not you," said Young. "Was he doing drugs? I know you don't."

"I don't remember him doing no drugs. I remember him drinking."

"Was he high?"

Again unwilling to portray his pal in negative terms, King repeated, "Drinking."

"I know," said Young. "Was he high? Did he get drunk?"

Observers grew increasingly impressed with this taxi driver's ability to skate around questions from highly educated lawyers. King said, "Well, we had two—a couple fifths of Rémy Martin. So you're going to get a little buzzed off of drinking a couple of fifths of Rémy Martin."

Turning to a different subject, Young asked about the woman who joined them in the room. King insisted that she came there independently; he had neither arranged for her presence nor transported her. The attorney, with eyebrows arched, asked, "You didn't bring her?"

"No, I ain't bring her. She showed up."

"Were you there when the television was damaged?"

This topic seemed to infect King with an attack of verbosity. "Well, you know, she was owed some money, and she asked for the money. And the way I . . . You know, at first I thought maybe he intentionally broke the TV, but I don't really know if he really intentionally broke it. Because she was a little abrupt with him, and he jumped up out of the bed and he kind of fell over the cocktail table. And I think when he was trying to grab . . . catch his fall, he knocked the TV off. I don't know. I was buzzed, and so couldn't really, you know . . ."

This verbiage hadn't produced what Young had sought. He tried to steer it back on course. "Was he angry?"

"Yeah, he was a little angry, but it wasn't like crazy with it."

Young gave up. "I have nothing further. Thank you."

* * *

Bobby Grace decided to have another try at pinning down this amazingly slippery witness. He asked, "Mr. King, so did you witness some sort of dispute between defendant Mahler and a prostitute who had come to his hotel room at the LAX Marriott?"

"Yes."

"Were they having a dispute over money that the prostitute felt she was owed by the defendant, David Mahler?"

"Yes."

"Did he specifically get mad at the prostitute regarding her asking for the money?"

"I think it was more the way she asked."

"Mr. King, whose idea was it to order room service?"

"I don't know. It could have been—it could have been mine, because I think I switched . . . I changed the subject. I said, 'Man, let's get some booze,' you know, whatever, you know. 'Let's get this party started,' and that's when we ordered up some booze."

"Did you order it, or did Mr. Mahler order it?"

"Dave did it."

At this point, it appeared that Bobby Grace had decided just to have some fun with King.

"Whose idea was it to offer the big tip?"

"His. He tip everybody."

"And who ordered the prostitute?"

"He did."

"And you observed him doing all this on the phone?"

"He was on the phone."

Grace's brief flirtation with fun turned to making a point. "And he was functioning well enough to use a phone?"

"Yeah."

"And as far as you know, he had driven himself to the LAX Marriott in the blue Jag?"

"Yes."

Bobby Grace shook his head again, and said, "Thank you. Your Honor, I don't have any further questions for this witness."

Larry Young turned down the opportunity for more cross-examination.

Most observers in the gallery were disappointed to see this man leave. Atticus King had been the most interesting and entertaining witness many of them had ever seen.

Judge Wesley called for a fifteen-minute break. In the hallway outside the entrance to his courtroom, a strange encounter took place.

CHAPTER 34
MISDIRECTED PROPOSITION

Insiders had been waiting eagerly to see the next witness, Michael Conoscenti. But before allowing him to be called in, Judge Wesley addressed a separate issue. David Mahler had requested the judge's intervention in a problem. Mahler wanted to be relocated to a different cell in the county jail because he had been receiving death threats from another inmate. Wesley issued a court order to have him moved to a safer location within the jail.

After that bit of business was settled, Bobby Grace called Michael Conoscenti to the stand. Not quite six feet tall, his short goatee helped mask a weather-beaten face, which was once handsome but now featuring deep-set eyes, slightly sunken cheeks, and the display of a missing tooth when he opened his mouth. The dyed hair looked too black for his age, fifty-six. A single, small gold loop decorated his left earlobe. Conoscenti wore baggy dark slacks and a loose-fitting, long-sleeved green shirt that revealed an indecipherable tattoo on the left side of his chest.

At Grace's request, the witness pointed out David Mahler and stated they had been acquaintances for "roughly about a few years."

"Would that be more than two years?"

"Yeah."

One of the prosecutor's assistants, Armine Safarian, entered the courtroom at that moment, bringing some documents for Grace. Even if her high heels clicking on the hard floor hadn't caught the attention of most men in the gallery, her exceptional beauty and figure would have. Nearly every day of the trial, she had been running errands for Grace. His assistant had recently graduated from law school and worked for the DA's office in preparation for a bright future. Among the men who stared at her was the witness Michael Conoscenti.

It would later be revealed that during the preceding break, Conoscenti had cornered Safarian in the hallway. Knowing that he would be the next witness, she maintained a courteous demeanor. He seemed somewhat flirtatious, and then he got to the point. "How would you like to be in a movie? I could arrange it."

Of course, Safarian knew exactly who this guy was, and what type of movie he meant. Her duties in helping the prosecution included advance work with witnesses. She had spoken to Conoscenti several times by phone, and had arranged his transportation to and from the court.

Safarian smiled, maneuvered her way around him, and said she would not be interested.

Directing attention to the screen on which a picture of Kristin Baldwin's smiling face appeared, Bobby Grace asked if Michael Conoscenti had known her. "Yes," he said. "It's

Kristi." He acknowledged meeting her sometime in 2006 and guessed they had been friends for about a year.

"At some point in time, did you introduce Kristi to the defendant, David Mahler?"

"Yes."

"During that time frame, were you renting and using a property as a film place in Los Angeles?"

"Yes, it was in the San Fernando Valley."

"Did you see the defendant during the last week of May 2007?"

"I did, at my house in the valley."

"Did Mr. Mahler say anything to you about requesting your help, or if you knew anyone who could help him with a service?"

"He asked me if I knew anybody that will do a disposal job."

"Was that on a day that you were filming?"

"Actually an evening. He came a little bit after the filming was over, and everybody was running back and forth. I didn't understand what he was talking about at first, and he wasn't being very clear about it. Every time I asked him, he just . . . he seemed like he was in a daze, you know. I never had seen him in that state. I was already upset with him because of something he did."

The gate-crashing incident to which Michael Conoscenti referred had no relevance in the trial, so Bobby Grace didn't give the witness an opportunity to explain what he was upset about. Instead, he asked, "Are you sure those were the words he used?"

"Yes, I am."

"After that date, did you become aware that he had been detained on these proceedings?"

"Yes."

Grace turned Conoscenti over to the defense.

* * *

In movie terms, Larry Young cut to the chase. "Did you sometimes use drugs with David Mahler?"

A shadow crossed the witness's face. He hesitated a moment and then said, "I've watched him use drugs."

"I don't mean to embarrass you," Young said apologetically.

"No, that's quite all right," replied Michael Conoscenti.

"What kind of drugs did you see him do?"

"Cocaine, but mainly he consumed a lot of alcohol."

Once again steering arrow-straight toward the destination of showing his client's possible incapacity to behave normally due to narcotics and booze, Young asked, "Have you seen him act in an unusual manner at all?"

"Yes, I've seen him irate lots of times, just out of control, completely out of control."

This answer seemed tailor-made to observers. Some guessed that Larry Young had probably interviewed Conoscenti earlier, and knew exactly what he was likely to say. He asked, "Did he sometimes fly off the handle with no apparent reason?"

"Yeah."

"Did he exhibit mood swings?"

"Yeah, I'd say that would be a close enough description."

"Did his actions seem to be of an extreme nature?"

"Uh-huh."

Usually, when witnesses use this colloquial affirmative expression, attorneys ask if they specifically mean "yes," but Young seemed happy to accept it. He moved on. "Now, you were doing some filming at one of your residences?"

"Yes."

"Was that when you were in the porno business?"

Michael seemed to stiffen briefly. "Uh, yes. I'm in the adult-film industry."

Larry Young had meant no disrespect. "Well, I meant the adult—"

The witness relaxed and said, "I'm actually in the entertainment business, which covers adult and—"

Interrupting, Young inquired, "Are you an actor in the adult business, or are you a producer or director?"

With a slight smirk, Michael replied, "All of the above."

The answer seemed to surprise Young. "Oh, you are an actor too?"

"Uh-huh."

"What's your stage name?"

"It's Damien Michaels."

Young's cheeks appeared to be slightly more crimson. He commented, "Maybe the young people in my office have seen you."

Conoscenti frowned. "I'm sorry?"

Leaping from the tangential digression, Young asked, "When Mr. Mahler flew off in an unusual manner, did he direct it at any person, or was it just in general?"

"Well, it's a pretty broad question. But it was just . . . depending on the situation, he directed his anger at certain people, including myself."

"Have you seen that happen more than once?"

"Yes, many times."

"Was it in connection with the drugs he was doing, or was it without drugs, if you know?"

"Actually, I don't think . . . I mean, I'm sure drugs had something to do with it, but think it was . . . I've seen him act like that with drugs or without drugs."

Grateful for the witness's help in tilting the scales toward his theory, Young said he had no further questions.

* * *

Bobby Grace wanted to rebalance the tilt. "Mr. Cono-scenti, the times that you saw Mr. Mahler mad, was he mad because of a specific reason?"

"I mean, you know, he was always like that with mood swings. It would be a specific reason or a reason he thought was important enough for him to get upset about. A lot of times, it wasn't."

"So, would he get mad in a business context?"

"Yeah."

"In those two years you knew him, did you see him use drugs during that entire period?"

"Yes." The answer might have been interpreted by jurors as confirmation of consistent erratic behavior for a long period of time. But Grace pulled an ace from his sleeve.

"And was he still conducting business, whatever business he was involved in, during that entire time?"

"Yes. Well, he said he did, but yes."

The implication was clear to spectators. If David Mahler had been using drugs for two years, and still carried out successful and profitable business transactions, his behavior could not have been as destructive as the defense wanted to portray.

Larry Young leaped up to repair the damage. "Did you ever see him associate with a girl named Cheryl?" The witness said he had. "Were you aware that at some point, they broke up their association?"

Michael said, "You know, she tried to do that quite often."

"Did you notice whether or not he used more drugs after that relationship ended?"

"I couldn't say for sure, you know. I know he was just using drugs on a constant basis. I don't know if it was a little more or a little less. I wasn't constantly with him. I'm sorry."

Perhaps disappointed, Young could only ask what kinds of drugs he had observed Mahler using. The witness repeated that he had seen cocaine, but mostly alcohol and "some kind of pills."

"Do you know whether or not he was doing methamphetamine also?"

"I mean, I've seen him doing it. I don't know if it was his main drug. Like I said, the cocaine was constant, and the alcohol was constant."

"Thank you," said Larry Young, with possibly feigned enthusiasm. Good lawyers know never to let the jury see them disappointed.

Neither attorney had any more questions for the witness. Judge Wesley excused him.

When Michael Conoscenti walked out of the courthouse on that warm afternoon of September 1, with smoke still soiling the sky from rampaging fires in hills, he had no idea that he would be dead within two months. On Tuesday, October 27, 2009, someone stabbed him to death in a motel on Ventura Boulevard in Woodland Hills. Investigators speculated that it had resulted from a drug deal gone bad. No one had been arrested for the murder as of August 2011.

The trial resumed on the following day, Wednesday, September 2, but not until one forty-five in the afternoon. Other matters had occupied the judge and lawyers all morning.

The first order of business involved a discussion between Judge David Wesley, Bobby Grace, and Larry Young, with the jury in their conference room. Wesley asked Grace if he still planned to pursue a verdict of first- or second-degree murder. The prosecutor affirmed those goals. Young stated that the evidence would certainly support nothing more than manslaughter, probably involuntary.

Wesley said they would proceed. David Mahler interrupted, asking if he could say something. The judge allowed him to speak, and Mahler thanked him aloud for arranging the change of jail cells away from an inmate who had made threats.

The first witness of the afternoon, Ralph Chung, a youthful-appearing man, told of his profession as an electrical contractor specializing in video equipment for both residences and businesses. He had installed eight security cameras at the home next door to Mahler's Cole Crest house. At the occupant's request in June 2007, Chung had transferred the hard drive's content to a disc and given it to an officer from the LAPD. His testimony lasted only five minutes.

A San Bernardino County sheriff's deputy, Eric Morales, came next. He filled in a few more details about the body discovery, and also spoke no more than five minutes. During his brief testimony, a photograph of David Mahler showed on the big screen, with some printed information below it. Larry Young hastily scribbled notes on a yellow pad.

At two o'clock, LAPD officer Bill Wilson, of the Hollywood Station, took the stand. He told jurors of being dispatched to a house on Cole Crest Drive at four o'clock in the morning. Along with other officers, he had entered the residence, invited in by a tenant named Jeremy Moudy. Wilson had glanced into the garage, illuminating it with his flashlight, and observed what appeared to be bloodstains. He had also noted additional spots on some stairs.

Later he and another officer descended to another level in the house while conducting a "protective sweep." Wilson said he noticed some movement behind material on an upper shelf inside Jeremy Moudy's closet, and then he discovered David Mahler hiding up there. They took Mahler into custody and placed him in a patrol car.

Wilson stepped down after fifteen minutes.

The next witness would amaze everyone.

CHAPTER 35

"HE'S BEEN TRYING TO COVER UP THE CRIME"

Detective Wendi Berndt replaced Bill Wilson in the hot seat, and turned out to be one of the most impressive witnesses ever seen by the jurors, spectators, and even lawyers.

Professionally and attractively dressed in a black suit, with a white blouse, minimal makeup and jewelry, she looked as if she had been sent by filmdom's Central Casting.

Answering Bobby Grace's first question, Berndt said, "I'm a police officer for the Los Angeles Police Department. I'm a detective supervisor with the rank of D3, assigned to the Hollywood Homicide Unit." Her excellent voice and crisp delivery further solidified the image of a star doing an important movie role. Berndt informed jurors that she had been with the LAPD almost twenty-eight years.

On June 1, 2007, she had arrived at the Cole Crest house soon after the discovery of Mahler's hiding place. "My job is to make sure that I have the resources necessary to process the crime scene. In this case, it was a very large residence with multifloors. First I made sure that we thoroughly searched it and collected evidence. I directed specialized people we asked to come assist us. We asked for criminalists because any time we have such an involved crime scene, we need their meticulous skills. They really are most important at that point in the investigation."

Responding to Grace's inquiries, Berndt said, "We had our photographers come to make pictorial records of evidence collected. In this case, I also requested a cadaver dog to go through the residence to see if any human remains had been concealed in there." Three teams of detectives, she recalled, had been assigned to search every inch of seven levels.

Grace asked, "When you did your walk-through of the residence, can you give us the highlights of what you observed?"

"When I first arrived, I noticed that you step down a walkway that leads to the front door, and from there I could see two vehicles parked in the garage. One of our officers, Bill Wilson, had seen what turned out to be spots of blood in front of the black Jaguar and more stains on the back of the car. Once you enter into the residence, and go down a few steps into the living room, we could see a blood smear near the bathroom going in almost a semicircle onto the carpet. Down those stairs, which lead to Mahler's bedroom, we saw what appeared to be more blood on the steps."

As Berndt spoke, Grace used a laser pointer to indicate, on projected color photos, the bloodstains to which the detective referred. Next he advanced the sequence of pictures to one of the garage interior where two Jaguars were parked. Berndt explained exactly where each trace of blood had been collected by criminalists.

Showing another photo, this one of Mahler's bedroom, Grace asked Berndt to explain. She said, "When we stepped into the bedroom, we saw a large spot on the red carpet that looked darker. Closer examination revealed that it was probably blood near the fireplace. We also noticed containers of cleaning fluids on the fireplace mantel and a plastic bag containing more cleaning materials. There was a robe hanging in the hallway, near the bathroom, and we found a bloodstain on it. On the sink in the bathroom, I recall seeing scrubbing sponges with red fibers stuck to them. It was our opinion that Mahler had used them in attempts to clean the carpet."

More photos showed the bedroom interior and a closet. Berndt said, "We found a holster concealed in a boot inside that closet. Regarding the bloodstains in that room, I was with the criminalist when we lifted the entire carpet to check underneath to see if blood had soaked through. It was apparent that some efforts had been made to eradicate the blood spots. Pulling up the carpet enabled us to see what had been impossible to wipe away with cleaning fluids and sponges."

Numbered placards could be seen at various spots on the carpet, and Grace asked Berndt to comment on them. "Those are placed by our Scientific Investigation Division people. When they collect evidence, they have to mark it. The numbers correlate with property reports of collected evidence and itemized explanations on police reports."

After a few more questions and answers in which Berndt identified the various brand names of cleaning products found in the house, Grace turned her over to the defense for cross-examination. Wendi Berndt knew exactly how to respond.

Larry Young asked, "In the exhibit on the screen, you have red dots showing what appears to be like a pathway of blood droppings on those stairs?"

Wendi Berndt answered, "The blood I saw on the stairs went from the living room down to the level where the office is and then down the stairs to Mr. Mahler's bedroom." Using the laser pointer, she said, "If you go up to the living room, the garage would be around the corner and down a hallway to a door that leads into the garage."

"Were you able to form an opinion if there had been a body in the bedroom, how it was removed from the house, based on what you saw?"

"It's my opinion that the body was dragged out of the bedroom, feetfirst, up the stairs to the landing where the office is, and then up the stairs to [the] living-room area, up another short flight of stairs into the hallway and the front door. There is a smear near the bathroom, so it appears that the body was apparently in the bathroom area at some point, but I cannot explain why."

"And is it correct, from all that you've seen, you could form an opinion that there's no way this was a careful, planned event that took place that night?"

Berndt raised her eyebrows, wrinkling her forehead. "I don't think I can make that opinion."

Undiscouraged, Young asked, "It certainly wasn't a careful, planned removal, was it?"

"Well, again, I don't think I could make that opinion because people make mistakes. And it's good for us, as detectives, when they do make mistakes, but that doesn't mean I would necessarily say that it's planned or unplanned."

"Does the mere fact that cleaning equipment is in a large house mean any inference can be drawn?"

With a little smile teasing the corners of her mouth, Berndt replied, "Well, yeah, it tells me he's been trying to cover up the crime."

"Did someone actually cover up the spots in the bedroom?"

"Yes, sir."

"But there was no attempt to cover up the blood spots on the stairs or in the garage or anything like that, was there?"

"Again, sir, suspects, thank goodness, often miss small details that we, as detectives, find."

Larry Young, an intelligent and effective lawyer, appeared

to be underestimating the witness's ability to debate a point. "But often when they're thinking clearly, they don't miss it, do they?"

"No, I wouldn't say that at all, sir."

A note of incredulity tinged Young's voice. "You don't?"

"No, I would not say that at all."

Persistent, Young asked, "If a person was thinking clearly, he wouldn't be more careful, more exact, more precise?"

Berndt held her ground. "You would think, under those conditions, that might be true. But the problem is that people do make mistakes even if they're trying to be very methodical. It's just a fact of life that they make mistakes. When murders occur, mistakes are made trying to cover it up."

"The sloppiness doesn't mean anything then, in your opinion?"

"I'm not sure I know what you think it should mean, sir, and I apologize for that."

In the gallery, observers leaned forward so as not to miss a single word of this clinic in how to testify. Young shot back, "Well, I was trying to see if you agree that it would show a lack of a clear mind, a lack of—"

Cutting him off, Berndt continued in her sprightly dissection. "Oh, I think there was a lot of clarity in this, in the fact that the perpetrator was trying to clean up the crime scene after the fact. This shows definitely a consciousness of guilt. . . ."

"A consciousness of . . . ?"

". . . in trying to cover up the crime."

Young's expression indicated a heightened respect for this detective's logic. Still, he needed to keep his theme on track. He countered, "But not in any intelligent manner, though, was it? I mean, the person leaves a blood trail going downstairs, upstairs, into a garage. I call it sloppy, and you just say it's a mistake?"

Cool and confident, Berndt pressed her own theme. "I'd say that people make mistakes when they commit murders.

And they don't always see the minute details that we, as detectives, later see. It could be lighting. It could be the color of the carpet. It could be the hurriedness of somebody's movements that they fail to give attention to. So there are a lot of reasons why a suspect wouldn't see what we see."

Circumventing the issue, Young said, "You've classified it in your mind as a murder. But you understand that's for the jury to decide, don't you?"

"Well, sir, I classified it in my own mind. Yes, sir. In my mind, this is a murder, sir."

"Did you investigate the circumstances of the shooting?"

"I investigated the crime scene and the available evidence about the incident."

"Well—the shooting, how did the incident happen?"

"If you are trying to see if I was an eyewitness . . . no, I was not an eyewitness. I was a supervisor who overviewed the investigation. In that overview, I was aware of a lot of witness's statements. I was aware of what the criminalists found. I was aware of what the coroner found. And that's what I base my personal opinion on."

"Without talking to anyone who was there?"

"Well, again, sir, there were witnesses at the location who were interviewed by my detectives. And I'm very familiar with their statements."

Young wanted specifics. "Did Mr. Donnie Van Develde explain what happened?"

Bobby Grace had listened with fascination to the testimony that turned into a debate, and skipped several opportunities to object. But he finally protested. "Your Honor, I'm going to object on the grounds of hearsay."

"Sustained."

Young quickly shifted gears. "Was there any attempt by your officers to prevent other people from entering the scene?" Perhaps he hoped to imply that evidence had been contaminated by outsiders.

Berndt was ready for this too. "When the officers went there and cleared the location, they secured it until we got a search warrant and returned to conduct the search."

"Was there any yellow crime scene tape put around there, blocking off sections of the house?"

"The crime scene photos would probably show that. If you mean sections inside the house, the answer is no, because it was secured from the outside."

"Did the officers go into an office that was in the location?"

"I wasn't there when the initial searchers went through the residence to clear it. And so I'm not sure where the officers went when they did clear the location prior to securing it." At last, Larry Young had exploited a tiny chink in this remarkable detective's armor.

"Are you aware of whether any drugs were found in the bedroom?"

Berndt had an immediate, unequivocal answer. "In our search after it was secured, there were no drugs found in the residence."

Hoping to exploit any possible oversights in the search, Young asked, "Was there any attempt to prevent personal belongings and electronic equipment from being stolen out of the residence?"

Bobby Grace thought this went too far afield and objected on the grounds of relevance. Judge Wesley sustained it.

Larry Young stepped over to the defense table, picked up some papers, returned, and said with a new air of confidence, "Did you say there was no evidence of drugs in the residence?"

"That's correct."

"Would it refresh your memory if I showed you a property report from the Los Angeles Police Department of the house on Cole Crest Drive purporting to show—"

Judge Wesley interceded. "Don't tell us what it purports to

show. If you are going to refresh her memory, show her the document."

Berndt studied the paper and started to say, "Sir, this is a search warrant of a different—"

Judge Wesley quickly stopped her too. "If that doesn't refresh your memory, just give it back to him and tell him it did not refresh your memory."

Sounding feisty, Berndt retorted, "It does refresh my memory, but he's incorrect."

"All right, then," Wesley patiently advised, "that's fine. Let him ask the question."

Now alarmed, Young said, "If I got the wrong report, tell me why this is wrong."

Berndt replied, "You do have the wrong report. That's a search warrant for a different location, sir."

Sounding chastised, Young uttered, "Not at the Mahler residence on Cole Crest?"

"No, sir. If you will read the report, further down it will tell you the location of the occurrence. It's about the middle of the page, sir."

"Oh," said Young, "down on Clark Drive."

"That's correct, sir."

All of the gusto had left Larry Young. Ironically, he had proven that even intelligent, well-prepared experts in their profession can make mistakes, as Wendi Berndt had stated. He could manage only, "I apologize. Did you search the office?"

Avoiding a display of triumph, Berndt replied, "Yes, I did."

"Just to be clear, I meant Mahler's office inside the house. Was anything removed by you or your officers from that room?"

The witness thought for a few moments and then answered, "My recollection, there may have been a letter on top of the desk, I believe, and some business cards. Because of Mr. Mahler's occupation (as a lawyer or broker), I was very aware of trying to not invade any personal files that could relate to his business. So I was not looking through paperwork or files. I was basically looking for evidence of blood or any other evidence of the crime."

"Thank you," Young said. "I have nothing further."

Judge Wesley excused Detective Wendi Berndt, who walked out through a gallery of new admirers for her remarkable professionalism and skill at fielding questions in a court of law.

Bobby Grace later expressed his admiration of Detective Berndt. "In terms of evidence collection and her presentation on the stand, she was one of the best witnesses I have ever seen testify in court. I've handled over fifty murder cases. Sometimes supervisors don't really have a detailed grasp of the events, but her attention to detail and knowledge of where everything was, and how the scientific aspects related, was extraordinary. Many detectives don't pay enough attention to the SID people to know what to say and what not to say on the stand—why certain things are important in terms of the scientific aspects. They can recite where evidence was found, but unless you can talk about it in terms of what conclusions may be drawn, they don't give a complete picture. Wendi made it clear the victim's head was dragged—where many investigators would have just said she was dragged. Some detectives don't get that they can testify to the logical flow of evidence. The way she framed it let the jury understand conclusions of what could have happened. She was so effective in her court presentation, and you can't put a price on the value of having a witness who is knowledgeable and comes off so well in front of a jury."

Grace made it a point to also compliment Ron Bowers's graphics. "Ron's diagrams helped Wendi too. We could take the victim all the way from the bedroom into the garage to the point where the jury could see blood droplets in the garage and on the car. This led to the inescapable conclusion that the victim was dragged all that way and placed in the Jaguar luggage compartment."

The de facto jurors in the gallery agreed that, so far, the evidence strongly pointed to David Mahler's culpability. He had obviously killed Kristin Baldwin. But defense attorney Larry Young had made significant headway in portraying his client as a drug-addicted, temperamental alcoholic whose erratic volatility could indicate symptoms of bipolar disorder. The jury might very well decide that he could not be held responsible for his actions. If so, they could find him not guilty, or come back with a guilty verdict of manslaughter.

CHAPTER 36
ANOTHER TRIP TO DAGGETT

Jurors next heard from criminalists Raphael Garcia and Wubayehu Tsega, who had worked together collecting the bloodstains Wendi Berndt had discussed. Color photos on the big screen and the use of a laser pointer made their testimony crystal clear.

On cross-examination Larry Young said to Tsega, "You have a wonderful accent, sir. What country were you originally from?"

"I am from Ethiopia."

"Did you do any lifting of prints or stains—tape lifting on any of the cleaning material or plastic bags found in the bedroom of the residence?"

"I don't recall."

"Is it correct that you recall the tape lifts and the cotton swabs from the automobile?"

"Yes, I did."

"Now, there were two automobiles, were there not?"

"Yes, there were."

"Did you do the other one also?"

"No, I didn't."

"Were you asked to do any examination of a trunk of a green taxicab?"

"No."

Young had no further questions. He had apparently been attempting to plant a kernel of doubt in jurors' minds by suggesting that fingerprints of someone else could possibly have been found on the cleaning materials. Or, perhaps, that Kristin's blood might have been inside Atticus King's green-and-white minivan taxi.

Another uniformed officer from the Hollywood Station, David Kim, spent about twenty minutes delivering testimony about the two Jaguars, using the laser pointer to eliminate any possible confusion jurors might have about which vehicle had made the long trip to the desert in the dark morning hours of May 31, 2007.

The courtroom clock ticked close to five o'clock on that Wednesday evening, and Judge Wesley announced the trial would not resume until Tuesday afternoon, September 8. He wished everyone a happy long weekend for Labor Day.

All murder trials, in which the bodies were found, feature testimony about gory details of the victim's autopsy, usually from the forensic pathologist who conducted the postmortem surgery and examination. Dr. Louis Pena took the stand at one thirty in the afternoon on Tuesday. A solidly built man, with salt-and-pepper wavy hair, rimless glasses, dressed in a gray suit, with a diagonally striped tie, Pena looked more like a stereotypical senator than a medical specialist.

He spoke of the difficulties in doing an autopsy on a dehydrated and decomposed thirty-one-pound body. Taking the jury through the whole process, he used the pointer to elaborate about inconclusive findings due to badly deteriorated internal and external organs.

One photo depicted the small tattoo of a blue dolphin on Kristin's lower abdomen. It had helped confirm her identity.

Jurors heard Pena's opinion that Kristin Baldwin had probably been shot in the upper right chest, rather than the face as indicated by previous testimony from Donnie Van Develde and Karl Norvik. Conradictory evidence from witnesses is not uncommon in murder trials. Which version the jury believed would have to be worked out during deliberations.

While Dr. Pena answered questions from both attorneys, David Mahler busied himself reading while frequently adjusting his glasses with his left hand. He appeared to be making notes on a pad of legal-sized yellow paper.

The testimony concluded with a photo of the bra and stained sheer white pants Kristin had worn.

A slim, dark-haired, handsome investigator for the district attorney's office replaced Dr. Pena as the next witness. Classic-movie buffs thought Ronald Valdiva bore a strong resemblance to actor Ricardo Montalban, who, in addition to scores of film roles, had starred on television's *Fantasy Island*.

After having Valdiva state his name and occupation, Bobby Grace asked, "At my request, did you and one of your colleagues take a drive from Hollywood, California, to Daggett, California?"

In a resonant voice, the witness answered, "Yes . . . to Daggett."

"When did you take that drive?"

"On July ninth, this year."

"What time did you start?"

"We started at two seventeen A.M. from the Mahler house on Cole Crest Drive in the Hollywood Hills."

Spectators who had been paying attention to previous testimony realized that the timing corresponded exactly with the security camera video of Mahler's Jaguar leaving his garage in the early morning of May 31, 2007. A map of their route to Daggett appeared on the large screen.

"What time did you arrive in Daggett?"

"The trip took two hours and four minutes. We got there at four twenty-one A.M."

"Did you immediately start your return trip?"

"No, not immediately. We delayed about six minutes." Jurors could be seen taking notes, perhaps observing that six minutes would allow enough time to dump a body in the desert.

"When you returned, how long did the drive take you?"

"The trip back from Daggett to the house on Cole Crest Drive also took two hours and four minutes. We arrived at six thirty-one A.M." Jurors again put pencils to paper. The Jaguar had been gone nearly five hours on May 31, and Valdiva's trip had taken four hours and eight minutes.

"What kind of driving speed were you doing?"

"From the Cole Crest address down to the main highway, which is Laurel Canyon—leaving at two seventeen A.M., it was dark, winding, and the roads are narrow, so the speed through that portion was quite slow, no more than twenty miles per hour. On the surface streets, primarily from Laurel Canyon to the 101 Freeway, I maintained a speed of five miles per hour over the posted speed limits. And freeway speeds were seventy miles per hour." A question might be in the minds of jurors. Had Mahler, carrying a dead body in the trunk, cautiously obeyed the speed limit to avoid being stopped? This would partially account for his trip taking about forty-five minutes more than Valdiva's.

"Did you encounter much traffic on the way there and back?"

"There was very little traffic on the way out. It increased on the return trip, but was moving along quite well and did not keep me from being able to maintain my speed. I just had to drive without the cruise control coming back."

"You spoke of difficult driving conditions between Cole Crest and Laurel Canyon. Does it require some kind of coordination or dexterity in order to make that drive up and down from Cole Crest to Laurel Canyon or the reverse?" (Grace might as well have asked, "Could Mahler have successfully done it if he had been under the influence of alcohol or drugs?")

Valdiva understood the implication and answered, "Yes, in order to avoid hitting something—yes."

His testimony ended the court's session on that Tuesday, September 8.

Wind-fanned flames still swept up hillsides in the Angeles National Forest on Wednesday, September 9, 2009, devouring brush, trees, and wildlife. News reports announced the firestorm only 60 percent under control. Temperatures downtown, though, had dropped to the high 70s.

In Judge David Wesley's courtroom, another type of storm roiled the proceedings. While the jury waited in their room, a hearing took place to air Larry Young's protests against Ron Valdiva's testimony the previous day. He stated that the investigator's assumptions in making the round-trip were full of speculations. Specifically, even if Mahler had driven to the desert, Valdiva could not have known the exact route used. There were five separate paths, said the defender, from Cole Crest to the freeway.

Bobby Grace had anticipated the objections. Early that morning, he had arranged for Valdiva and his colleague to drive each possible route, including the one Ron Bowers had discovered on his trip up to Cole Crest, involving the use of what appeared to be a private driveway. In fact, the narrow passage provided access to Blue Heights Drive, which connected to Sunset Plaza Drive. The man riding shotgun had videotaped all five of the drives.

Judge Wesley gave permission for Grace to show the tapes to the jury.

One other matter occupied about twenty minutes of heated discussion. Larry Young planned to call only one witness for the defense, a psychiatrist. To accommodate the doctor's calendar, Young had received permission to bring him in before the prosecution rested its case.

Bobby Grace wanted to be certain that no "diminished capacity" testimony would be allowed. This tactic had been commonly used for decades to convince juries that the mental states of defendants had made them incapable of forming the intent to commit a particular crime. Unlike a plea of insanity, which could result in a verdict of not guilty, diminished capacity could lead the jury to believe the defendant could not form the necessary intent to commit murder, thus could reduce the matter to manslaughter. But California voters had outlawed this type of defense in 1982 due to a notorious trial in San Francisco.

A former city supervisor, Dan White, had shot and killed two victims, Mayor George Moscone and Supervisor Harvey Milk, in 1978. The defense portrayed White as being under diminished capacity resulting from the consumption of too much junk food, largely Twinkies snack cakes. Despite other evidence of premeditation, the jury found White guilty of manslaughter. The story was told in the 2008 film *Milk,* for which actor Sean Penn won an Academy Award.

Larry Young argued that he wanted to show the long-term

effects on Mahler of drug abuse and alcoholism. Judge Wesley ruled that Young's psychiatrist, Dr. Samuel Miles, could testify but would not be allowed to offer an opinion indicating so-called diminished capacity.

During the discussion, David Mahler sat at the defense table with an angry look on his face, lower lip protruding and eyes glaring.

With the jury seated once again, Bobby Grace showed the videos of Ron Valdiva's five varying routes. It took an hour, and did not make for good theater. Jurors looked sleepy, and observers seemed restless. But it produced a finding of Larry Young's objection being overruled. A lunch break afterward revived everyone.

The next two hours would change everything.

Chapter 37

Swordplay on a Psychiatrist

Dr. Samuel Miles came forward at one forty-five that afternoon to answer questions. He would fit most casting directors' idea of a psychiatrist. With a high forehead, receding gray hair, a matching goatee, deep-set eyes, and wearing a gray suit, with a dark tie, he looked the part.

Jurors appeared particularly interested. This testimony could be crucial in deciding the verdict.

Larry Young asked, "Dr. Miles, what is your occupation?"

"I'm a physician. I specialize in the evaluation and treatment of psychiatric disorders and substance abuse disorders."

Young said, "We called you now, out of order, and you were able to cancel your appointments and duties you had for today?"

"Yes."

"As a matter of fact, sir, are you under appointment to examine the defendant, David Mahler?"

"Yes." Following that answer, the witness spelled out his education and work history, called a curriculum vitae, or CV.

"Can you tell the jury what procedures you used to render an opinion or diagnosis?"

"In general, I rely on history, observations, and tests. In a case like this one, I obtain information from interviewing the defendant and from records provided to me. I may also ask for some testing." He had requested some psychological and neuropsychological tests to confirm impressions gained through examinations. In addition, said Dr. Miles, he had tried to obtain hospital records from David Mahler being "psychiatrically hospitalized" when he was seventeen years old. Unfortunately, they had been destroyed.

"Did you have a chance to review police reports on the incident for which he has been accused?"

"Yes, I did."

"In going over the testing and your observations, did you find that there was any type of mental disorder that you would characterize as being present in this gentleman?"

Spectators, lawyers, and jurors leaned forward, determined not to miss a single important word.

"Yes," said Dr. Miles. "His presentation is consistent with bipolar disorder."

No one on the prosecution team wanted to hear those words. The statement could undermine all of the investigation, accumulation of evidence, and testimony up to this point.

The witness continued, "It used to be called manic-depressive illness. It is also consistent with cocaine dependence, which at the time of the examination was in remission in a controlled environment. . . . He did not have cocaine and didn't have access to it. He had cognitive deficits. His ability to think and reason and planning was impaired because of his chronic use of drugs."

Observers thought that Larry Young must be ecstatic. This witness had placed a golden crown in the defense case—exactly what Young had needed. The defender asked, "Did you find any type of mental deficit due to what you say is the chronic use of drugs?"

"Yes, the deficit is in the ability to plan and reason. He is easily derailed by impulsiveness and by emotion. . . . On his IQ test . . . he did very, very well on the verbal parts. On the performance parts, he did really not very well. This is significant. It's the kind of difference we see in people who have difficulty with brain functioning, with planning and figuring out what to do. He's able to talk well, but not able to do very well."

Mahler watched and listened with rapt attention. A pink band encircled his left wrist to signify the new jail cell location.

Asked to explain bipolar disorder for the jury, Dr. Miles replied, "It is what we call a new disorder. It's a major mental illness. It's chronic, can be episodic, where a person suffers from changes in mood that are not related to the environment. The changes for bipolar disorder are different from straight depression in that there's at least one episode of mania.

"Mania is sometimes thought of as the opposite of depression. Instead of feeling real bad, someone can feel real good for no good reason. But more often, there's a kind of irritation that goes with mania. So there can be lack of a need for sleep. There can be a feeling of being on top of the world, or a feeling that one is better than everybody else. The person can be speaking more rapidly, maybe thinking so fast that they can't keep up with themselves, easily distracted. In an extreme, we get to a kind of a speech that we call a word salad, where someone can't finish a whole sentence because they get distracted by things around them."

The doctor's words seemed almost to be a picture-perfect biography of David Mahler. Was he really the poster definition of the mental illness?

Continuing his riveting definition, Dr. Miles said, "So, if someone has at least one episode of that, we call it bipolar disorder." Observers wondered about that statement. Most people can recall having at least one episode of feeling terrific, followed by a period of depression. Did that make them bipolar?

Obviously delighted with the doctor's definition, which appeared to be a mirror image of the defendant, Larry Young asked, "The irritability you mentioned—can you explain what that is?"

Dr. Miles explained that the condition is a defense against depression encompassing a feeling of being all powerful, denial of vulnerability to being hurt, and a need to attack any threatening event or person.

Young wanted even more. "In a rage attack, can that be a momentary thing, or is it something that goes on for a period of time?"

Rage, said the expert, will generally burn out in a short period of time, while irritability might last for days or weeks.

"When it burns out, does the person realize what they said or did?"

"Sometimes, if they've got the evidence in front of them, they might realize that they've broken something they valued."

"What if you add to that episode the use of cocaine?"

"Stimulants make mania worse. Drugs like cocaine and amphetamines, on their own, cause irritability. Alcohol impairs judgment. . . . People who are bipolar, in the course of their lifetime, about two-thirds of them, will at some point suffer from substance use disorder . . . to the point of losing control either periodically in a binge of abuse."

"And you state that Mr. Mahler has been doing that since he was seventeen?"

"Yes."

"How old is he now? Do you recall?"

"In his midforties." (Mahler would be forty-five on his next birthday, in March.)

"If someone is in such a rage, could they be doing a gibberish-type vocalization?"

"That might happen, yes."

"And could they also be screaming?"

"Yes." The exchange brought to mind descriptions from Donnie Van Develde and Karl Norvik of David Mahler screaming at Kristin Baldwin shortly before her death.

Young elicited from the witness statements that he had studied a personal history of the defendant and had collected information from his childhood onward. Dr. Miles said, "He had a troubled childhood. His parents were divorced. He was kept from his father for a while, but he felt a close relationship with him. He had behavioral problems in school and started using quaaludes in his teens."

Mahler's relationship with his father had been portrayed differently by other sources who knew him. They had portrayed it as strained and full of anger.

"In your examination of Mr. Mahler, did you go into his remembrances or impressions of what happened in this incident?"

"Yes. His description was consistent with a period of being out of control. He explained that he had some interactions that evening—actually, he'd been kind of in an altered state for a while up to that point. But somebody had come by who wanted some money from him, and he was irritated by that and also threatened. He went to an ATM machine and got the money and this was around eleven thirty at night. He came back to the room and found Kristi with one of the tenants." The witness presumably referred to Donnie Van Develde but did not use the tenant's name. Jurors would have to decide the meaning of his words. "He was irritated by that and told the tenant to leave. He said he later realized the tenant wanted some drugs."

"Did he indicate what the money was for?"

"He had asked this [other] person to help him scare a

woman by planting some drugs on her and have a corrupt police officer make like he was arresting her. Mr. Mahler had decided not to go through with that and told the guy to call it off, but the guy was now wanting money and saying he had gotten other people involved and needed to pay them off. He was irritated by that. He felt threatened—like if he did not give the guy the money, that he would be injured."

At the defense table, Detective Vicki Bynum glanced at Bobby Grace with a skeptical look. This alleged trip to an ATM had never been brought up in any of the previous statements. The entire story sounded to her like more of Mahler's duplicity.

Young asked, "What happened then as he explained it to you?"

Dr. Miles's continued account left out any reference to the individual allegedly at Cole Crest who was there demanding money. He seemed to have vanished. "Well, Mr. Mahler asked the tenant, you know, 'Why are you here with the door shut?' And then he argued a little with Kristi. Donnie left and then the argument was over. He was calmed down and he was naked in bed doing some cocaine. And he felt it was time for Kristi to do her thing."

"Did he mention whether or not he had been screaming or yelling at any point that evening?"

"He did not. He called Donnie back to find out what he had been there for, and it turned out Donnie wanted drugs. He asked Kristi if she had any with her, but she didn't respond. He asked her eight or ten times, and she still didn't answer. He felt irritated. He snapped. He picked up the gun thinking, you know, this is—this will scare her and him into, you know, answering the question. And then he doesn't know what happened next, but the gun went off. He doesn't know if it went off when Donnie was trying to get it from him or whatever. He had not shot a gun since he was ten years old in camp."

Urged by Larry Young to continue, Dr. Miles said, "Well,

at the point the gun went off, Donnie left and [Mahler] doesn't remember what he did next. But eventually he put his suit on because he wanted to get into the frame of being more organized—that, if he had a suit on, then he's a lawyer and he's organized and he can think. Without the suit on, he's a drug addict and he's all over the place and can't think."

To Vicki Bynum and several spectators, the story seemed increasingly bizarre, too pat, and hard to believe. A case could be made that David Mahler had taken bits and pieces from testimony at the preliminary hearing and built a patchwork narrative for the doctor. He had woven self-serving, made-up details around verifiable facts to create this scenario of an unfortunate man driven by bipolar disorder.

Young seemed to like the image of him donning a suit. "Boy, that's almost like Clark Kent putting on a Superman suit, isn't it?" The psychiatrist agreed. Young asked, "Now, was this consistent with your diagnosis of a bipolar individual?"

The answer may not have been what the defender expected. "It was, and it wasn't. It was, I think, something very unusual about him."

"Wasn't it somewhat of a grandiose fantasy?"

"I don't think of it in those terms, because, in fact, he was a lawyer. I thought it represented his insight into the fact that he wasn't thinking clearly and needed to, because he was confronted by something awful."

Young followed up with a few more questions to reaffirm the manic and the depressive aspects of Mahler's behavior, plus the possibility that Mahler felt remorse about the event.

If Las Vegas had put odds on a verdict of murder versus manslaughter at that moment, there would have been a long line of gamblers placing tons of money on the latter.

With that, Larry Young turned the witness over to Bobby Grace.

* * *

The prosecutor first established that the evaluation by Dr. Miles had been developed after conversations with the defendant. Then he asked, "When was the first time you spoke to him?"

Dr. Samuel Miles said it took place on September 16, 2008, and again on June 30, 2009, about two months before the trial started. Most of Mahler's account of the killing had come during the June 30 meeting.

"Doctor, how long would you estimate the defendant has had this bipolar disorder?"

"He may have had it all his life, but the first symptoms he described might have occurred during his adolescence. After that, it was fairly quiet or masked by his substances."

An air of confidence seemed to radiate from Bobby Grace. He had the appearance of a swordsman testing the edge of his blade. "Did the defendant tell you that he graduated from college?"

"Yes."

"Did he tell you that he graduated from law school?"

"Yes." Observers could sense the importance of these questions.

"Did he tell you that he passed the New York State Bar the first time he took it?"

"Yes."

"Did he tell you that he passed the New Jersey Bar?"

"Yes."

"Did he tell you that he practiced law on his own in the New York area?"

"Yes."

"Did he tell you that once he came to California, he started doing day trading?"

"He may have. I don't recall that specifically."

"Well, did he tell you how he supported himself during his time in California?"

"I'm pretty sure he did. He was practicing some law. I

don't recall if he also talked—oh yes, he did talk about some kind of stock trading. I don't recall if that was day trading or not."

"Did you do anything to confirm any of these uses of drugs that the defendant reported to you, other than the testing that you described?"

"The only confirmation I had was contained in the police reports with interviews of various people who described the drug use."

"So, did you personally talk to anybody that said they saw him take drugs?"

"No."

"Did you watch [a DVD] of the nine-hour interview the police did with the defendant after he was arrested in connection with this case?"

"No, I did not."

A feeling hung in the courtroom that Bobby Grace's sword had already scored "touché" several times, and the defense was going to need a good supply of bandages.

"Have you heard of a term called 'malingering'?"

"Yes. 'Malingering' is the conscious faking or exaggeration of symptoms in order to gain something."

"And when you talked to the defendant about this particular incident that occurred in May of 2007, he had a law degree?"

Perhaps feeling a little feisty, the doctor snapped, "Yes, he did. I don't think they take that away from you."

"Nope, they don't," Grace happily agreed. "Doctor, about how many people in the United States suffer from what you call bipolar disorder?"

"It's about two to three percent of the population."

"And of these two or three percent, do many of them function on a day-to-day basis . . . being able to pass a couple of bar examinations?"

"Yeah."

"Practice law?"

"Yes, most commonly, bipolar disorder is episodic, and between episodes people function fairly well."

"And, as far as you know, from the defendant's reports, he had been using some kind of drugs since the age of seventeen?"

"Yes."

"He told you that it was just about six months prior to the shooting that he started using meth, or speed, as you referred to it?"

"Yes. At one point, he said that the only drug he had used in the last twenty years—or ten to twenty years was cocaine. And then he later corrected himself, saying that over the last six months he was using speed from time to time because of a woman he was involved with."

Bobby Grace, pacing back and forth, nodded and said, "Well, let's talk about that. In your interview with the defendant about the actual shooting, did he indicate to you that he was upset with Kristi because she didn't respond to him quickly enough regarding his questioning if she had any drugs with her?" Yes. "As a result of that, did he tell you that he went and got a handgun from somewhere in the room?" Yes. "At some point, did he tell you he loaded the weapon?"

After a short volley with equivocation from the witness, he finally said, "He didn't tell me how the bullet got in there. He said, 'Before you know it, a bullet was in there.'"

His voice a notch higher in mock confusion, Grace repeated, "'Before you know it, a bullet was in there'?"

"Yeah. Now it's not clear from my notes whether he was saying to me, 'Before you know it, the bullet was in her' or if it was in the gun."

A few cracks had seemingly appeared in the previously solid bulwark of the doctor's story. Grace said, "Well, actually, that sentence, or phrasing, comes before any discussion of the gun going off. Isn't that correct?" Miles agreed. "Then the defendant told you that he specifically got the gun out because he wanted to scare both Donnie and Kristi?"

"Yes."

"And the defendant told you that he got progressively more upset or irritable because Kristi was not responding to his questioning?"

"Yes."

"And that he asked about eight or nine times?"

"Yes."

"Did he tell you he immediately realized that Kristi was dead after the gun went off?"

"He didn't say."

"Well, did he tell you that he immediately went for help from Donnie and Karl to try to help him get rid of the dead body?"

"He didn't say that he did that immediately."

Allowing a tiny bit of sarcasm to color his tone, Grace said, "Oh, I forgot. He went and put a suit on first, right?"

"Yes."

"Then he went to Karl to get help to move the body?"

Sounding like a professor speaking to a misguided student, Dr. Miles corrected Grace. "He went to Karl and told him to look at what was there, look at the body, and then Karl went back to his room."

"And Karl wouldn't help him?"

The answer rang with defiance. "Karl offered no assistance."

"He told you that from there, he called some other people who he described as losers to ask them to help him with his situation?"

"Well, he called a lot of people asking for help and he describes them all as losers. And he berates himself for not calling people he knew were not losers who might have provided him with some reasonable advice, like call the police."

To a few spectators, the testimony seemed to have morphed

from a doctor's professional opinions to that of a friend trying to rationalize an alibi for Mahler.

"By the way," said Grace, "did he ever tell you that he called the police?"

"No."

"Then eventually does he tell you that he placed Kristi's dead body in the back of his [car] trunk?"

"Yes."

The jury, at last, had heard an admission of this important part of the case. Mahler had also told the doctor of driving for hours.

"But he doesn't know what happened after that?" Grace questioned.

"All he knows is he was arrested the next day."

"No," Grace said, "I'm asking if he told you what happened after he drove that distance with the body in his car."

"Yes. He pulled over and put the body somewhere. I can't read my handwriting as to what he did with the body there." It seemed strange to listeners that the doctor knew so many details about Maher's behavior, but couldn't recall hearing about the dumping of a dead body without being able to read his scribbled notes.

"Did he speak about putting the body somewhere?"

"I don't know if he dug something or if he just put it at the side of the road. I don't know. I can't read my handwriting."

"All right. So did you get the impression that he had no idea where he was driving to or where he put the body after the shooting?"

"He said, 'I have no clue what I was doing.'"

"When did he tell you his version of how this occurred?"

"That was June 30, 2009."

"In the police report, did you read that detectives had interviewed the defendant for over nine hours on June 1, 2007?"

"Yes, I read it, but I didn't recall that date."

"And didn't you think it was important to hear what the

defendant had to say in that interview to see if it matched what he later told you?"

"Well, in retrospect, I would have liked to have seen the videotape of that."

Bobby Grace returned to the issue of malingering and asked the same question: wouldn't it have been important to compare the interviews?

Dr. Miles partially agreed and commented about his concern that Mahler was "malingering mental illness."

"Can people who have bipolar disorder lie?" Grace queried.

"Yes."

"So, in terms of you evaluating this case, don't you think it would have been important to try to figure out if the defendant was lying to you, by comparing what you heard from him to what he said in the police interview?"

The doctor's confidence appeared to be cracking. His faltering answer seemed cloudy with doubt. "Well, it would have been helpful to have that data and look at that data. And that, I think, would have been, you know, in retrospect, I wished that I had thought of that—thought of seeing the videotape. And the videotape could have given more information than just what he told the police."

Bobby Grace holstered his sword, having inflicted significant wounds to the bipolar/drug usage excuse. "Thank you, Your Honor. I have no more questions."

Larry Young rushed in to perform some triage. "Doctor, you mentioned that you thought he had worked for some law firms. Do you have any basis for that?"

"He mentioned working for a law firm, but I don't recall the name."

"Do you recall if he told you that he couldn't keep a job working for other people?"

"Yes, he said that he couldn't."

"Now, an inability to keep a job—is that at all consistent with the bipolar situation?"

The long, convoluted answer amounted to a definite maybe.

Young asked, "The police reports you have read, isn't it true they included a synopsis of this nine-hour interview?"

"Yes."

Everyone in the room realized that a synopsis, whether a few sentences or a few paragraphs, would not provide a reasonable comparison.

"Would you classify a drug addiction as a disease or a moral defect?" Young posed.

Another lengthy answer sounded nondefinitive.

With the defense's case hemorrhaging credibility, Larry Young had no more questions.

Bobby Grace, apparently satisfied, chose to let Dr. Samuel Miles leave.

CHAPTER 38

"HE'S A VERY SELF-CENTERED, ARROGANT MAN"

On Thursday, September 10, 2009, Bobby Grace had only one more witness to conclude the prosecution's case, Detective Tom Small. With the morning used up by other matters for the judge, Small took the stand at one forty-five P.M. and would testify for only one hour. Responding to questions from Bobby Grace, Tom Small told of his twenty-five years with the LAPD and fourteen years as a homicide detective. He confirmed that he and Detective Bynum had conducted the long videotaped interview with David Mahler, which took nearly all day on Saturday, June 2, 2007.

Most of the detective's tenure on the stand would be used up by playing segments of the videotaped interview Tom Small and Vicki Bynum had conducted with Mahler. A full transcript, nearly four hundred pages, was given to each juror.

Prior to the playing of each clip from the video, Grace validated it as evidence by having Small state that he and Bynum had asked those questions.

Grace signaled for the tape to stop, and inquired of the witness, "At some point in time, did you take a break in your interview with the defendant?"

"Yes, we did."

"And was there a way to monitor him when you were not in the room?"

"Yes. There's a side room where the equipment is, and there's a video screen and audio in there."

"Was your attention called to something the defendant was doing while you were not in the room with him?"

"Watching him on the monitor, I saw that Mr. Mahler was up and around in the interview room. He was in the corner and seemed to be contemplating something. He initiated an action that was, at the time, rather comical to us. What he did is—he set up a faint, knocked some furniture into the wall, and then laid down under the table."

"Did you go into the room to see that he was okay?"

"Yes."

With the judge's permission, Grace played the video segment showing Mahler going through his unconvincing charade of pretending to faint.

As everyone in the room watched the childish ploy, Mahler stared straight ahead, perhaps embarrassed but clearly angry.

With the screen again blank, Grace said he had just one more question. "Detective Small, at any time, did the defendant admit to having killed Kristin Baldwin?"

"He did not admit to killing her."

Larry Young's final turn at cross-examination brought him out of his chair. After courteously greeting Detective Small, he asked, "Would you characterize his behavior as somewhat bizarre during that interview?"

Tom Small, like his supervisor Wendi Berndt, had testified in more trials than he could remember, and he knew exactly how to handle it. He replied, "I would characterize him as very unusual."

The defender inquired, "I mean, there were times he was laughing out loud. We hear that one loud 'ha, ha, ha, ha.' And at other times, he would speak quite loudly. Isn't that unusual, in the context of the conversation?"

"Are you asking for my opinion?" Detective Small responded.

"Yes, sir."

"My opinion is that he's a very self-centered, arrogant man."

"Do you think he thought he could outwit you—that he could be the best person you have ever talked to and negotiate with you and walk out? Don't you think that's what he was trying?"

"I believe you would have to ask him."

"He just thought he was the greatest thing going, didn't he?" Small didn't bother to reply. "Did you notice how even some of his words were very, very rapid, weren't they? Remember, he said, 'I'm sorry if I'm going too fast'?"

Unexcitable, in a level voice, Small replied, "I don't find that unusual."

"And the bizarre language he used, or that he wrote in those notes, didn't you find that a bit unusual?"

"My opinion was that he's very proud of his training as a lawyer and he tried to exhibit that, put it on display for us."

"In your opinion, a real lawyer wouldn't have written that?"

"I don't know. He did."

"And what was this about? 'The body was left near a hospital'? Did you find a hospital out there?"

"I didn't recover the body. I spoke to the detectives who did."

"Was there a hospital there?"

"The area where the victim was found was in a remote section of the desert."

"So it wasn't true that there was a hospital there?"

"That I don't know. When you say 'there,' you'd have to—"

"Well, the location."

"As far as I know, it was a rural road, very remote location, near the I-40, and several miles east of Barstow, near Daggett."

Young ended with a brief exchange about what Mahler wore in his bedroom when Kristin Baldwin was shot, and then he sat down.

A short redirect by Bobby Grace drew the final testimony to a close. He announced, "The people rest." Larry Young followed suit with "The defense rests."

David Mahler, however, had no intention of resting. He asked the judge for permission to speak, and presented a Marsden Motion to fire his attorney. It surprised no one. All morning, his whispered arguments with Larry Young could be seen by everyone in the room.

Granted the opportunity to speak, Mahler complained of the psychiatric diagnosis and said the testimony had been too short and inadequate. It should have covered long-term effects of drug usage. He wanted to be hypnotized to show his mental problems. A court case he had handled in New Jersey, Mahler claimed, would be relevant. He demanded that he be given an MRI or CT scan. And records of his behavior in jail should be admitted. He said, "I feel the jury has heard an inadequate psychological defense."

Judge Wesley ruled the Marsden Motion would be denied, since Larry Young had presented a spirited, well-thought-out defense case. The other issues could be addressed in post-trial appeals.

* * *

On Friday, September 11, 2009, the eighth anniversary of a tragic day in U.S. history, jurors and spectators filed into Judge David Wesley's courtroom to hear Bobby Grace and Larry Young present their final arguments. Outside, the sky had cleared considerably as firefighters continued to work in the Angeles National Forest to bring the devastating flames under final control.

Dressed sharply in a navy blue suit, pin-striped white shirt, and an iridescent blue-red tie, Bobby Grace accepted the judge's 10:45 A.M. invitation to begin. Still observing the un-written rule of keeping a one-yard buffer between him and the jury box, he first paid a moment of respect to the memory of 9-11-01.

Without the use of notes and speaking directly to the jury in a folksy tone, often crossing his arms or placing his left hand in his pocket, Grace told them of Mahler's living the "Hollywood lifestyle."

Since the jury would have to wrestle with decisions re-garding murder or manslaughter, Grace commenced with ed-ucational definitions. He nodded to the courtroom clerk, who, according to plan, dimmed the courtroom lights. The jurors' and the audience's eyes focused on the large screen above David Mahler's head. The first slide set the tone with a larger-than-life photo of Kristin Baldwin. Bobby Grace next used graphics to explain the concept of circumstantial evidence versus direct evidence.

The slide show moved on to clarify witness credibility. Grace knew the unusual cast of characters who had testified might not have impressed jurors as completely reliable. He wanted it understood that the world of a killer is not populated with angels.

After spinning a positive image on the parade of people who had known David Mahler, Grace walked the jurors along a path of education about levels of homicide, starting with first-degree murder and proceeding to the least severe crime of involuntary manslaughter. Explaining that he wanted to focus on second-degree murder, Grace underlined that Russian roulette, as an intentional act dangerous to human life, constituted murder—even though explicit intent to kill might not be present.

When prosecutors argue this type of implied malice, they may seem to be giving a mixed message. Jury instructions define "murder" as requiring "malice aforethought," which generally means the defendant must have the *intent* to kill. But another jury instruction states that "malice" is implied when a person commits *an extremely dangerous act*. This is an acceptable substitute for the intent to kill. Grace's use of graphics on the screen helped jurors grasp the subtle differences.

Shifting to the key points of his argument, Grace summarized testimonial evidence from the witnesses, emphasizing the events in David Mahler's bedroom that took Kristin Baldwin's life, the video of his Jaguar being gone the amount of time required for a trip to Daggett, Mahler's attempts to find help in disposing of the body, and his callous behavior at the Marriott, including liquor, meals, and the use of a prostitute.

Anticipating what Larry Young might say, Bobby Grace attacked the psychiatrist's testimony as inadequate to prove that bipolar disorder or drugs had driven him to kill Kristin Baldwin. The doctor had quoted David Mahler saying, "I contacted every loser I knew to get someone to help me get rid of the body." This demonstrated consciousness of guilt.

Illustrations of every point appeared on the screen in full color. All of the evidence, said Grace, pointed unequivocally to a finding of second-degree murder.

Mahler's facial expressions turned from eager spectator to defiant opponent. He furiously scribbled notes on a pad, moved his glasses from his forehead to the bridge of his nose and back again, and glared at his own attorney.

A lunch break interrupted the show. At 1:45 P.M., Grace resumed his presentation, often backed up by a projected photo of Kristin, with a soft smile on her face. At two ten, he gave the jury an earnest look and slightly above a whisper said, "The people thank you."

Larry Young's argument got off to a bad start with a technical malfunction. His aide flipped the on switch of Young's computer to project PowerPoint images, but the battery had died. Unhappy with a possible delay, Judge David Wesley suggested to Young that he connect it directly to an electrical outlet. Embarrassed, Young groaned that he had left the power cord in his car. Frowning, Wesley asked if the DA's power cord could be used. Bobby Grace quickly unplugged his cord and handed it to Young's assistant. She said, "It won't work because I have a Mac."

Judge Wesley offered one more solution. Could Mr. Young use Mr. Grace's computer? But the assistant didn't think the Mac slide show was compatible with the PC equipment. Wesley informed Young that he had about ten minutes to solve the problem, or he must proceed without the graphics.

Armine Safarian, the comely young woman who had been propositioned by Michael Conoscenti, came to the rescue. She offered to help the assistant convert Young's digital show to a Mac format, and said it would take only a few minutes.

While Safarian worked, another drama took place at the defense table. Mahler and his attorney had been exchanging grumbling words. Young's voice grew loud enough to be heard in the gallery. "I'm the one who will talk, not you!"

Mahler snapped back, "Who the hell do you think you are?"

In a low growl, Young replied, "your lawyer."

The quarrel continued, in sotto voce, until Armine Safarian announced after only ten minutes of expert assistance that the conversion was done.

* * *

Relieved, Larry Young rose to make his final argument. His voice combined the qualities of a radio announcer and a preacher—easy to listen to and, at the same time, reassuring. Not to be outdone by Bobby's mention of the 9-11 tragedy, Young amplified the significance of this special day and how all deaths are tragedies for all concerned. David Mahler contemptuously stared straight ahead.

After reminding jurors of witness statements that illustrated Mahler's "out of control," bizarre behavior, his frequent temperamental outbursts, and long-term drug usage, most of Young's speech and graphics centered on the psychiatrist's testimony. He insisted that Mahler was the classic example of someone afflicted with bipolar disorder. "Dr. Miles provided some of the best psychiatric testing you can find."

In his recap of events leading up to the killing, Young suggested that Kristin Baldwin might have been a "call girl." At the prosecution's table, Bobby Grace scratched out rapid notes.

Young shifted the jurors' attention to the various forms of homicide. Using PowerPoint, he aimed at minimizing the evidence of second-degree murder. Relentlessly, Young hammered away at the merit of such a verdict. He told jurors that "doing an act involving a high degree of risk of death without due caution" was involuntary manslaughter.

To demonstrate his understanding that Mahler deserved no sympathy, Young described his client as the "whacko from New York living in the Hollywood Hills." Jurors' eyes zeroed in on Mahler expecting his short fuse to be ignited. Surprisingly, no explosive reaction occurred. Mahler sat stoically in his place staring at counsel table. His attorney spoke of Mahler "living in the fast lane," using hookers for his pleasure and abusing drugs in the process. At no point did Young say anything complimentary about his client. He concluded his presentation after fifty-five minutes.

Bobby Grace stood to deliver his rebuttal. Larry Young's insinuation that Kristin was a call girl ignited a fire that burned Bobby's ire. He wanted to come out swinging, angry that the victim had been unfairly diminished. Known for his aboveboard relations with defense attorneys, including Larry Young, Grace felt that the "call girl" reference had struck below the belt. However, his desire to dispel the image could not be heard by the jury. The law holds that the victim's character is irrelevant in a murder case, so the prosecutor had no opportunity to present evidence about that.

Putting aside Young's comment, Grace refocused the jury's attention on the definition of manslaughter versus murder. He then turned to the issue of David Mahler's behavior. For the sake of argument, Grace conceded that Mahler may have had a form of bipolar disorder, but he pointed out again how it apparently hadn't limited his work in the legal or financial professions. And, said Grace, Mahler had never been arrested for any drug violations. On the screen, a slide appeared to reinforce that statement. Unfortunately, just below the bold print words *No prior incidents,* another image could be seen. It showed a faded arrest report.

Larry Young leaped up and shouted, "Objection! May we approach the bench?" Grace searched the screen, wondering what he had done to trigger such an outburst.

Judge Wesley seemed curious too. At sidebar Young complained that the prosecution had projected on the screen, in full view of the jury, one of Mahler's prior arrest reports. References to previous offenses—which are unconnected to the current trial—are generally prohibited.

Grace explained that the graphic had been included as a generic illustration, and that Mahler's name, plus the facts of the arrest, had been blurred out. Nothing prejudicial could be seen, nor was it intended.

Young vehemently demanded a mistrial, which would require a repeat of the entire process. Judge Wesley denied the motion, admonished the jury to ignore the slide, and told Grace to continue. Still, Young had established an issue to be raised on appeal.

Grace remained composed and returned to finishing his presentation. His final slide depicted Kristin smiling down from the screen as though she were in a Higher Place. In a soft but firm voice, he told the jurors that Kristin did not deserve to be murdered, and justice demanded that this defendant be found guilty of murder.

Judge David Wesley turned to the jury, read aloud the legal instructions, and sent them to their conference room to begin deliberations.

It would take them until Tuesday, September 15, including a weekend, to decide David Mahler's fate.

CHAPTER 39

"SHE WAS A PERSON"

During the interminable four-day wait, debates flared among lawyers, investigators, and court watchers. Some argued that David Mahler would be found not guilty and walk out a free man. Others presumed the jury would convict him of involuntary manslaughter, the lowest form of homicide. Even fewer insiders would bet on a verdict of voluntary manslaughter. And the number of people who believed he would be convicted of either first- or second-degree murder could be counted on one hand.

On Tuesday afternoon, Judge David Wesley's courtroom filled up rapidly. A brief hearing on another matter treated the standing-room-only crowd to an added attraction. The principals in a highly publicized case filed in and stood before the judge. Celebrity Anna Nicole Smith had died of an apparent drug overdose, and charges had been filed against several people in her coterie. Judge Wesley heard their complaints and ruled that a trial would be postponed.

* * *

At two o'clock, a bailiff called court to order for the David Mahler case. All parties were present, with one major exception. The chair in which the defendant had been sitting since late August sat conspicuously empty.

A deputy sheriff, who ordinarily would have escorted Mahler into the room, told Judge Wesley, "Mr. Mahler said he didn't care, and he went back to sleep in his cell."

Unperturbed, the judge stated that Mahler's attorney was present and could represent his client. The verdict hearing would go on as scheduled, without the defendant's presence.

It is commonly said that spectators should watch the eyes of jurors as they file in after deliberations. If they look at the defendant, it might indicate a verdict of not guilty.

In this case, the old theory did not apply, with Mahler choosing to stay in his jail cell.

With the twelve people seated, Judge Wesley asked if they had reached a verdict. A husky young man, with short blond hair, rose from his chair in the front row and said they had. At the judge's instructions, he handed the forms to a bailiff, who brought them to Judge Wesley's desk. After reviewing them, Wesley passed the filled-out documents to his court clerk. She read aloud:

"'We find the defendant, David Mahler, not guilty of violating *Penal Code 187(a), murder in the first degree.*"

At first, the two crucial words "not guilty" chilled a few people, until they realized that the verdict applied only to first-degree murder. Several possibilities still remained.

The clerk read from the second form:

"We find the defendant, David Mahler, guilty of violating *Penal Code 187 (a), murder in the second degree.*"

A collective gasp rumbled through the courtroom. The jury had accepted the evidence presented by Bobby Grace's prosecution and rejected the defense's theory of mitigation through bipolar disorder and the influence of drugs. Some knew that the penal code calls for imprisonment of fifteen years to life for second-degree murder, perhaps more with additional charges.

Judge Wesley's clerk hadn't yet finished. The jury also had found true the allegation that Mahler had personally discharged a firearm causing death. This would add more prison time to the sentence. In addition, they had nailed him for assault with a firearm, as related to the threat of shooting Donnie Van Develde, adding even more time in prison.

The sentencing, Judge Wesley announced, would take place on Friday, October 9. And David Mahler would have no options about attendance. His presence would be required.

In the San Gabriel Mountains, above Los Angeles, the disastrous fire had been snuffed out finally. From August 26, it had roared across canyons and peaks, through forests, meadows, and residential settlements, taking two human lives and countless wild animals. The blaze had lasted from the beginning of the trial, burning for the same amount of time it took to mete out justice against the man who had taken Kristin Baldwin's life.

On sentencing day, October 9, 2009, the courtroom again filled. Three deputy sheriffs escorted David Mahler in from a side door, and stood guard near him during the entire sentence hearing. He wore jail-issued gray coveralls, slippers, and handcuffs. A thin shadow of newly grown hair decorated the space between his upper lip and nose.

After a bailiff called "order in the court," Judge David Wesley allowed a hearing on the defense attorney's motion for a new trial. Larry Young had based it on several issues, including the brief, inadvertent flashing on the screen of a prior law violation by the defendant. Wesley ruled that it had not been proffered as evidence, was accidental, barely visible, had not included the defendant's name, and was harmless. He had admonished the jury not to consider it.

He also denied the request for a new trial, saying that the evidence had been sufficient to support conviction for second-degree murder.

Another issue, said Young, involved David Mahler's claim that he should have been allowed to replace his counsel during the course of the trial and defend himself. Wesley explained he had not allowed it because Mahler had filed incorrect and inappropriate motions repeatedly. And Mahler had sabotaged himself by refusing to come to court on the verdict day. Wesley called that childish decision by the defendant "absolute vindication of the court's decision."

Mahler stood to make a personal appeal, but his lengthy speech failed to convince the judge. The convicted killer even tried to negotiate with Bobby Grace to postpone the sentencing, but without success. Judge Wesley put a close to that portion of the hearing, which had consumed nearly an hour.

Bobby Grace asked, "Your Honor, before you pronounce sentence, we do want to present some victim impact statements." Wesley concurred.

Grace said, "The victim's family was kind enough to put together a short DVD slide show of photographs of the victim in life that we would like the court to view prior to a representative of the family making a statement."

"All right, that's fine," the judge said.

Larry Young objected to a slide show. "That's too much like a memorial service. I don't believe that's proper in a sentencing."

Judge Wesley said, "Well, your objection is overruled."

The silently screened photos of Kristin Baldwin, from early childhood to her adult years, crept into the hearts of observers and brought tears to the family's faces.

Bobby Grace stated, "At this time, we'd ask Robin Henson to come forward."

* * *

Robin Henson rose from her place in the front row, where she had been sitting with her daughter, her stepfather Peter Means, and Jennifer Gootsan. She walked with elegance and grace through the swinging gate, up to the lectern. Robin carried what appeared to be a mahogany wood treasure chest, about ten inches long.

With delicate care, she placed it atop the lectern and softly said, "This is my sister."

Goose bumps dotted the arms of everyone in the room. The silence was broken only by the soft sounds of sniffling and weeping. Everyone realized the chest contained the ashes of Kristin Baldwin.

Even Vicki Bynum couldn't hold back the tears.

Robin's voice trembled, but she held her emotions in check. Her daughter openly sobbed, while stepfather Peter Means struggled to maintain composure.

"This is Kristin," Robin explained. "I just wanted to say that my family's life has been completely turned around to a point of pain and suffering because my sister is gone. It affected my kids, my family, and my friends.

"Everyone who knew my sister loved her. They thought she was funny, annoying—just like a normal human being. And then one day, she's just gone, way too early in her life. She didn't experience marriage or her own kids, or all the trials and tribulations of being alive and having a life.

"There's absolutely nothing that I can do to change the events that happened. And I would just like to say that a person who could do this needs to go to prison for a very long time if only to protect others from him."

Robin's eyes welled over and tears spilled down her cheeks. "I'm sorry I'm so upset," she apologized. "But this is just the hardest thing that I've ever had to do in my life. I love my sister and I miss her and I want her back." She could say no more, except a heartfelt, "Thank you."

* * *

David Mahler, as usual, couldn't let anyone else have the last word. He asked to speak.

Judge Wesley allowed it.

Mahler began by saying he didn't have much to say. "I don't have to say anything. I could just sit here and my sentence is going to be the same, despite the sister's crying and the family crying. So I don't have to say anything right now—but, nevertheless, I feel it's my obligation. I want to say to the family that I'm sorry this happened. . . . It happened and I'm taking responsibility. And I am going to jail for a very long time, don't worry.

"But, nevertheless, it's important to me and maybe it means something to you to let you know that I'm extraordinarily regretful. I can't tell you how sorry I am. If there's anything I could do, I would do it. . . . Anything I can do to try to ease the pain of the family because you deserve that, and you don't deserve this, and I'm sorry."

Reaction in the gallery was divided. Some thought Mahler sounded sincere. Others thought it was a typical example of his belief that he could negotiate for everything. Perhaps if he expressed his regrets, the judge would hand down a lighter sentence.

Judge Wesley said, "Thank you, Mr. Mahler."

Without hesitating even a brief moment, he continued.

"The court finds that Mr. Mahler is ineligible for probation. It is therefore denied. On count one, for violation of *Penal Code 187, murder in the second degree,* the defendant is sentenced to the term of fifteen years to life.

"The jury having found true the enhancement that the defendant personally discharged a firearm causing death, the defendant is sentenced to the term set by law of twenty-five years to life to be served consecutively to the fifteen years for a total of an indeterminate sentence of forty years to life.

"On count two . . . assault with a firearm, the court selects the middle term of three years. This is a determinate term. Upon its completion, he is to serve the indeterminate term of forty years to life."

Next the judge gave Mahler credit for the time he had already served since being arrested in June 2007. In addition, Mahler was ordered to pay a restitution fee of $10,000, plus a $5,000 "State Court Construction penalty." At the expiration of his "period of incarceration," forty years, he would be eligible for parole in his mideighties.

Judge Wesley also advised Mahler that if he wished to appeal, he must file a written notice within sixty days. He concluded with, "The defendant is remanded without bail to the custody of the Los Angeles County Sheriff's Department of Corrections, forthwith."

Later discussing the case, Vicki Bynum acknowledged that she cried when Robin Henson said, "This is my sister."

"I was very touched by the victim impact words from Robin," Bynum said. "I've been to a lot of murder trials, but this one got to me. We tend to become a little cynical in this business, but sometimes cases like this adjust the perspective for me. I remember hearing a judge once say the criminal justice system is exactly that—justice for the criminal. The victims often take a back burner to the system. At the end of it all, we did this for Kristin, because she was a person."

ACKNOWLEGMENTS

From the moment a lightbulb flashes on above a nonfiction author's head with the nucleus of an idea for a new book, the project becomes a matter of teamwork. Each member's contributions ultimately determine whether or not the idea will finally reach the hands and eyes of readers. Our championship team of regulars, draftees, and volunteers couldn't have been better.

Michaela Hamilton, editor in chief, not only opened the starting gate, but also gave us her usual warm and welcome advice.

Susan Crawford, literary agent, connected the logistical dots for us.

LAPD detectives Vicki Bynum, Wendi Berndt, and Tom Small were absolutely terrific in friendly discussions, giving us a guided tour through the iconic Hollywood Station, and coming through with inspiration.

Robin Henson, Peter Means, and Robin's twin brother, Rick, generously spoke to us about their beloved Kristin, as did her best friend, Jennifer Gootsan. They also provided photographs we desperately needed. Robin and Rick faced another devastating loss on November 9, 2010, when their mother, Marie Dionne, passed away from natural causes at age sixty-one. She sat next to the author during the trial on the day before her sixtieth birthday and shared personal memories about her family.

Bobby Grace, the prosecutor, gave us insight into the legal process and delighted us with his story of the elephant eating his jacket.

Larry Young, Mahler's defense attorney, graciously chatted during breaks at the trial.

Stacy Tipton overcame her fearful reluctance to provide essential background information.

Armine Safarian and Lea Malit-Crisostomo, assistants for Bobby Grace, filled in important blanks.

Sherry Quenga, court reporter, worked overtime to provide essential trial transcripts.

We are also grateful to the most colorful cast of characters ever to populate a true-crime book. We have changed a few of their names to protect privacy.

Finally, a particularly inspirational woman deserves our heartfelt acknowledgment. In the words of Ron Bowers:

"In this story of Kristin Baldwin and David Mahler, my wife, Rosemarie, proved to be incredibly valuable. I talked her into accompanying me to the desert where Kristin's body was found. She is accustomed to such adventures, but would prefer to avoid trekking through murder scenes where rattlesnakes, lizards, spiders, and coyotes might be lurking. Courageously, she joined me to explore the site near Daggett, and came up with a startling theory. We wondered how Kristin's body had wound up mostly under the low bridge. Rosie surveyed the scene, noticed the gradual slope downward, west to east, and suggested that the corpse had been dumped on the other side of the bridge. In her theory, a flash flood had moved the body to its discovered location. We are still debating it, but she deserves admiration for not only this input, but for her many years of support in dealing with horrific crimes."

POSTSCRIPT

In September 2011, an unexpected and explosive decision in the David Mahler case changed everything. The California Court of Appeal, Second Appellate District, issued an opinion that stated: *We are compelled to reverse the murder conviction because the trial court improperly instructed the jury on felony murder. . . . The conviction is reversed and the matter remanded to the trial court.*

When Ron Bowers and I heard this, we were amazed. It had been our impression that Mahler had missed the deadline for filing an appeal and that any legal maneuvering would occur sometime in the future. I contacted several members of Kristin Baldwin's family, her friends, and other individuals involved in the story to ask about their reactions to the reversal.

Robin Henson, Kristin's sister, choked back tears as she said, "I'm stunned and sick to my stomach. I just pray that justice will ultimately come about."

Peter Means, Kristin's stepfather, stated, "I'm dumbfounded and shocked. I certainly hope a new trial takes place soon and that Kristin's killer is kept behind bars."

Jennifer Gootsan, the close friend of both Kristin and Robin, couldn't believe it. "I'm sick, appalled, and disgusted. I can't believe so many tragic things can happen to Kristin and her loved ones. This just makes it worse."

Dreading the specter of a new trial, or the possibility of Mahler being released, Karl Norvik said simply, "Here we go again."

The court's decision made no mention of David Mahler's guilt or innocence, nor did it deny that he had shot and killed Kristin Baldwin. Instead, the three justices focused on an obscure provision in the instruction defining second-degree murder that Judge David Wesley had read to the jury before deliberations began.

The instruction is intended to define felony murder and to

inform jurors that the defendant can be found guilty even if there is no evidence of malice aforethought. It points out that when the killing is accompanied by the commission of a felony—such as rape, kidnapping, robbery, or assault with a firearm—these facts can supplant the evidence of malice, allowing the jury to reach a verdict of guilt even if the killing appears to be unintentional.

As observers of Mahler's trial had seen, the evidence left no doubt that he had used a handgun, and that Kristin Baldwin had been killed. So it appeared that Mahler's waving the weapon around, and repeatedly pulling the trigger while pointing it at both Kristin and Donnie Van Develde, could be interpreted as felonious assault with a firearm. This would certainly appear to meet the definition of felony murder.

In a twenty-two-page explanation of the court's decision, Associate Justice Laurie D. Zelon disagreed. She referred to a 1969 decision by the California Supreme Court that stated: *[When] the felony merged with the homicide [it] cannot be the basis for a felony murder instruction.*

Trial judge Wesley, regarded as one of the finest legal minds in the Los Angeles County court system, was no doubt familiar with the California Supreme Court ruling. He may have considered Mahler's pointing the weapon at Donnie Van Develde, and pulling the trigger, as a separate assault, not "merging" with the crime against Kristin Baldwin. The appellate court, however, rejected that logic.

As an experienced prosecutor, Ron Bowers was perplexed by the reversal. He noted, "Bobby Grace did not argue the issue or even mention it to the jury. The defense attorney neither discussed the rule in his arguments, nor lodged an objection to it being read to jurors."

Regardless of any controversy, David Mahler's conviction was overturned. Several legal experts suggested that the reversal was unwarranted since the appeals court could certainly have classified the questionable jury instruction as "harmless error."

* * *

The Los Angeles County District Attorney, along with the Superior Court, faced several options, including releasing Mahler, offering a plea bargain that would reduce the sentence but still keep him in prison for several years, or initiating a new trial.

The long, complex process began on January 5, 2012, with a "pre-trial" court hearing, indicating the District Attorney's intention to once again prosecute David Mahler for murder. Everyone involved in the case dreaded the forthcoming ordeal of endless hearings, another bruising court battle, and the possibility that a new jury could make an inexplicable decision.

Kristin Baldwin's tragic death had been marked with a staggering number of strange twists. Yet another stunning event hit the news in early March, 2012. David Mahler entered a plea of guilty to voluntary manslaughter!

For reasons known only to Mahler, he made the decision to accept a sentence of two decades in prison. Perhaps he thought it far better than facing a potential death penalty.

A collective sigh of relief came from Kristin's family and friends; from investigators and witnesses; and from two authors. Robin Henson's prayer for justice had been answered.

Don Lasseter
March, 2012